Joy Street

Joy Street

A Wartime Romance in Letters
1940–1942

MIRREN BARFORD

AND LIEUTENANT JOCK LEWES

EDITED BY
MICHAEL T. WISE

FOREWORD AND COMMENTARY BY
ALAN HOE

Little, Brown and Company
Boston   New York   Toronto   London

First American Edition

ISBN 0-316-94767-9

10 9 8 7 6 5 4 3 2 1

HAD

Published simultaneously in Canada by Little, Brown & Company
(Canada) Limited

Printed in the United States of America

ACKNOWLEDGEMENTS

Two people have earned my specials thanks: Christopher Barford, my uncle and Mirren's brother, for his hospitality during my visits to Britain, for his unflagging efforts at proofreading the manuscript, for his tireless help in researching family and military history, and for his insistence that I clarify obscure but important details; and Dr David S. Lewes, for his extraordinary enthusiasm and support throughout this project, for giving me access to family documents, and for the welcome he and his wife Daphne have given me at their home in Pavenham.

John S. Lewes, David's son and Jock's nephew and namesake, has shared freely of his own ongoing research into his uncle's life.

Thanks also, for their enthusiasm, support and diverse help, to: Mary Charlotte Angelica Guyon de St Prix ('Angel'); The Rt Hon. the Earl Jellicoe; Daniel Francis Verdery; Angela Kaufman; my agent, Michele Rubin; my editor at Little, Brown, Catherine Crawford; and to The Consigning Women.

This book is especially for Mirren Louise Stegman-Wise. May she one day know – even briefly – the love her grandmother knew.

EDITOR'S NOTE

Mirren Wise died in February 1992, and shortly after her death I discovered this collection of letters tucked away in the back of a drawer in her desk. They were not hidden, as her love for Jock Lewes had never been hidden from me and my brothers – or my father – during my childhood. She had told me quite openly that my older brother John had been named for Jock.

As I began to read through the letters, I thought that my brothers would like to see copies and began to transcribe just a few. But the task caught hold of me, ran away with me, and the letters begged for publication. I admit to a feeling of guilt as I prepared to make these intimate writings public, until I came across Mirren's letter of 30th August 1940, in which she says, '. . . one day I hope my great-grandchildren will take the trouble to have them published, for many people would read them gladly if they had the chance.' I had been given her blessing.

The transcription itself was an adventure of discovery. I worked mostly late at night, recognising some of the characters from my mother's stories of her youth. But where was Joy Street? I thought at first it must be an allegorical representation of a specific place, but came to understand that it described Mirren and Jock's individual meetings. Who was the 'beggar priest', who threatened their procession along Joy Street? Only after many, many weeks of working on the manuscript (as it was becoming) did I recognise Lust.

But my greatest discovery was of Jock. 'He is what Alcibiades should have been, perhaps,' wrote my friend Daniel Verdery on reading his letters. He was the consummate warrior. His intellect complemented his passion, his obvious courage and dedication to duty were matched by his tenderness. He loved, but he did not hate. I began to feel almost a part of his family, and I determined to try to find his brother. Jock mentions (24th July 1941) writing a letter to David '. . . to congratulate him on being a doctor', and during a visit to Britain in 1992 I tracked David down through the British Medical Registry. When I first met David in 1993, his daughter was visiting from Australia, and she said that Mirren's name had been a household word during her own childhood. The circle was complete.

This collection appears to be almost complete except for a seven-month period from March to October 1941. Because Jock left Mirren's letters with his parents when he went to North Africa in February 1941, they were saved, and they were returned to Mirren after the war. Her letters to him from the time he went overseas until early October of that year have been lost, but those sent after 1st October 1941 have been preserved.

Almost all of the letters are dated. Those which are not can generally be placed by their content within the context of a particular 10-day period, and I have tried to do so.

Michael T. Wise

MIRIAM ESMÉ BARFORD was born in India on 8 December 1920, the daughter of Luther Holden Barford, an Indian Civil Servant, and Mary Sheila Todd-Naylor, daughter of a District Commissioner in Burma. She was raised in India and Italy until the age of about 11, when she moved permanently back to England.

Mirren's parents underwent a bitter divorce when she was about 15, and her mother married Herbert J. Paton, known as 'Hamish', a professor of philosophy at Oxford. From then on she lived with her mother and stepfather in 14 Merton Street, Oxford, and in Nether Pitcaithly, Bridge-of-Earn, Perthshire, also spending much time at the several homes of her aunt Esmé, including Cowcroft and 50 Bryanston Court. She came to be called 'Mirren', a Scottish variant of Miriam, and reversed her first and middle names, so that by the time she met John Lewes she was known as Esmé Mirren (or Miriam) Barford. Her brother Christopher was four years her junior and lived with their father. Her closest friend was Angelica Galpine.

Mirren spent one year at St Andrew's University in Scotland before entering Somerville College, Oxford, in 1939. After getting her degree from Somerville in 1942, Mirren joined the Service and worked for a military intelligence unit.

JOHN STEELE LEWES was also born in India, in 1913, the son of an English father and Australian mother. He was raised and schooled in Australia and then, in 1933, entered Christ Church College, Oxford, where he was renowned for his prowess as an oarsman. Jock worked as a member of the British Council (similar to the U.S. Information Agency) after finishing at Oxford. He joined Tower Hamlets Rifles as a reservist, when he saw the approach of the War in 1939, and later transferred to the Welsh Guards.

Jock was not content to be a regular soldier, and even his joining a Commando force in 1940 and the action he saw in North Africa during mid-1941 left him frustrated, as he thought he could organise better ways of using small forces. In August 1941, David Stirling asked him to help form what was to become the S.A.S. – Special Air Service, the most famous and perhaps most successful British commando unit both during and since the war.

Jock's sister Elizabeth had preceded him at Oxford, and his brother David followed. His parents had returned to England prior to the outbreak of war.

Mirren met Jock and David at Elizabeth's wedding in August 1939.

FOREWORD
by
Alan Hoe

'Never run; once you start running you stop thinking, now remember that!'

Lt. John Steele Lewes, 'L' Detachment, SAS Brigade

I never met Jock Lewes, but I can easily imagine that I did. I interviewed so many people who served with him during the early days of the SAS in North Africa that I feel that I know the 'Jock' of those times – the warrior. It is a privilege to introduce this collection of wartime letters which show his other faces – the romantic, the philosopher and the humorist.

The SAS – Special Air Service – is still Britain's most secret, daring and romantic military force. It requires a different type of leadership from any other form of the profession of arms, and this was as true during the campaign in the North African Desert in World War II as it was in the Gulf War fifty years later. Working as small patrols, unsupported and often at perilously long distances behind the formal lines of battle, places strains on the best trained of soldiers. For the officer the pressures can be even greater.

During the formative stages of the SAS three 'hostilities only' officers dominated the scene. All were undoubtedly courageous, dedicated to winning the war and had deep religious convictions, but in most other respects they were very different. Lieutenant Blair 'Paddy' Mayne, a huge red-haired, volatile Irishman, was a renowned athlete who approached the war with enormous enthusiasm and the courage of a lion; to the forefront in any battle, he had the knack of making his men feel invincible. Lieutenant David Stirling was a tall, broad, softly-spoken Scot who issued his orders almost apologetically but with the sort of quiet confidence that made men believe that with him they could achieve anything. But what of the third officer, the oldest of the three – what of Lieutenant Jock Lewes?

A highly successful product of Oxford University, Lewes was working for the British Council when, without waiting for the call to arms, he joined the Tower Hamlets Rifles as a reservist prior to enlisting in the Welsh Guards in 1939, where he was quickly selected for commission to the rank of Second Lieutenant. In his chosen regiment, his reputation as a fast-learning enthusiast and perfectionist was quickly gained.

Although he did not know it at the time, Lewes was suffering from some of the same frustrations as Stirling and Mayne during those early days of military training. A clear-thinking man who had appreciated the technical advances in weapons and military transport systems, Lewes found it difficult to come to terms with obviously experienced instructors who insisted on teaching the tactics of World War I.

It was these frustrations with the outdated training and tactical methods that led eventually to the collaboration between David Stirling and Jock Lewes in the formation of a new, special unit – which, ultimately, became the most elite in the British army, the SAS.

Jock's letters to Mirren are remarkable in that he seems to have been able to separate himself almost totally from the war for most of the time. It is true that his various frustrations show through, and occasionally it is possible to detect a touch of bitterness, but he does not dwell on these things.

FOREWORD
by
Alan Hoe

'Never run; once you start running you stop thinking, now remember that!'

Lt. John Steele Lewes, 'L' Detachment, SAS Brigade

I never met Jock Lewes, but I can easily imagine that I did. I interviewed so many people who served with him during the early days of the SAS in North Africa that I feel that I know the 'Jock' of those times – the warrior. It is a privilege to introduce this collection of wartime letters which show his other faces – the romantic, the philosopher and the humorist.

The SAS – Special Air Service – is still Britain's most secret, daring and romantic military force. It requires a different type of leadership from any other form of the profession of arms, and this was as true during the campaign in the North African Desert in World War II as it was in the Gulf War fifty years later. Working as small patrols, unsupported and often at perilously long distances behind the formal lines of battle, places strains on the best trained of soldiers. For the officer the pressures can be even greater.

During the formative stages of the SAS three 'hostilities only' officers dominated the scene. All were undoubtedly courageous, dedicated to winning the war and had deep religious convictions, but in most other respects they were very different. Lieutenant Blair 'Paddy' Mayne, a huge red-haired, volatile Irishman, was a renowned athlete who approached the war with enormous enthusiasm and the courage of a lion; to the forefront in any battle, he had the knack of making his men feel invincible. Lieutenant David Stirling was a tall,

broad, softly-spoken Scot who issued his orders almost
apologetically but with the sort of quiet confidence that
made men believe that with him they could achieve anything. But what of the third officer, the oldest of the three –
what of Lieutenant Jock Lewes?

A highly successful product of Oxford University, Lewes
was working for the British Council when, without waiting
for the call to arms, he joined the Tower Hamlets Rifles as a
reservist prior to enlisting in the Welsh Guards in 1939,
where he was quickly selected for commission to the rank of
Second Lieutenant. In his chosen regiment, his reputation as
a fast-learning enthusiast and perfectionist was quickly
gained.

Although he did not know it at the time, Lewes was suffering from some of the same frustrations as Stirling and
Mayne during those early days of military training. A clear-
thinking man who had appreciated the technical advances in
weapons and military transport systems, Lewes found it difficult to come to terms with obviously experienced instructors
who insisted on teaching the tactics of World War I.

It was these frustrations with the outdated training and
tactical methods that led eventually to the collaboration
between David Stirling and Jock Lewes in the formation of a
new, special unit – which, ultimately, became the most elite
in the British army, the SAS.

Jock's letters to Mirren are remarkable in that he seems to
have been able to separate himself almost totally from the
war for most of the time. It is true that his various frustrations
show through, and occasionally it is possible to detect a
touch of bitterness, but he does not dwell on these things.

Very few soldiers were able to resist passing on to their families some of the flavour of 'specialist' operations, and for me it has been most interesting to read this very personal record of correspondence whilst knowing what some of Jock's activities would have been at the time of writing.

Portrait of Jock Lewes by Rex Whistler
Photographed by Dr David Lewes

TRAINING BATTALION – THE WELSH GUARDS

In April 1940, the recently commissioned Second Lieutenant Lewes was newly transferred to the Welsh Guards Training Battalion. He had arrived via the Tower Hamlets Rifles, one of many such reservist units into which those eager to prepare for the coming war could enlist. As reservists they were given only the most basic of uniforms and part-time tutoring in foot drill and basic tactics.

The move to Sandown Park represented one step nearer to the front line, as this camp was used for final training and equipping prior to moving overseas and into action.

Mirren Barford was in her first year at Somerville College, Oxford, reading Modern Languages. Her time was spent in college and at the homes of her mother and stepfather in Merton Street, Oxford, and Bridge-of-Earn, Perthshire.

BEF READY FOR ANY ATTACK
THE TIMES Friday 12 April 1940

Tyn-Y-Coed
Arthog
North Wales
14th April 1940

Dear John,

I have an unpleasant feeling that I never posted an answer to your very welcome letter. I had such a busy time in a Cotswold village, trying to persuade the local policeman that I really wasn't a spy, that I guess your letter was never sent.* And now I shall have to get your brother David to forward this, since I don't remember your address.

I doubt that I shall be in Town again till after the summer term, so if you come to Oxford before then, please come and find me at Somerville. I so much want to see you slightly bemused by champagne and murmuring – there

*Mirren and her friend Angel (Angelica Galpine) were staying at a country inn, practising their French, German, and Italian, and were apparently overheard by local residents. They were detained briefly and questioned by the local police.

was an old lady who swallowed a fly . . .! Dear John, do you remember that end to a very happy day? No, but seriously. I'd be glad to see you again, so come to Oxford if you have time and inclination, and we'll have a happy time all over again.

Write when you will,

Yours,
Miriam

HOLLAND ON THE ALERT
THE TIMES Saturday 20 April 1940

8 Tudor Court
Castle Way
Hanworth, Middx.
Saturday, 20th April

Dear Miriam,

I am at home for the weekend for a change, and intend to employ very profitably some of the precious moments in thanking you for your letter, a thing which I should have done immediately upon its welcome arrival, had I not had during the last four weeks more to do than my limited ability and endurance could possibly cope with. Your letter penetrated this militarist monochrome and shed colour around: it reminded me of the possible continued existence of a side of my life to which at one time I attached considerable importance, but which disappeared with the coming of war. I have led a positively monastic life, at any rate since transferring to the Welsh Guards, not so much from necessity but because I thought that the most important thing for the moment was to turn myself into a good soldier as quickly as possible.

Now that I am at any rate a better soldier than I was and I look around and see what a jolly good time much worse soldiers are having, I begin to wonder whether I may not have been just a little too keen on things military and a little too regardless of the major pleasures of life. But whatever it would have been wiser for me to do, the fact remains that I have now succeeded in landing myself with an admittedly very responsible job, but one which demands all the time and energy I have to vie, and more. My ventures into the civil life are therefore, infrequent and brief, and when they do materialise are rather naturally centred around the ancestral hearth.

I don't expect to get away next weekend, and if I do I must come to London, but the weekend after that looks more hopeful and I shall make a real effort to reach Oxford and say hallo if you are visible – it would be fun and I hope that the powers in whose hands these matters rest will move to my advantage. The only thing I am afraid of is that our next meeting will be postponed for so long that you forget the tale of the old lady who swallowed a fly and the happy day which it ended. It delights me to think that you haven't, particularly as I had forgotten telling it. What a story to tell at that hour – it goes on and on! But still I might have done worse and at any rate it had the merit of being whimsical; my childish sense of humour, especially when quickened by champagne, delights in whimsy – it is warmer and kinder than wit.

And now I must apologise for the length of this letter. I am one of the few remaining people who like letter writing and practise it, however ineptly, as an art. I am afraid I often inflict my efforts upon friends and acquaintances who, probably very rightly, prefer the more modern conveniences of the telephone and telegram. If you are among them, then please take this letter to be a verbose and belated telegram, which, with due regard to the national necessity for economy would run somewhat like this:

'Glad you glad meet again anxious repeat champagne story etcetera earliest opportunity.'

Love (that's conventional),
John.

P.S. My 'business' address in case you want to slap my face for this is:

Training Bn. Welsh Guards,
Roman Way Camp,
Colchester.

[Page 1 of the following letter, which appears to have been written shortly after Mirren's letter of 14th April 1940, has been lost.]

. . . I don't at present know how much of it there will be, that is to say how much of your priceless time you will be willing or able to lavish upon this worthless one's attentions.

If there is a good play or review on please get me some tickets on Friday or Saturday night, and the rest can be left to the inspiration of the moment which is always more pleasurable because unexpected. Get good tickets because I hate half-baked pleasure.

When you write, tell me how it was that even a village policeman could be so obtuse as to entertain even for an instant the idea that you are a spy. You'd make a very good one as a matter of fact, a second Mata Hari.

Dave told me of the frustrating miscarriage of mail which caused each of you to think grievous thoughts of the other.

I hope that in spite of that annoyance you enjoyed the evening. Dave certainly did.

Yours,
John

Somerville College
Oxford
Friday

Dear John,

I expect that you will go to Christ Church first of all so I hope you find this note waiting for you. I didn't book seats again, however, because I thought maybe you'd rather go on the dream-wrapt river, instead of listening to the dreams of others in the theatre. Anyway, we can fix up something when we meet.

I shall be in College from six o'clock onwards so you ought to be able to find me all right.

Addio!
Miriam

Somerville College
Oxford
2nd May 1940

Dear John,

I'm so sorry I shan't see you this weekend. I'm spending tomorrow night in London and I had thought we might travel down together on Saturday. But still come the weekend if you can, and before that I'll write you a long letter because I want you to enjoy it even half as much as I enjoyed yours.

But look you John, if you are coming, give me warning if it's possible, because then I can organise my work maybe and avoid an essay crisis.

A bientôt, and I'll write again,
Yours,
Mirren

Wednesday [*8th May*]

Dear John,

My work is well under control, and my dates too. I'll be ready for you all day long after 11 o'clock on Friday and most of Saturday except for a tutorial at 10 a.m. and the late afternoon – possibly; I may be going to a dance that evening, but it's likely to prove a frost. So either let me

know where you want me to meet you or leave a message at
the Lodge for me, and I'll come and find you. I got two
tickets for 'The Two Bouquets' with Leslie French at the
Playhouse – it should be good.

And now I must clutter off to a lecture.

A bientôt,
  Mirren

Training Battalion
Welsh Guards
Roman Way Camp
Colchester
[undated – April–June 1940]

Miriam,

There is no hope left for next weekend. Here I'll stay and
there you will be in London. I am sorry for I should like to
have seen you. How absurd it is that even in times like
these one should go on saying only a tithe of what one
feels! But of course, my dear, we must remember propriety.

Miriam, there is one great service that you can render to
this country and to the world. Persuade everyone you meet
that we will and can fight not to the end but until we win.
Any thought of anything less than complete and final
victory is traitorous; and I hate to say it but women are
amongst the worst renegades because they can't bear to see
individual suffering and agony, and are inclined to think
that any sort of life is better than the agony of total war.

That is untrue, for to give one's life and one's happiness in a cause like this is to win for oneself in a future life which certainly awaits us all – even Hitler – such ecstasy as we in our wildest dreams wot not of.

I have been reading Auriel's 'Journey In Time' with very great pleasure. I wonder if you know it. Probably not. Philosophy and introspection have little feminine appeal.

Do you know and do you possess Robert Bridges' Anthology 'The Spirit of Man'? If not, may I give it to you please?

    Au revoir (the mark of the optimist)
        Fairly completely yours,
            John

FRENCH HOLD FIRM UNDER NEW ATTACK
THE TIMES Thursday 6 June 1940

Training Battalion
Welsh Guards
Roman Way Camp
Colchester
6th June

Dear Miriam,

This is just to remind you that if ever I get leave again you are going to dine and dance with me in London. Don't bother to answer this; it is written only because the Air Force are doing so wonderfully and the Army so poorly that I thought I had better attract attention somehow.

I hope you are standing the strain of success as gracefully as when I last observed you. I'm not going to add to the strain by telling you why I sometimes think of you.

Yours,
John

(However little)
(modest afterthought)

Somerville College
Oxford
8th June

Dear John,

This is just to tell you that I don't like me very much for
not having written to you long ago. That book you sent me
is good to have. Thank you for it. But it was unpleasant of
me not to write and I hope my humble apologies will be
accepted generously.

Oxford is in such a strange way, John. People are
working themselves blind tired over Examinations; they get
drunk, murder each other, sing, play, dance and cut their
own arteries in the bath . . . so messy! You should be very
glad not to be back this year; the Oxford you knew is dead
and gone.

Angel and I have decided to leave Oxford. We find we
must go and Serve Our Country, which sounds pompous
and romantic, but is, in fact, the truth. It's intolerable here,
with the very foundations of the University cracking, and
all the lovable people we know going away. Besides, I don't
personally know how I shall ever adjust myself to seeing
familiar names in the casualty lists complacently, and if one
is going to do good book work, one must have tranquillity
and a real eagerness. Study as a form of desperate escapism
is abominable and I don't think very worth while. So Angel
and I hope to do Government work until we can find
something rather more active and dangerous.

But still, Angel and I are making the most of our time
here. Curiously enough our work seems to get better and

better, which would seem impossible if you knew the way
we were going giddy giddy around. Angel flips off from
one thing to another enjoying everything wildly and
immensely till she comes back into College sleepy and
rather dreary. She is somewhat like a slightly intoxicated
may-fly trying to drag feathers from a peacock tail, but she
is a darling all the same. And I'm rather like a poplar leaf
turning and twisting in the wind, feeling a million new
things each day, but still rooted to my ancient belief in
understanding, generosity, beauty, love, and other such
impractical ideals.

John, I didn't mean to write to you this way at all. It must
be the effect of the hesitating thunder and an urgent desire
for sleep which will not come and swathe me in the land of
dreams. Oxford in thundery weather is disturbing. Things
look so metallic and yet they seem to be misted over so that
shapes and sounds become almost blurred. It's all very
confusing, or maybe it's only the after-effects of an essay on
Rabelais which are confusing. I don't know and anyway it
doesn't much matter.

I'm writing on my knees – hence the erratic
inscriptions – wondering if we should have another air-raid
warning tonight. Last night Somerville was given a
preliminary warning and we all had to tumble out of bed
and wait in pitch darkness. Women aren't very attractive in
the sudden night hours. Knotted up in hair curlers, dressed
in their silks, satins, clothes or rags, with pale faces washed
of powder and rouge they look strange enough. I would like
daughters, but I do hope the little gods allow them to look
soft-eyed and rumpled, and not bleak and bemused as most
of these women do. It makes me laugh, the way you men
are ensnared by powder and paints. You can only tolerate

an untidy woman when you love her so much that you will accept her in all ways. And defend yourself if you can, friend John, but don't tell me that it doesn't take you all some time to estimate whether this goodly apple woman is rotten to the core or not. An attractive woman has the most immense disadvantage – it's hard for her to tell whether a man is only enchanted by her looks or whether he really likes her for herself too. But this is bad: I seem to be getting acid, and your letters are always so bonny, blithe, good and gay. I think you had better write fairly soon, because I like your letters and I want one!

The thunder won't come but I think sleep will now I've written this sullen letter; next time I'll write gaily when the sun shines.

    Goodnight and blessings on you –
      Mirren

I've forgotten your rank so don't forget to tell me.

CRUCIAL STAGE IN BATTLE OF FRANCE
HEROIC RESISTANCE TO NEW GERMAN
ONSLAUGHT
THE TIMES Monday 10 June 1940

Training Battalion
Welsh Guards
Roman Way Camp
Colchester
10th June

Dear Miriam,

I like you for wanting to serve our country: I like you
even more for saying so in as many words. True, it sounds
pompous and romantic but there is the tragedy of our
generation – it has learnt to laugh at that sort of pomp and
romance. The pomp of the mightiest kingdom and empire
that has ever existed for the good of the world, the
romance of unselfish service in the cause of impractical
ideals: impractical only because we, or rather our fathers,
have set them so high that we cannot hope ever to attain
them. Since those days we have learnt to be modest in
estimating our national characteristics and to jeer at the
overweening pride in their nationality displayed by our
elders. We have also learnt to be modest in the estimation
of our saintliness and so we abandon to monks and nuns
and other professionals the more alpine of our ideals, and
are content to sit and dream within the footlands of our
spiritual strength.

The strength which our mothers and fathers gained, they acquired by trying their powers up to, and indeed beyond the breaking point – it was the strength of endeavour, not the weakness of attainment and we, smug little malcontents, seeing how often that endeavour failed, dubbed them wicked old men and awful hypocrites. We have forgotten what they knew: that we must work for happiness.

This I could almost forgive, for I'm such a hedonist myself, if only we had remembered what they also knew: that we play for pleasure. But we have got it all topsy turvy (and I could have said much worse than that) for instead of working for happiness as the ultimate goal and taking and tasting the full flavour of the world's playful pleasures, we work and strive to attain pleasure and so ruin the finesse and delicacy wherein alone its virtue lies, and moreover think that happiness – the ultimate reward of human virtue – will fall into our languid hands by a little playful titillation of some of our rather commonplace desires.

And now who was talking about bitterness? Your letter (which I loved and thank you) was flowing with milk and honey in comparison with this gall and wormwood that I am pouring out. It's partly the Italians, of course, for they have emphasised the senseless tragedy of the war. Against Germany it has a meaning and even romance: good against evil. But the Italians aren't evil, just misled and foolish, which is exactly what we have been for the last fifteen years, and yet they will suffer most terribly for it. I am very sad because it is not part of the necessary conflict in which I am proud to be sharing.

And so let's cleave fast to our impractical ideals of understanding, generosity, beauty, love; above all let's be

unafraid to admit and even preach them: God knows they
stand in sore enough need of a few faithful defenders in
deed rather than shamefaced word alone.

What a sermon! But that is why I liked your decision to
go down; apart from that it is a good thing because Oxford
is unbalanced and quickly going mad; their Ophelia will
soon be drowned. But how right you are to enjoy it while it
lasts: 'Gather ye rosebuds while ye may.' Both you and
Angel (to whom please remember me with kind words)
seem to have a positively American delight in living, which
at any rate shows a sense of appreciation and gratitude.

Somerville in an air-raid must be a weird sight indeed –
strange enough to female eyes who know the secrets of
woman off her guard: an absolute fantasy to masculine
imagination. And yet it is the sudden night hours that are
the touchstone of truth and beauty. What has been
discerned by human foresight can be prepared for by
human artifice. Art and artificiality are among the most
entrancing adjuncts to human pleasures: they are not either
truthful or beautiful. At best they are only the human, and
therefore material expression of their spiritual realities,
truth and beauty; at worst a vain albeit very human attempt
to conceal their absence. There are those people whom, if
their art is good, we highly estimate correctly, because –
except in the sudden night hours (I like that phrase) – we
never see the core of the goodly apple.

There is my excuse, dear Miriam, which, I admit, is self
accusation rather than self defence. The task of apple
tasting is sometimes too sharp for us, but I have a system;
for every mark you give at a party, give a hundred in a
crisis. Thus:

No. 2,249
Barford E.M. (I think) Miss (I hope)
Ball Room Beauty   90[†]
Air Raid Rumples   9000[†]

[†]Unverified Estimates

At the opposite extreme to the heartless harpies who
practice their deception upon us are the little children who
know no artifice; true because they know no deception,
beautiful because they know not ugliness. To them every
event is unforeseen, every substance a touchstone. They,
being sincere, shew to the world – and everyone and
everything is 'the world' to them – no kind of artifice, but
themselves simply, as the great god has made them, soft-
eyed and rumpled: your daughters. Artist, what a picture!
That is near too much for me whose heart has always
belonged to little girls: little girls before they know what it
means to be attractive, when they still talk of being
beautiful.

   The more attractive they become as they grow up, the
greater is their danger from us ham-fisted men. They look
for an idea and they find a stark reality, they look for
something fine and good and are greeted by gross
pusillanimity, they look for love and find eroticism and yet
if they can swallow that vomit they will have their reward,
for there is nobility in man although he knows not where it
lies. God made woman to regard first the end and then the
means and man to see the means before recognising the
end. Woman the idealist, man the materialist.

   To most men an attractive woman's looks are her entire
self: he does not see the self that you mean, not until much

later, not perhaps until too late when woman is disgusted
by his lechery. And so the world goes on: how wise god is!
for without this strange complexity, this paradox, this
unequal division of labour in the first and second instance,
the slightly sordid process of reproduction would not
continue, would be abolished by mutual consent. And so
the world goes on, because man and woman cannot agree.

This is quite the oddest letter I have ever written and if I
go on much longer I shall have to start calling it a treatise.
It was started as you can see from the date on the 10th of
June; it is now the 13th. It has been written in little bits and
pieces and in all sorts of moods – in the drunken evening
and the sober morning, at leisure and in haste, with a sad
heart and a gay one but always with pleasure. So even if it
bores you stiff, shocks you, just leaves you cold or does any
of the many unfortunate things I shall imagine it doing
once it is in the post, it still won't be entirely wasted
because it has been fun to write – my fun at your expense, I
know, but even that is better than no fun at all.

Leave is still not being given to the Training Bn. so that I
just can't say about the 22nd. I wish I could, but if you
would give me a few days' grace there is just a chance it
may be granted as we are expecting to move very soon.
Both our 1st and 2nd Battalion have been here, re-forming
after rather a nasty time in France. They have taken all our
men and many officers and once more I have been passed
over – I hate it and am doing my best to get out of this job
of mine which is entirely responsible for my not having
been in from the start. What really shames me is to see all
these men with wives, children, homes and a hundred
family responsibilities being risked in the battle before me
who am completely unattached, without ties, dependants or

responsibilities. It's not that I'm impatient – I'm just ashamed.

My rank is 2nd Lieutenant, an Ensign as it is called in the Brigade, but any rank below Captain is never used in one's civil life, so I'm just J.S. Lewes Esq. and bid fair to remain so for the term of my natural life, which, in spite of that most signal disadvantage, I would not change for any other, however promising.

Well, my little aspen leaf: I hope you flutter across my rather turgid path in the very near future. Whereunto shall I liken myself? I wish I could think myself the boisterous wind trying to carry you away from your ancient anchorage: I'm afraid the nearest I get to such a likeness is in my unrivalled production of hot air. You had already thanked me for the book when I promised to send it to you in Oxford so please go on liking yourself; you're all right really, I promise you.

Goodbye, Helen,
    Yours,
        Paris

BRISTOL CHANNEL AREA BOMBED
11 DEAD IN SCOTLAND
THE TIMES Tuesday 2 July 1940

50 Bryanston Court
George Street W.1.
2nd July

My dear John,

Your letters tickle my conscience – I'm so bad about
writing to you. But I do thank you for both your letters and
will answer them properly as soon as I stop being fevered
about shopping and train time-tables and other such
intricacies.

You know John, a lovely woman was Helen, but she was
bad, wild and bad. Her lips drew forth the soul of man, her
beauty launched those thousand white-sailed ships, and she
deceived man into believing she could bestow immortality
on him. She may not have been as bewitching as Cleopatra,
but she was wondrous and had supreme power in that she
could raise men to a mighty conception of love – or so some
think. Maybe she wasn't very bad, but her power was awe-
inspiring and such power is dangerous. All the same, I like
Helen, and when I next see you I will wear royal purple, the
colour she surely wore. But I'm not really Helen, nor you
Paris, for I don't belong to anyone, and thus cannot be swept
away on the strange wings of wind. I must be Penelope,
wondering and weaving – yet my husband is but imaginary.

But bother you, John, why do I ever write these letters to

you? I've only met you twice, and I'm quite sure the old-fashioned world would think this correspondence most improper!

And now I must go pack and return to an Oxford crowded with soldiers and women in slacks cheering sweets up the Corn and down the High.

Addio . . .
    Mirren

Officers Mess
Training Bn. Welsh Guards
Sandown Park
Esher, Surrey
Friday, 5th July

My dear Penelope,

I thought you were throwing a pretty shuttle last night – a fine piece of tapestry we wove (I say we because I can't help feeling I was the shuttle) and I only hope that you won't follow the classics too closely and undo it all in your secret chambers.

You told me carefully and very quietly last night exactly what your movements for the next month will be but I have forgotten, so please do write a tiny note and tell me again. I must see you at the very next opportunity. I shall press home the attack until I have penetrated the barrier of no-confidence; what the outcome of the subsequent infiltration will be I cannot tell except that it will be happy.

8 Tudor Court
Castle Way
Hanworth, Middlesex
6th July 1940

My dear Mirren,

I wanted to write to you on Friday while our pleasure was
still fresh to the touch; I tried just after lunch but it was
then that sleep came drawing through the garden of my
mind, and I had to drive her away with brandishing a
shovel on the miniature range I'm building. This morning I
read through what I then wrote; I had started, 'To Penelope
in Purple', and had made much play with your weaving,
your shuttle, which seemed to be we, and the web we wove
on Thursday, which I hoped you wouldn't unpick, since
besides being a loss in itself, that would delay Odysseus'
homecoming very considerably if he were to stick to the
classical time-table.

And then it seemed to me that I was making light of an
occasion of some gravity so I determined to start again in a
less hilarious mood. And here I am at home, certainly less
inclined to be merry at Thursday night, but also less
convinced that laughter is out of place. For after all what
have I, or rather we done that is so serious as that? I have
said I'm in love with you, but I knew that was going to
happen a year ago and you knew at our second meeting.
You have refused to let me kiss you on the strength of it,
but that will make a kiss from you all the sweeter when it
comes, and in any case I know kisses what they are worth, a
glass of good wine or a little sunshine on the river. I

wouldn't grow a horse's-mane moustache if I were
misguided enough to wish to specialise in osculation. Either
I'm no gentleman or else the song's all wrong, for a slap and
a tickle hold no satisfaction for me and are a very mild
statement when taken alone.

But I feel that there is one aspect of our joint experiences
on which I must bring a serious mind to bear for a moment
to the exclusion of my mistress' laughter. I have realised
that when a man knows his own mind as surely as, at least
in this case, I know mine, it will always be difficult to
convince anyone, and most of all a cultured woman, that
his decision is the result of deliberate choice and not
merely the dictation of desire. If after he has said, 'this will I
do', desire falls upon him with violence and says, 'this shalt
thou do a damn sight quicker', his sincerity will be even
more suspect and difficult to establish. And even if his calm
decision originally required speed in execution, yet the
upstart urge may so colour his methods as to make a more
conventional tempo absolutely essential to ultimate success.

The above is in the nature of a soliloquy which will
probably disturb you by its cold reasoning, but it's only
because I know what I want that I can bring my reason to
bear on the means to attaining it.

The golden rule of war is 'Don't drift into battle.' In my
war I have no intention of drifting with the wind or tide
into friendship, even into acquaintance, much less
friendship, or out to any deeper seas but will. I shall steer
my little ship by the star which the wise men followed with
all the finesse at my command. The star is faith in God &
what he and others have made of me; finesse is just reason
at its top. Together they raise man from brutality to the
likeness of divinity. That is why I am steering straight at

you; instinct tells me a good thing will come of it and I would rather do a good thing on purpose than by accident.

And now the question is when am I going to see you again. I would like you to come and stay a weekend here when you can. You would like our diminutive flat and humble life: here is no glamour and black velvet, sparkling wine or bowing servants. Just Mother and Father and much quietness. Do come; next weekend if you like, or the weekend after, or just for a day if your plans are made for too long ahead.

With love,

O Johnnie ♪ ♪ *

UNCEASING BLOWS BY R.A.F. AND NAVY
GERMAN SHIPYARDS AND
BASES BOMBED
THE TIMES Monday 8 July 1940

8 Tudor Court
Castle Way
Hanworth, Middex
Wed., 7th July 1940

Dearest Mirren,

It was a new experience talking so close to someone on
the telephone; it was like our dancing, it ran on with a
smooth easy motion of its own broken only by quick
spasms of realisation of the motive and harmonising power
behind and within it.

And so Somerville is reaching out a sinuous hand and
chilling your prophetic bones with misty premonitions. I
shall say at once, that is, before I forget my better self, that
I should grieve to underrate the value of discipline in our
lives, and yet the prospect of your devoting two whole
years of the life which has taken on for me more meaning
that I can grasp and understand simply deflates me, it is so
huge an abrogation to ask of so small a store of self-control
as in these matters I possess. I once boasted that when it is a
question of waiting upon events outside my control I have
the patience of an elephant – little did I think that the
impatience of desire could be equally elephantine. And yet

I refuse to swallow my words and would almost welcome the opportunity of putting myself to the test. It would certainly do me more good than anything else that could happen to me unless my weakness were to turn discipline into frustration. And that is what I am still afraid of for you. If you go to Somerville in spiritual revolt you can hardly help bringing frustration and with it moral deterioration upon yourself.

Whenever I look at this matter objectively, when I step outside myself and just observe, I realise with a horrid impersonal calm that the wisest and indeed the most daring course would be for you to return to Somerville, absolutely free of any sort of engagement or understanding either implicit or express with regard to me. No promise made, no gages either given or received, you a free agent, to enter as fully into the life to which you are to devote two precious years as that life indeed deserves: war or peace, hysteria or calm, Oxford still has more to give, and therefore more to be most lovingly preserved from danger, than almost any other institution in which the legacy of Britain is and will be for ever stored. While the light of reason and the warmth of wisdom have still a few moments to flicker before being swallowed up in the blanket of desire, let me propose this course to you as being that which we should adopt, we I say because I cannot now separate myself from your destiny until such time as you bid me go. Darling, are you willing to risk our jewel in this gamble? Are you willing at once to submit it to the severest test of absolute worth – two years of time – and to work and fashion for it a setting worthy of its brilliance – two years of the most civilised experience that world still has to offer? Are you equally willing to run the risk of the setting predominating the

jewel, subordinating it to such an extent that the rôles
become reversed and my little jewel-stone simply takes its
ordered place in the setting to something of even higher
value, the existence of which, I hasten to say, is
unimaginable to me now?

Are you willing? Or do you just not look at the matter
this way? Is it now or never for you? Right, let it be never.
Christ, how I shall regret saying that if I ever send it!

I have argued the diametrically opposite case in a letter
to you before, with perhaps an equal show of wisdom and
reason. I am not afraid to admit I was wrong but I am
terribly afraid that you will suspect an ulterior motive to
this persuasion of a kind with the one which inspired me to
advise its opposite in the first place. I wanted you to go
down because I thought that only by that expedient
could I ever hope to win you. I now want you to go up
because I believe that only by that means will I
succeed in winning your love as well as your desire and it is
your love I want, your *love* I want, none other and nothing
short of it.

John (with Jock about to attack me with all the fury of
his violent desire)

                    10 a.m. Train to Perth
                    11th July

'O Jonny, o Jonny' . . . and so sing two Canadians as they
play rummy opposite me. You won't like this letter of mine,
John, because I'm not going to answer your letter as easily
as I answered the one afore that. There is an immense

amount of what you said that I could analyse, criticise and argue about, but knowing you even briefly as I do, I guess there is no point in trying to show you where you are wrong. All I can do is to ask the Seventh Saint to show you wisdom; how else should you be taught that I'm not really as lovable as you think I am. Maybe one day you'll learn that, John; I hope you will because I hate to be like Helen and to enchant people with that curious power of deception she had. But I don't like writing this way about us – it makes me nervous.

I'd have answered your letter sooner, but it's been chasing me all over the countryside. For the last three weeks I seem to have done nothing but whisk from night-clubs and champagne to wild strawberries and sun warmth in Wiltshire. And now I'm on my way up to Perth in a dank train which should be lonesome if it weren't for a little boy of nine, opposite me. He and his burly mother have taken the place of the soldiers, and I like the little boy because he doesn't much mind if I go on scrawling to you while he talks to me. He has huge brown eyes and has spilt purple ink in his eye and he looks fascinating.

These two bits of paper smell like a train and I don't like it at all at all. You needn't bother to read them, because as far as I can make out, most of what I wrote was nonsensical. And now I'm at home and feel rather like a parlour maid with two free hours between lunch and tea. I arrived up here to find that Mummy had thrown a heart attack an hour before I came. She didn't recognise anyone and talked rubbish, and since then I feel like murder. Maybe, if I can hate like the damned and be as bitter and as unforgiving as a child of the fiend himself.

Whether I thought you loved me or not I wouldn't

have kissed you, John. Unlike most young women of my
age, I take kissing seriously, perhaps too seriously.
Kissing, as a result of a mutual desire to do so, is lovely.
Kissing for the sake of it is nauseating; a kiss in sheer fun
is delightful. But surely you realise that if I had let you
kiss me that evening the whole thing would have been
shabby and unpleasant. I won't kiss people if I'm sorry for
them because that's cheating them; I won't kiss a man
who is serious about me, and I not about him, because
that would be an unpleasant sensation for me and I'd get
nervous and feel cheap. Besides, it frightens me to be
kissed against my will and you'd not have wanted that
either. Men can send me into a panic when they are
nearer to me than I want them, and that's a fear I've learnt
to control but not to destroy. Do the fears that have
walked by my side for exactly ten years make you smile,
friend John?

I shall go South again in two or three weeks time. Then I
hope that I might be able to visit your parents for a
weekend because I like them. Anyway, I'll let you know
when I am going to London again.

I think you know Alan Tysen, a Trinity rowing man – or
he knows you. I know him fairly well and like him; and it
seems he has put in a few good words for you. Do you
mind if various people come and challenge you for a duel,
because by now, all Oxford knows that I am acquainted
with a handsome Guardsman. Sometimes I wonder if a
woman is only a butterfly wavering amongst a multitude of
clutching hands, or whether she really may be considered
as an independent, individual creation of the good God.
They say that women are possessive, more possessive than
men, but I wonder, indeed I wonder.

This is a tiresome letter, dear John, so you had better write to me instead, and soon, for one is very stranded up here.

Blessings,
Mirren

Officers Mess
Training Bn. Welsh Guards
Sandown Park
Esher, Surrey
Tuesday [*16th July 1940*]

Dear Mirren,

I have been trying to write since I had your letter, but words will not come.

I am distressed at the news of your mother's illness and your own state of mind when you wrote, but both will pass. And I write now simply to assure you of my affection and desire that you would be happy, or at least amused, and not content to be opaque and dulled. I still believe in faith that we acquire more merit on this earth in doing gladly those tasks set us which are least attractive than by any amount of enjoyable labour. This, however, is cold comfort: how I wish I could bring something warmer than philosophical platitudes!

I shall write you a letter very soon: this scrap is sent because very soon is not soon enough.

Bless you,
Jock

Nether Pitcaithly
Bridge-of-Earn
Perthshire
Scotland
17th July 1940

Dear John,

I've written to nearly everyone I know at all, and now it seems to be your turn again. Did my last letter make you feel all prickly and cross and restless? I hope it didn't, but I guess that if I'd had one like that I should have been fretted enough. You know, I haven't spurned you or any such thing, but you don't know me and my ideas very well yet, and I thought it would be wise if you begin to get acquainted with some of those things.

O Jonny, if you only knew how it was raining and raining, if you only knew how this melancholy jazz music throbbed through the room you might know too that I so much want to be anywhere but here. You couldn't guess how I disapprove of flattering mankind, but I do approve of being honest. Thinking back on it, I don't know when I've ever danced as easily, carelessly and happily as I did that evening with you.

I've just been getting tea and now I'm listening to Vic Oliver on the wireless – he really is the most preposterous man. And soon I must go look at a chicken and wonder how to cook it. I've fixed up a beautiful hors d'oeuvres, but I'm not quite sure how to make the chicken taste beautiful too. I like chicken breast with cream and pimento, but I couldn't make this horrid raw creature taste that way.

I spent a night with a darling friend of mine who was married about a year ago. She and Betty are staying in a farmhouse near to their husbands' camps and they are the four happiest people I've ever seen. Bill and John are only allowed to go home one night a week, but mostly they can have all their meals at the farmhouse. We sat in that dusty room watching July's night sky which never goes really dark in Scotland. And John, till then, I've never been so wholly aware of the complete unity between two people who love each other. Joan and Betty are both going to have babies in seven months' time, and the knowledge of that and the complete silence, was one of the most overwhelming things one could feel. I don't know whether it was sentimentality, but it almost seemed sacrilege to be in the same room. From time to time they became aware of me curled up in the arm-chair, and it was dreadful disturbing the peace of that dark room. Now I understand why a person is never at peace within himself when the other they love is not there. To obtain that rare thing peace, one must not yearn nor desire, not demand anything nor indeed be conscious of anything except the supreme fulfilment of those hidden yearnings.

I'm glad I understand a little of the way they must feel, or perhaps I should say that I'm glad I've been conscious of this their peace. Bother, I always manage to write something private to you, which I'm not at all sure that I want you to know of, anyhow. But still, I guess I could control my pen enough to write you a charming, formal letter if I really wanted to. It seems though I didn't want that, and besides you never let me feel shy about what either you or I say, and that is good. I must have started writing to you about babies and peace, because I was thinking of chicken, and when I had supper with those four, we had a hectic time trying to cook their chicken.

I enjoy writing letters too. Just now, you are welcome to criticise them all you wish, but I warn you that one day I may get a spasm of nervousness and henceforth my letters will be dreary and my words will sound like the taste of dust.

Write when you will, John, because I like your letters.
Blessings on you,
Mirren

NATION'S FOOD
NO FEAR OF SHORTAGES
HOPE OF MORE TEA AND SUGAR
THE TIMES Friday 19 July 1940

Esher
Friday, 19th July

Dear Mirren,

This is written in my smelly office (it's next to the cookhouse) on horrid government paper which ought to be in rolls, not sheets, and in houses which should be devoted to the work of national importance (yes yes). It is so written in order that I shall reach you as quickly as may be and tell you that your letter was a delicious surprise. I'm afraid I carried my last letter to you in one of my pockets for a day after writing it; you did not get it, therefore, when I intended that you should. Perhaps that is a good thing, because then you might not have written when and as you did.

Your other letter chastened me but did not nettle. What sting it carried was salutary and most thoroughly deserved, for I made a false step that evening which was as bad in taste as it was in policy. I didn't mind your gentle rebuff to my quite understandable advances – on the contrary I like you the better for it – but it was my reply that was unworthy. Still, even the surest foot slips at times, and I can harbour no regrets for any part of that evening, no, not even for me at my most puerile: I'm glad you've seen it, because you won't get another chance if I can help it and, oddly enough, I want you to see me as I am (as no doubt you do) and not as I play up to you; but I think you will admit that the play is fun. It is different from the peace which you describe. It is full of unrest, sinuous desire, artifice, control, abandon, careful thought and sudden impulse, action and reaction.

It is no far-fetched metaphor, to say that you have only known me at war. At our first meeting I had all my armour on and my weapons to hand; since then I have been waging war on your affections. At first it was simply waiting for the opportunity, which I knew would come, to declare war; then I tried to develop a Blitzkrieg, but my Fifth Column let me down. There was no capitulation, not even a break through, and so what? What now? A Sitzkrieg? A war of frightfulness? A Peace Offensive? I will threaten them all, invasion included, and perhaps try them all, and then one day, if I succeed, the play will fade before your eyes and there will stand someone whom you hardly recognise: I hope you will like the change.

(Now I'm in my dressing gown in the wee little room I have been given for a billet by my maiden lady hostess; and now I'm out of my dressing gown, for I found it over warm, and in my baby-blue pyjamas, you know the ones with royal blue facings. But no, of course you don't know – must have been two other people.)

Damn! now my flippant interpolation has bereft this letter of the last vestige of coherence

And now I leave you, to meet again shortly, God willing,
    and bless you
        John

KRUPPS WORKS RAIDED BY R.A.F.

THE TIMES Saturday 20 July 1940

Nether Pitcaithly
Bridge-of-Earn
Perthshire
20th July 1940

If I go on writing to you like this, Jock dear, soon I shall
have little more to say. I was glad when I fetched your letter
from the post office yesterday.

I want to see you again for I don't know you well
enough and that is disconcerting, especially as you are so
purposeful and deliberate. But misfortune has befallen us
and I can't get south on the 25th as I had planned. It's all
too complicated to explain in a letter, but with one hand
I'm more or less holding my mother's and with the other I'm
fluffing up soap suds. The family have decided to go back
to Oxford a week later than they had originally planned,
and they don't want me to be alone in the Oxford house.
Besides, they've discovered I can be some use in the house if
I want to be, and I don't like to leave Mummy with too
much on her hands. So please, if your parents can have me,
may I come the weekend after the one I suggested? I'm
sorry to be so tiresome, but it's difficult to organise things
otherwise.

Will you give me some good advice, Jock? You well
know that I left Somerville because I thought it selfish to
stay on. I've been looking around for a job to do, but the

openings in the Air Ministry, Chatham House, the War and Foreign Office are now non-existent. The family doesn't want me to join the WAAFs nor indeed any of the women's services, because then I should have to sign on for duration unless I got married. They very much want me to go back to Somerville, and though I see reason to their arguments, the whole plan seems intolerable. They think that I ought to go back while there is any money at all left, so that I can train my mind and get the degree which will help me get a job when war is over. They say that if I married a poor husband, if I had a degree then I could go get a job as well. But Jock, I'd stay at home under such probable circumstances, and look after my own babies and my own house, rather than get a job and pay servants. I'm old-fashioned enough to believe that a woman can't satisfactorily have young children and a house as well as a job at the same time. Moreover, I think it's morally wrong to go back to Somerville. I don't want to go because it's a luxury these days; besides, I don't believe that the individual is as important as all that, at the present moment, unless he or she is doing specialised work or indeed training for it.

And yet there is wisdom in what the grown-ups say. When war is over there surely will be use for people with trained minds, for people with degrees. Then the necessity for the reconstruction of sanity will be as urgent as the need for the destruction of insanity of today. A job, with the qualifications of a degree might be an immense advantage – I may well never marry, be left a widow, or indeed, even if I were married, maybe there wouldn't be enough shining silver for children anyway. O yes, they are wise and cautious and reasonable and from the theoretical point of view, I agree with them entirely. And yet it's hard for the young to look ahead as much as all that. Harder still the idea of thinking of books alone for two years, for if one did not do that, all sorts of feverish and curious thoughts would surge up and disturb steady and worth-while study. Of that, at least, I am certain. And Jock, I want to join the WAAFs. The discipline may be hateful, the work tedious and the idea of being in the Service for duration disconcerting. Yet the more I learn of men, and the way men go through with war, the more assured do I become that women should and indeed could withstand these comparatively trivial difficulties.

Please tell me what you think about it, because your ideas are important.

I wonder why you found it difficult to write. Will you tell me?

Goodbye for a little while, and blessings,
    Mirren

Officers Mess
Training Bn. Welsh Guards
Sandown Park
Esher, Surrey
Sunday, 21st July 1940

If you go on writing to me like this, dear Mirren, I shall soon have so much to say to you that, failing your speedy return to London, a journey to Perth would be the only way of getting it all and adequately said.

I must occasionally write better letters than I think. To bring you to a moment of contentment was the utmost I had hoped for from that unstudied note of mine. Even then I thought I was flattering myself.

Of course it will be all right about next weekend and the one after. Come then, or whensoever it arranges itself, as it assuredly will. I have the patience of an elephant when it comes to waiting upon events outside my control.

It must be extremely disconcerting to have a stranger courting your affection quite so openly and unashamedly as I am and I think in the circumstances your only course is to get to know me better and find out what it is all about. Of course our grandmothers would not have been quite so disconcerted; they reckoned they knew what it was all about and would have replied quite simply: 'Oh, Mr Lewes, how you do run on!' We have learnt to be a little more generous with ourselves, to give a little of our private thoughts even to a comparative stranger, without feeling that a proposal of marriage must inevitably follow.

And now Miriam, my love, you do me the honour of asking my advice. Here it is, but you must judge whether it is good. Don't go back to Oxford unless you intend to put your best into your work. Here are your own words quoted from memory 'Study as a form of desperate escapism is intolerable.' I hope, therefore, that you will not decide to put your best into book learning; you would be doing your spirit violence, your heart would not be in it, you would be escaping from your destiny which, as I see it, lies elsewhere, though certainly along no smoother road. If you follow that road you will not need a degree, and in following that road you will help your country best.

It is a modern affectation among women to act as though

they had no intention of ever getting married, to try and
carve out a career for themselves in competition with men
instead of in co-operation with them. The old system was
good: the man shall earn enough for two and for children
when they come, the woman shall build and beautify the
house. That which menaces it is bad: each earns enough for
one. If two wish to marry they still have enough for two but
no home is built and children can't help being an
encumbrance. Here are the seeds of sterility for they are
sown in selfishness, the unwillingness to sacrifice
independence. Husband and wife may be devoted to each
other but unless they are jointly devoted to something
greater than their two selves their union is sterile.

Even if you accept what I have written, the question still
remains, 'What to do now?' Sit and twiddle your thumbs
until someone who repels you comes and with fine words
says, 'will you marry me,' and you in a moment of
desperation or misguided devotion say 'yes'? Of course
what you must try to do is to find the finest work of which
you are capable. If, however, nothing approaching that
standard is offered, then take the best thing that is.
Washing eggy plates with the WAAFs would only be
unworthy if you can do something which required your
own special qualifications and not just a coarse sense of
touch and a willingness to work. Having to sign on for the
duration means a tremendous sacrifice of independence but
it still leaves open what I believe to be your true vocation –
marriage.

To that you reply 'I may well never marry.' Then I don't
know you. 'I may be left a widow.' And so may every woman
who marries either in war or peace. This risk, together with
that of insufficient money, are risks that have to be borne by

someone in these days if our race is to survive. Are you unwilling? Oxford, and indeed the WAAFs for the duration would be a smoother road than yours with such a burden of risk, but which is the finer and more worthy?

Again I have been sending you cold comfort, but I would delight in the opportunity to be of more practical assistance.

Yes, I will tell you why I found it difficult to write you before, but you must remember when you read it that you asked to know and that I should not otherwise have written it.

Because your letter written in the train and its continuation at your home made me want to do something to help you stop feeling like murder – it was horrid hearing you say that though I'm glad you can – and yet when I put pen to paper I could do nothing but rant and rave about my own tempestuous desires, and say things about the shape and colour and feel of your body which could only have infuriated you.

A bientôt,
Jock

Bryanston Court
7th August 1940

When I went to bed last night I couldn't sleep at once, for I was trying to remember some lines of poetry. Even now I don't recollect them properly, but I think

The night rolled out like velvet, as we drove from inn to
   inn
We drank a little purple wine, we drank a little gin –
I leant my sight 'gainst yours, and saw what lay within.

Take a chance on a trance; your dancing girl's a fool –

Listen to the moan and groan of the saxophone,
Night was not made for those who have to be alone,
Night was made to keep the flesh from remembering the
   bone.

No, I don't remember it accurately, but I was so possessed
by the chance on a dancing girl's trance that I nearly
jumped up and wrote you a fevered letter. But I'm glad I
didn't, because the velvet night, a little gin and the moan
and the groan were too important just then.

But it's so different this morning – no glamour, no face of
yours in the half darkness, and no overwhelming feeling of
urgency and need. Assuredly I couldn't help but write
steadily and restfully this morning. The air is so heavy and
opaque; the whole atmosphere is so breathless and still.
This must be the kind of warmth which presses on and
rounds off the smoothness of peaches and grapes; it blunts
the dome of the peas and folds itself round the flowers so
the petals can't drift from the blooms. A curious kind of
day, but the right kind of day to be born from those drier
hours of the early morning.

Because everything is so motionless and even the blood
bemused, I can write to you now, the way I couldn't speak
to you yesterday. After last night your idea of me is sure to
have changed a good deal – you may think I am a wanton

wench or a wise child. But Jock dear, you are wise; you must have sensed ages ago that I was acquainted with the powers of physical proximity. From the movement of your hands I knew very well that they had moved in such a way before. Of that I am so glad; it's the way it should be. I'm so utterly sure that being with you last night was good and right that what you think of me now doesn't matter. I don't mind if you think I'm 'easy', too urgent, lacking in modesty. I know that you did something so immense for me, that all your disdain, bitterness or regret couldn't ever alter its importance.

You have just rung up and I can't possibly write seriously now. Darling, I don't know that you had ever better ring up again because it puts me into such a fever of impatience – it's dreadful. Aunty Esmé came into the room just as your father came downstairs and looked at me rather quizzically as I rang off. She even had the temerity to ask whether we were engaged or not. And I used to think that I could have secret thoughts and not let people guess about what I was thinking – well, well fancy that. But I was very vague and casual and said anyway I couldn't get married for two years on account of Somerville, and that by such a time you'd probably have grown out of the habit of wanting us to be together. One thing is that even if this is only a béguine, I know that I shall be able to go back to the George,* look at our table and be so glad that once, in our eager youth, we there ate crêpe suzette. Yet I don't know that I shall be very good about going back to the 400 Club – that does belong rather privately to us. Maybe when I'm older and wiser I shall be able to go back and smile there a little acidly. But

*The George Hotel in Oxford.

maybe the only time I shall go back there will be with you anyway, because I think I rather want us to be married. Yet I'm not accepting the highly unromantic proposal ventured in a prickly field with the chorus of winged creatures adding to the glamour of the situation – not just yet.

The disappointing thing is that we'd have to have a concrete covering for the wedding cake instead of icing, and I did not want to cut a beautiful cake with your sword. Instead I'll have to shoot through the plaster of Paris with your pistol and that will be so noisy and smelly. May I have bridesmaids or must I be married in a stark frock with no veil and train at all, at all? Darling, the peas in the kitchen want me to attend to them so I must stop writing such nonsense because I'm not going to get engaged to you yet anyway.

Blessings, and with them some kind o' love which I don't understand,
   Mirren

Officers Mess, Training Bn.
Epsom Race Course
Thursday
[Probably 8th August]

Dear Mirren,

I'm feeling like a tramp. I know I look like a tramp because I have just been told so, and I expect I smell like one only my best friend won't tell me. This is the first of the trials of the knight errant in search of his fortune and a lovely maiden. He has not yet left his father's kingdom but the hospitality of one of his vassals compares ill with the sumptuous life he has just left. I have been troubled all day by the letter I sent you: not that I think what I said was regrettable; just ill expressed, that's all.

This town in full of Canadians. They are ill-behaved and drink too much which is a pity, for they are good soldiers. I am glad you said you didn't want me to be always a soldier because sometimes I feel I ought to be, and then I think I might become a great soldier and lose all my capacity for happiness. What great military genius that you can think of could you say possessed a happy nature? The expression on the face of Napoleon and Hitler is enough to tell us about them. The Romans were essentially soldiers: few of them were happy though many were pleased. Hindenburg, Foche, Kitchener, Gordon all betrayed the pain of their profession in their eyes and the set of their mouths.

I am tired tonight and I can't help my mind dropping its subject like a sleepy child's toy and listlessly picking up another. I still want to know what you recognised as happening last night. You nearly told me then and perhaps you have done since, but I shall not get your letter till tomorrow afternoon when I go home. I shall go to bed and hope to dream the answer. Did you visit Stephen?* Did he guess, darling? Did he see two children playing in the sun, two serious faces searching for the truth, two sentimental drunkards, two pennies and two slot machines, some chewing gum, a glass of wine, a game of chess, a butterfly

*Stephen Foster, a London clairvoyant.

and grasping hands, an aspen leaf and a strange strong wind? What was his vision of the present? I care not what he prophesied.

Goodnight.

BRITISH FIGHTERS MISSING
53 RAIDERS SHOT DOWN IN CHANNEL
THE TIMES Friday 9 August 1940

---

8 Tudor Court
Castle Way
Hanworth
Middlesex.
[undated – probably Friday, 9th August 1940]

This is Friday and I have just been talking through the
partition to a shapely comely colourful voice all warm with
awareness and proximity. *L'amour, c'est le contact de deux âmes et
deux peaux.* That was told me by the red-headed girl in
Berlin. Our souls touched all night, but, because they were
going in opposite directions, only for so long as it took
them to bounce off again.

She taught me much wisdom and not a little knowledge
and I am truly grateful to her. I deeply regretted my callous
remark about her the other evening and I ask her
forgiveness from you. I was cruel and bitter because it was I
who wronged her when the end came: it is ever the wrong
doer who bears the malice.

Has my idea of you changed after the night? Assuredly,
but the way you think? Your second thoughts were best, O
Queen, O shrine of beauty. Ages ago I sensed, yes sensed
indeed that you were acquainted with the powers of
physical proximity. To be more precise, on the evening of
4th August a year ago I had my hand tentatively on the soft

skin of your arm and underneath I felt a muscle tighten.
That told me nothing then, except perhaps that you
wouldn't get up and leave the theatre if I took your hand,
but because I remembered it I have known you better and
found you ten times more attractive. Thereafter you gave
me nothing, almost less than nothing. I was thrown into a
panic of fear at moments when I thought of you as
altogether beyond my sordid reach, and shrinking in
disgust from the hairy paw should it ever stretch so high.
You a wanton wench? Not yet my darling, but I have high
hopes for you. Don't marry me if you are afraid of being
wanton. A nice child? Well, who isn't? (you probably) or do
I judge the whole world by myself? I have had twenty years
of practice, before even I knew what it meant or where in
my body that stinging thrill came from. I could produce the
food and drink of passion, the ecstasy of love. You will
wonder how I can say this so shamelessly. It is not
shameless, but neither is it shameful. I have fought a
thousand battles against this thing which was more of my
doing. I have lost them all, right up to the end which is
now in sight, which now is, when that which was called a
perversion becomes an act of devotion.

That, my darling, is how my idea of you has changed.
You have saved me and cleansed me and freed me from
something more than fear. You release all the strength and
power of will that have been immobilised in this internal
conflict for concentration on the task in hand. And now,
Mirren, if what I have said upsets you with its groupist
confessionalism, you are still enough of a friend to put it
aside without comment. Accept it for the tremendous
compliment that it is and reject the rest from your memory.
I write this only because I am convinced beyond the reach

of reason or human persuasion of the inevitability of our union and the unbounded horizon which it will open to us. We have the chance to rank with the world's greatest lovers, with Romeo & Juliet, though perhaps they are great only because they loved but did not live. We shall live and love and the world shall be better for our stay. Our love shall fashion our lives, and our lives shall build a home and our home a world. Many are called by the god of love but few are chosen; we shall be among the chosen in Elysium, God willing. Whatever we touch will be hallowed for us and for those who see us. Our table at the George, the 400, Freda's home and the river – we give the world a meaning as we go.

Darling, your letter was wonderful. I think I rather want to be married. Yet I'm not accepting the highly romantic proposal ventured in a prickly field with the chorus of winged creatures adding to the glamour of the situation. That thrills me with pleasure. So it does. Instead I'll have to shoot through the plaster of Paris with your pistol. Yes darling, please have lots of bridesmaids, most beautifully dressed. Your own gown must be Spanish in inspiration, with lace and fine needlework. Yes, we shall need a lot of money, so perhaps you had better not go and get engaged to me yet anyway.

Shall I ring you up when I arrive in Oxford, at about 6 o'clock? I don't know how you are going to get this letter before you see me again, but love will find a way.

Your love makes mine,
Jock

ITALIAN THREAT TO EGYPT
MECHANIZED FORCES MASSED
THE DESERT RAMPART
THE TIMES Saturday 10 August 1940

Saturday, 10th August 1940

Goodness I'm clean – I've just had the most delicious bath – and now I'm sitting on my bed saying words to you which you will hear on Monday. That will be fun, I won't say anything about it when I see you and I shall be able to talk to you after I have gone and say that I love you still, whatever had gone between, love you mightily whatever you may have thought of my last letter, of me at our seventh meeting and our words and ways there.

I have been looking at the moon tonight – so have you. I have just looked again and seen its waxing shape through the filigree of a great chestnut tree. It's a magic night – God grant such a one for No. 7 Joy Street. The number seven pursues me. Today is the seventh anniversary of my leaving school, not that the particular event is of importance, but they say one's whole body changes in its entirety every seven years. I have served my apprenticeship to freedom. Soon I shall have known England for just seven years – as a guest. Soon I shall be one score and seven years in age, just seven years less thirteen days older than Penelope, high priestess of my cult and my devotions. But tonight holds something deeper than I see, something Egyptian, ancient, exotic and inevitable. I see no Penelope, modest and industrious. I see Cleopatra and slaves and the infinite grace of studied movement in their gold-brown bodies with lovely ankles and knees and shoulders and wrists.

When you read this the safety curtain of absence will have fallen between us again. But no partition can be of more than paper breadth while you write with your present brilliance and read with the eye of charity. Our separation is no more formidable than paper. It is a filter which rejects all that we most desire and passes on clear and clean all that we shall value most. We are children and must be disciplined and schooled, and beaten when we are horrid. We have got to start growing up all over again: we don't know how to behave in Joy Street, few people do because they think that they know already; they either think that the rules are the same as in the rest of the roads, or else that there are no rules at all.

We are two charming children; before us stretches youth, maturity and age: it will be our fault if they are not full of beauty, full of love and full of grace and understanding. If we believe that, fate cannot harm us, just as fate cannot harm a child except through the media of grown-ups. We shall never grow up in Joy Street and no grown-ups will be allowed in, so we shall be safe. When we go visiting other streets we shall be so grown-up that people will think we are positively platonic.

Darling,
   Goodnight.

GERMAN AIRCRAFT DESTROYED
ATTACKS ON WEYMOUTH
AND PORTLAND
THE TIMES Monday 12 August 1940

Written at Epsom
Monday, 12th August 1940

Mirren darling,

This is a bad beginning to our chaste absence, to my
experiment in belief and to yours in biology. This bitter-
sweet breathless relationship cannot continue indefinitely –
I shall have to mean something different by Mirren darling
if we are to make a success of it.

My parting from you was more than faintly ridiculous,
such a courtly gesture with such a visible accompaniment.
Perhaps it was an act of God, a finger post to the way, for
we can't possibly take each other as seriously as I meant
'Mirren darling' for two years: that would be ineffably
boring after the first couple of months. But I at least can
and will be serious about the memories which seven brief
meetings have left to me, though I shall do my best not to
live too much in the past. In moments of idleness and
repose only shall I tell over the places to myself, the
venture in a prickly field, the romantic passage of a
window, the 400, the river oh so warm, 24, 14 and two
specially mellow and sincere recollections – a staircase in

the year 50 B.C.* and dear Freda's dear garden. (You were right about the calligraphy of Freda, I had just misremembered.)

Goodnight and bless you,
     friend of seven seekings
to whom this is sent with the memory
     of love.
          Johnathan

14 Merton Street
Oxford
Monday, 12th August 1940

Blessings on your way, Jock darling, and thank you for making me happy while you were here. Tomorrow I shall go and buy an immense quantity of books, because otherwise I shall get so restless. Indeed I shall go now, talk busily, and then come home to sleep soon. I think I could almost tolerate your toenails this evening.

Be good and happy, Ulysses –
     Penelope

*Probably a reference to 50 Bryanston Court.

TRAINING WITH 8 COMMANDO

Lewes was an early volunteer for what was initially known as the Guards Commando. The principle of Commando work was still new and revolved around the classic use of boats to approach coastlines in secrecy, followed by lightning raids against enemy defensive installations before withdrawing through a predetermined position back to the boats. Lewes may not have known it at the time but 8 Commando — as it was to become — was earmarked to spearhead the main assault force in the capture of the island of Rhodes and most of the training was geared towards this.

In October 1940, the unit moved up to Scotland to begin a much more physical series of manoeuvres. Lewes revelled in this move closer to action. As October passed and then November with no hint of a departure date, Lewes began to question his presence in the Commando. He wanted action but all he was getting was training — training in the mountains, at sea, and sometimes a return to the lecture room. Had he remained with his original unit he felt that he would have seen action long ago.

The Guards Commando became 8 Commando, which became part of the Special Service Battalion, but it was not until February 1941 that Lewes' unit became part of Layforce, and set sail for the Middle East and the sound of guns.

BIG R.A.F. RAID IN ITALY
MILAN AND TURIN BOMBED
THE TIMES Thursday 15 August 1940

8th Commando
c/o Army Post Office
15th August 1940

Soon I am going to succumb to the temptation of ringing you up. It will be fun falling, but hell getting up again. Until I do I shall continue to exult in a growing sense of release from myself. It has been a strange experience, this awakening to the realisation that your presence simply hurls me down the precipice of self-absorption. The nearer you are the less account I take of you or your feelings, while the remainder of the world becomes as good as non-existent. Instead of delighting in your conversation, I wish simply to make you the passive record of my murky past and my obstinate opinion. I would have you understand me, admire me in spite of myself with an undignified, slave-like admiration, admit the superiority of my beliefs, however hypocritical, and rest the full weight of your soul's responsibility, for which I seem to care nothing, so be it. I enjoy the sense of personal power it brings upon my imperfect knowledge and appreciation of the world.

I say smugly that I believe in belief in the churlish hope that I shall by this subterfuge gain your verdict without having to submit all the facts to full investigation. If I honestly and without reserve believed in belief and also

sincerely held the conviction that our marriage is certain,
how could I possibly have failed to take you at your word
and marry you tomorrow. That was a touchstone of my
good faith, which shows in you a genius which perhaps you
don't suspect, and in me craven confidence in a self which,
as long at least as I remain under the spell of my own
importance induced by your presence enjoys the divine
right of kings.

As I slowly shake off the effects of this spell I find myself
liking you more and more as Mirren and decidedly less as
the mirror of myself which my conceit desired. Your
generous spirit which will do things in a big way or not at
all, your independence which forbids you to subscribe to a
view or belief which has not satisfied your own instinct or
your own reason, the sincerity which makes you so open-
hearted and open-handed, the taste whereby you embellish
with more art than artifice, all these appeal with growing
strength to the awakening John, though they do not please
the stupid Jock so well. He, mean spirit, wants a monopoly
of generosity, independence, sincerity and good taste.
Others, and particularly you whom he has singled out as
the clay in which he shall model himself and not, as is more
appropriate, the pattern to which he shall work, you should
desire these things in order that you shall admire him in the
possession of them, whence it follows that in order to
admire him as he desires – the word perhaps is envy – you
may not yourself possess the coveted attributes.

Mirren darling, Jock has been trying to work a
confidence trick, trust honest John who has neither the
confidence nor the trickery to do it. John may be dull but at
least he is trustworthy and clings to the vestiges of chivalry.
Jock, when he fails to excite, as in the end he inevitably

must if not at the beginning, is gross simply.

Jock says I am convinced beyond the reach of human reason or persuasion of the inevitability of our vision. John has hardly dared broach the subject yet, he just longs for a shared conviction that it would be wrong not to marry. He has no desire to make a show of borrowed confidence which must be repaid later by forced loan, a spiritual bondage, unless the gamble succeeds.

Tomorrow is the anniversary of a wedding, 18th August 1911; 29 years ago mother and father were married. I sent them a pair of chickens and a knuckle of ham from Fortnum and Masons as a little thank offering for that day. They will give it all away, of course, but if they didn't I would know they did not value it. They have the true generosity which gives only that which is valued and despises the gift of no worth to the giver however gladly received. That is just exchange, good riddance to bad rubbish.

Our letters will not be subject to censorship here but it is impossible for me to give you detailed news of my doings in case the letter were to go astray. Suffice it so say that we arrived here today and intend to spend till Sunday settling in. On Monday training begins in real earnest and I expect will be very exacting. I hope so; I hate to feel my body so full of strength and endurance, at the height of its powers, yet remaining unused and untried.

A man is talking in his sleep in the next bunk. He sounds so deliciously sleepy that I fear aural hypnosis will overtake me before I can say goodnight darling Mirren whom I like.

Jock

8th Commando
c/o Army Post Office
16th August 1940

Dear Mirren,

I have just finished a long letter to mother & father. Just
as I was about to say goodbye, it turned suddenly serious
and ran on for another four pages. It was the most
spontaneous thing that has ever happened to me. It is a
terrible letter: it lays bare the full horror of my finances, my
birthright squandered on a mess of pottage, my future
secured only by the body and mind which I have received
from my parents. It must be quite shattering to father
whose ideas on money and saving are higher than this
selfish brat can aspire to. He and I live in different worlds as
regards the saving of money, though we are unexpectedly
agreed on the question of spending.

But I have not altogether abandoned the struggle to set
up for myself my father's ideal; the letter that I have just
written proves it and though I make no good resolutions
nor promises, yet I am more resolved and committed to the
first steps in the building of my own fortune than if I had
taken a thousand vows and signed away my soul to the
devil.

I am terribly lucky to have escaped from the Training
Battalion to this. A pretty hard-bitten lot are my new
associates. Some are young, but not much younger than I,
the rest are old and tough and 'interesting'. That is a
peculiarly Teutonic expression: *ein sehr interessanter Mensch*,
and it's high praise too from a German. The difference

between that and the French method of expressing approval of a man is enlightening: *voilà une intelligence!* And the English? They are just fatuous and quite meaningless: a jolly good chap! charming man!

We are three extraordinarily interesting nations; the Germans represent experience, the French intelligence and we humanity. These are terribly sweeping generalisations, but they pretend to truth only in so far as they catch for a moment a certain effect of light on the character of the nations. In the most general terms there is truth in the statements that the Germans are a nation of empiricists, the French intellectualists, and the English humanists or else just plain unromantic utilitarians. Of the three I think the German character is most difficult to fix because it is the least formed. That nation is still growing, indeed it has hardly started in comparison with the French and ourselves, and so it exhibits the greatest paradoxes and contradictions. Germany, the birthplace of protestantism, almost the cradle of freedom, is now the shrine of what may be termed prostratism. But it will grow out of this youthful paganism and become a great nation, perhaps the greatest the world has yet seen, provided that it finds an ideal greater than the magnification of human reason and efficiency. Germans have other ideals besides these, but they betray the youth of the nation more surely than the rest. Their conception of love is sentimental, they worship success and despise failure like any schoolboy, so that true sympathy and understanding are almost unknown as ideals, and their beauty is the beauty of power, or else its corollary, rest and contentment, for rest comes only to the strong in this world, who don't need it, and success to the successful, who don't appreciate it.

I don't know why I have delivered myself of a homily on the German nation, particularly to you who do not like them I am sure. It is because I like and respect them that I do it, so please bear with my garrulousness while I say just one thing more: my liking for them, tempered as it is by what I am vain enough to call understanding, makes me far from sorry to be assisting so actively in their education, even though it should have taken on such a terrible form and aspect as this present war.

Tell me of the Italians, please. I have no pleasure in fighting them, and at present I can only despise them for what I conceive them to be and for having fallen, or so it would seem, from what I know them at one time to have been.

I shall finish this letter tomorrow. Now I owe myself some sleep and as the bailiffs of my bed are already knocking at the door of my eyes it is unprofitable to either or both of us for me to disobey the summons.

Goodnight.

Saturday

I have been infuriated by the discovery that no Army Post Office exists as yet; almost anything may have befallen such mail as was directed to me in care of it, and, in order to prevent the possibility of further losses or delays, I have given instructions for mail to be forwarded direct to me here.

Your mother answered the telephone when I rang this evening, and she kindly took down the address and will hand it to you. I hope you will find the time and inclination to write occasionally.

Sunday

The third attempt to finish this letter is now about to commence. The responsibility for its pigeon-holing must rest on the indolence born of nothing to do more difficult than lie in the streaming sun and on becoming more than bearably infused with its living warmth, to slide into the quickening water and swim and swim and swim against a racing tide, until the native watchers on the bank are so firmly convinced that I am struggling for my life that they on one occasion sent a dinghy to rescue me. I spurned it, and swimming safe to shore won much kudos for my prowess. Such was the impression which I made upon one wee lass that she came up and spoke to me later, as I was sitting in the big open window of the officers' mess, which is shoulder high to the six-foot-wide 'front' of this delightful township. She said, 'Do you know me? I'm Elizabeth Dane.' I said 'What?' in my usual stupid way, hearing perfectly what she said, and she repeated, 'I'm Miss Dane.'

'Oh!' I said.

'My father's Captain Dane.'

'Oh yes.' I thought he must be the captain in a highland regiment whom I had seen in the bar shortly before, though I discovered later he was the naval captain of all shipping in these parts. After a considerable pause she ventured:

'You're a good swimmer. So are you,' she added by way of consolation to a man who had been swimming with me that morning. 'We saw you this morning swimming right over the other side. They all thought you couldn't get back.'

I said something appropriately and fatuously modest and she went on to ask if I would be swimming again tomorrow morning (that's today). I said I would be so we decided to go swimming together. While we were sitting in the sun before going in this morning she let me knit a couple of rows of the dress she was making for her 'Australian bear'. It was two purl and two plain – I nearly always got it wrong though I can knit much faster than she.

This is really a game I'm playing, because now you have got to tell me how old Elizabeth Dane is, what she looks like and anything more about her that you can.

Your mother was quite charming when I rang up yesterday; she renewed her invitation to come and visit her any time. I shall certainly do so when next I am in Oxford. Would you ever like to stay at home when you are in London? Dave will be there most weekends and if he's not somebody else often is. Do go if you'd like to, or do Mama and Papa rather frighten you? They would take it as an enormous compliment if you did, just as they do when our friend Donald Graham comes. Write and ask them, or I'll get Mother to write and ask you, if you would really rather not.

Eighty-odd German bombers passed over us today in faultless formation which we had the pleasure of seeing smashed by our fighters. A few bombs were dropped then, without casualties to us here. I could hear a German 'plane circling round and round overhead. Once I heard it come in on its run to the target, but it climbed out again without dropping its bombs and took up its circling once more. Then I heard it coming in again, followed this time by the wail of falling bombs; first one exploded and then five in quick succession. Ter-rump-rumble-rumble: that's the noise they make. The windows rattle and the curtains blow into the room in a flutter, then bits and pieces begin to fall with bumps and a patter, the 'plane circles once more and flies off. One or two guns have a crack at it but they haven't a chance, not tonight.

It makes one feel tremendously important being singled out like this. I hope they have done no damage – I shall see tomorrow.

Goodnight darling,
    Jock

GERMANY'S HEAVIEST AIR DEFEAT
140 MACHINES SHOT DOWN OUT OF 600
THE TIMES Monday 19 August 1940

Journal to Mirren
Burnham
19th August 1940

It's working! it's working like a charm! That young fellow
Lewes' is rapidly assuming the recognition of reality. A
pleasant man called Barkworth, with whom I pass many of
my leisure hours, fell into the trap which the bland expanse
of my innocent face lays for the unwary. I think I remarked
on the enormous amount he had already managed to do in a
short life and he replied by way of modest consolation that
he expected he was a good deal older than I, having, as he
put it, attained the ripe age of 25! He rather deprecated such
antiquity, saying that it was on the wrong side of half way to
50, to which I replied non-committally that I thought it on
the right side and that I didn't care how soon I was 50 since
life begins at 40 anyway. I regret to say (regret, that is, my
duplicity) that I left him in the pit of his error.

I have a perfect specimen of a German incendiary bomb
on the table beside me. Its entrails have been removed and,
though very imposing to look at, it is no more than a
harmless husk in reality. If you would like to give it to
Christopher I'll send it to you: but perhaps he has no interest
in these ordinarily youthfully exciting things. It is about 15
inches long and 1½ in diameter, all beautifully shining
aluminium except for its neat olive green tail. It is most

beautifully machined and finished and bears all the marks of
German scientific genius and engineering skill. Perhaps you
would like it as a symbol of the delayed action incendiary
bomb which dropped between us in the 400 and elsewhere
and which, unless some vandal rips the guts out of it first,
will doubtless one day consume us both with incandescent
heat. What a ghastly reminder to have about the place.

Today I received letters from Mother and Father in reply
to what he called my 'runaway letter'. They were infused
with love and understanding such as are granted to few to
share. My financial sins are forgiven and I shall not weary
you with an account of them, but besides confessing them I
had written as directly as I felt able of them and myself and
how matters stood with us. If in doing this I have presumed
upon your graciousness or betrayed a confidence then I ask
your pardon and crave your patience until you discover, as I
have done, that nothing confided to my mother and father
could ever be betrayed.

Father wrote of the wisdom of your refusal to become
engaged to me. 'The interval of quiet steadfast work and
waiting,' he said, 'will be a real touchstone of happiness. I
do not say that lightly, as if it were an easy thing to do:
nothing worth while ever is easy: but out of my own
experience I do know its wisdom. Your mother and I only
met for a few days and then were separated save for letter-
writing: and it was three years before I could go down to
Australia to ask her to marry me.

'I was well over forty before I was in a position to
marry – far be from you such an ordeal of waiting. When
that happy day comes that you bring us a new daughter in
your wife, you know without the saying what a loving
welcome always awaits you both.'

This is the last time that I shall drag you down into my mine. Henceforth my letters will be 'bonny, blithe, good and gay' as you called those which were written while the deeper feelings were yet untroubled, but having written thus I can now rest assured that you will never underestimate my determination to marry you, come what may short of your engagement to another and, I hope, worthier man. This is no dog-like devotion, neither is it an attempt to bind you to me by any obligation of etiquette either real or implied. It is simply an attempt to establish a 'comradeship, a living and frank exchange of the best in both, with the deeper feelings untroubled.' I would never presume to suggest this had I not your own word for it that you have never known the friendship of a man such as would recognise an individuality of your own and did I not believe that you would welcome such a relationship. More than make the attempt I cannot do since friendship is a plant that grows and not a mechanical phenomenon induced by swearing. Moreover, it's a plant that won't be forced; it recognises no urgency: if urgency there is, then that's a separate matter, it cannot accelerate the growth except by inducing frankness, it cannot retard or blight except when it gives way to exaggeration & insincerity.

Only one cavern of my mine remains still unexplored: having dragged you through it I shall bring you into the sun-lighted world again where you may breathe fresh wholesome air. What of this urgency? How, in the light of all the pomp that has gone before in the procession of this night's writing, are we to regard this beggar priest of another god who has the power to turn this solemn pageant in a single moment into a primitive tribal rite, all woad and tom-toms (if the two ever mixed)? First of all what if he should disappear from the procession? Are we to regret him? Attempt to recall him? Go through the motions of his rite without him? Do you answer no as emphatically as I do? He will come of his own accord or not at all, if he comes we must learn to accept him and his madness for as long as he stays, and if he stays for good and becomes the priest of the household that too we must accept and bow to his imperious urgency. Should he disappear we must accept his absence, not as final and complete, any more than his presence, but simply as a fact governing present behaviour. And lastly, what if we get mixed up in other processions, or other rites with other beggar priests or perhaps gorgeously attired? Our little procession will have to halt temporarily until it is clear whether the new priest has come to stay or passes on taking his béguine with him. If he stays our procession will have somehow to form the body of the new; if he goes we may go forward again undisturbed.

I shall not send this letter till I have heard from you. I feel I shall do so tomorrow. The priest sits over my bed, filling my head with times and scenes which have strange meanings to my heart.

Goodnight

Wednesday

Your dear letter has arrived – I wish your map of Joy Street would too. I haven't read your letter except just the beginning, cannot read it now in this rush off to work and what I have read makes me ache so I just send this

with love.

14 Merton Street
Oxford
19th August

John dear,

I'm not exaggerating when I say that this is the seventh
letter I've started to write to you this afternoon – I'm
waiting over anxiously for your criticism of my verbal map
of Joy Street's wynds and gateways, or perhaps there is so
very much I want to say that I don't know how to begin.
And I can't begin, Ulysses, because it seems as if you had
been away ten years already, so that I have almost forgotten
when I knew you at all. This coming and going is very
strange. When you are away I can write to you about
Leicester Square in words I could never speak to you. But
now my head is so full of things I want to tell you and I
can't write them, because even now you are a stranger. We
passed through Joy Street, but you've never hesitated in the
Brig o'Dread and watched all hell's little devils prancing
before us. One day, dear Saul, I'll tell you about the Brig
o'Dread, but I'll have to know you very well indeed because
it's a very unsteady bridge, and you probably wouldn't like
to know about it at all. One of the little devils has done his
deed so well that we've had to send Mummy to a nursing
home for a week or ten days. She goes tomorrow, so once
more I shall gird on my belt heavy with the keys of
domestic duties and jangle them with officious delight. I
enjoy housekeeping, and I shall enjoy it even more this
next two weeks. Hamish dines out four nights a week and
Mummy will be away, so I shall read my books, avoid the

ghosts and cook my own supper if I can be bothered. But I won't have to do much washing-up because Laura comes in every day, so I shall dry up for her instead.

I must stop writing at once because the evening is dangerous if one is sleepy, and I am very sleepy. So I'll go to my bed now instead of writing a letter which I'd be too shy to send you in the morning. I must write to you about telephones tomorrow, but now I shall drone the first half of the sentimental dirge to the moon. Then I shall sleep and dream of most people except yourself – it always happens that way. Blessings.

Tuesday

Your letter came this morning, but obviously the one I sent to the Army Post Office still hasn't reached you. I wish it would because it makes me feel uncomfortable knowing that you haven't yet read it. But now I must talk to you about telephones. Is it really impossible for me to ring you up sometimes? I suppose it would be difficult to get hold of you, but one day you'll have to send me the number of a public telephone, tell me what time you'll be there, and then let me talk to you for quite a long while. One of the joys of peace is the possibility of being able to ring up people knowing that if they aren't at home today, they'll be there tomorrow. It's sheer torment the way people pass beyond the reach of one's eyes and tongue; you have 'disappeared'; officially others are somewhere on the seas or the sky and you are all so hopelessly unobtainable. It's mad and bad.

I needed you so much that evening you rang up. I was very busy trying to persuade a slot machine to turn into

scrap metal so that it could be recreated and go bombard
the heart of some other worthy spinster. But it's a very dear
and stubborn machine and refuses to stop pouring out its
hundreds and thousands till I can say I'm in love with
someone else. But I'm not in love – only ashamed. I wish
you could drink the waters of Lethe and forget that Helen
or Penelope existed. I am being most sincere when I say
that I have never minded the idea of hurting any man, as
much as I dread the possibility of hurting you. Don't let me
do it, John – please go away before the possibility ever
comes near to being a probability. Bother! The bad fairy
who came to my christening is flying round the room
trying to make me morose; wait one moment till I blow her
out of the window.

There, she's gone, but as I puffed her out of the window I
saw that the leaves on the trees are growing yellow already.
I hope it's only the drought and not autumn which is
making the trees look tired. When I work I sit on the
window sill, and when I get bored I look at the trees. If I
were a cripple for six months I'd sit and watch trees and
write a story about them. If you listen to them and pretend
not to, if you watch them and pretend to read you can see
and hear all sorts of sudden secret forms and sounds. It's
curious how creatures, be they young leaves or human
beings, hate to be stared upon. I suppose it's because every
single thing wants to keep its certain ways and thoughts
private. Some people resent interference passionately –
these are the arrogant unsympathetic and cruel creatures.
Some pretend not to resent interference because they are
afraid of themselves – they have no pride, no vision of
power, or if they have they benumb it, because they are
more scared of other people, mean minds, than they are of

death. Then there are still other people, but I couldn't explain how they feel.

If ever we are married would you interfere with my choice of friends? Warn me if you will, but don't command me because I'd rather learn of my own accord whether or not my choice were bad. If Mummy weren't ill, and if Hamish weren't dreadfully worried I should have been defiant and rude when they asked me to give up seeing a friend who has had seven lovers and an abortion. As it is, I was gentle and shall be deceitful. Diana has an ill mind, and if only people could possibly realise that they are condemning themselves by drawing away from her, they would be able to do so much for her. Diana is neither damned nor doomed, but she will be if people whom she likes and admires stop having anything to do with her. Then she will know the deathly feeling of desolation, then, in hopelessness she will indeed abandon herself to the pastimes of the harlot. She is uncontrolled and weak but she isn't cheap. She is coming to lunch today and when she tells me about the eighth man – as she probably will – I'll see again her expression of loathing and despair.

Nothing on earth will ever make me despise Diana, and though I can help her little enough I think you can guess how she feels when more and more of her friends drop off. They leave her because they are vain and afraid. Not one tenth of them are virgin in spirit or mind, though they may be in body – but they think they are 'nice' moral people, and Diana is not 'nice'. They are afraid they will get a bad reputation from going around with her, and they have the vanity of the mean and narrow-minded. Diana never lies; she is as generous with her money as she is with her emotions. She's honest, quick-minded and fine enough to be so ashamed. Oh, people make me so sick with their petty condemnations, their hypocritical prudery, their deceits and their baseness. Dear Diana. I wish she could have a really happy life, but she will get over her particular Big one day, even if she has to be pushed and dragged over.

Elizabeth is either five or seven years old – not six because then she'd have had no front teeth, nor eight or nine for then she'd be too shy. If she is five she has hair which looks mouse colour in the shade but brilliant and quick in the sunlight. She wears a very short pink frock and a Shetland cardigan which is long enough to make her frock stick out in a brief, ridiculous frill. She hasn't any brothers or sisters because otherwise she would have suggested that they should swim with you too. She has the self assurance of a very little girl who is adored by her parents and everyone she meets; she takes everything for granted because she never heard of insecurity; she isn't vain, but proud that she is Captain Dane's daughter, but she does accept with conscious pleasure the homage paid to little girls whose skin smells sweetly and whose hair is soft and cool to the touch. She isn't at all shy of you because people always have been enchanted by the freckles dusted under her eyes and across her nose, and they've always wanted to go on smiling at her wide, solemn, grey eyes. When she is older she will be called 'grey-eyed Athena', for she will be tranquil and lovely to know. She will be afraid, but only for others, for she will have known the supreme blessing of a house which is at peace.

If Elizabeth is seven she has long legs and toeless sandals. Her hair is straight and dark, braided into two stumpy pigtails. Her movements are sudden and she wants to cry when she hears music only she doesn't let anyone guess that. The way you swam excited her and she wants to tell

everyone that she talked to the big man who couldn't
drown. She is rather vain for her father is important and so
she is important too – besides, it's a good thing if the
servants call her Miss, and if strangers are told she is Miss
Dane. Later on she will want you to call her Lisbeth very
much because you did like her bear and even if you are
clumsy at knitting at beasts it's funny to see you wield the
needles. She is disdainful but very honest and was gifted
with the ability to make friends with friendly people. You
like Elizabeth because she is very sincere and you know
that when she is tired of talking to you she will say
goodbye graciously because she was taught beautiful
manners. You were self-conscious when she first spoke to
you, because you and all others will be startled by the
sweetness of a wide smiling mouth and the vivid eyes of a
child which has begun to grow up.

Was Elizabeth twelve, fair, shy, and rather silly after all?

It's now almost six o'clock and I'm trying to entertain one
Sam Stubbs. He is making a dreadful fuss of me, won't let
me write in peace, and has a distracting tendency to rub his
cheek against mine. A most persistent, tiresome and lovable
young man. I would like to kiss him but he smells of pepper
instead of hair oil, and sneezing would make my eyes water
so that I couldn't write to you. Dear Mr Stubbs; he is very
sweet but he has more fleas than I ever saw on a stray kitten
before. They aren't the ordinary black hopping fleas, but
slow-moving pale yellow ones with tiny brown heads. The
black fleas don't like humans but I'm not at all acquainted
with this kind – I hope they won't be annoying because
otherwise I shall need to have a bath in Lysol. But he is grey
and soft and fascinated by his reflection in the mirror.
Generally cats aren't interested in their reflections but Mr

Stubbs is fascinated and astounded. I'll need a kitten when I'm married; they are the most consoling creatures alive for you can complain and moan to them and for all their affected sympathy you know that they don't care at all which is a good thing. A dog knows and minds when someone feels morose, and it's a pity to have two morose creatures. You may hate cats, darling, but even this plain beastie couldn't fail to entertain you. He is rampaging to and fro from the glass, trying to catch himself out, beating his own reflected face, sneaking out from behind the mirror and astonishing his own eyes. Now he is hustling about in the rustling tissue paper which is really my paper pattern for a dress – he's torn it to shreds.

This is a very bad letter because I want to talk to you very badly and I can't write the words I would say. So all I have written now is of secondary importance, thus unsatisfying for you and for me.

I'll answer your letter tomorrow I hope, but I must post this now because you didn't have my last letter and you'll begin to think I'm disinterested already.

Blessings on you and don't drown nor get in the way of bombs because I want you to come back as soon as you will –

Mirren

Tuesday, 20th August 1940

John, dear John, it is very late and I can't sleep. I must pretend I know you very well or else I'll never swing down again from the mighty windswept regions, where the nerves quiver like the tautest string of a fiddle and whither a thousand unseen hands press you down to the quicksands of memories. The air hums with the silence of night, and each movement has the harsh, dulled tone of a goose quill pen fumbling its way over parchment. My mother's enormous pupils, Hamish's sorrow and the sounds coming fast, one after another, wedge me away from you whom I need so much tonight. The throat of bitterness is as keen as a sword and the sour taste of subtle lies cloys the tongue till one aches to drown in the waters of reason and peace.

If Man would never let himself be swept away to the wind-filled regions, he would still believe hell is but an everlasting fire. Do you know what one is taught in those wind-filled regions? The god of chastisement beats on his bellowing drum the eternal message that without desires we are made conscious of the absolute barrenness, the desolation of existence. With increasing desires, life becomes more significant for the spirit of man is restless and his only joy is the stirring after some unknown things. And in the mighty region we are confounded because we know what we desired, and yet we have been frustrated by our own weakness, our baseness and blindness. We reached, we almost grasped and then failed through no other power nor fault but on our own. And the voices clamour and deride us for we know as well as they that the believers shall be choosers. We believed, we knew, but failed, because we had not the strength to overpower the innate rottenness and meanness of our own spirits. And so I turn to you who have faith, to you who sleep tonight undismayed, unselfish and dear.

Yet I would not forget the powers of the wind-filled regions, for though change is the essence of life, it is death.

All things drift away – we flow from birth to death. But dear heaven, let us never forget sorrow nor joy, for, if we are acquainted with tragedy, nothing is more tragic than the ending itself which we are too willing to accept. The relief we derive from its ending is merely the measure of our weariness, our failure of spirit. Calm after storm, the death of passion, all such things are horrible, for they are signs of exhaustion, reminders of vacancy, indications of nothingness.

So let us never accept the annihilation of memory; even now may it remind us that Eight Joy Street will be all the more joyous, because the endless motion of life has sent you there and has left me here, only to move us together again some time, one day.

I'm sleepy now – goodnight, John, and thank you.

[This letter was sealed with bits of 'stamp paper' and the following was written on the back. It was enclosed and sent with a letter dated the following day.]

I stuck this up with stamp paper because if I'd read it again I'd never have sent it. As it is, I think you ought to convert it to ashes at once and just remember that I did once say night was a silly time to write – why, I can't even remember what I said now. Probably something melodramatic and foolish, but you may as well be forewarned of my weaknesses!

M.

THE ROAD TO VICTORY
U.S. HAILS GERMAN ATTACK
THE TIMES Wednesday 21 August 1940

Merton Street
21st August 1940

Good morning dear John; did you sleep soundly and
well, were you delivered from things which go bump in the
night? I hope you are feeling lively enough to go swimming
with Miss Dane this morning, though such an idea does
tickle my sweet store of jealousy.

I suppose that I did write to you in the quiet hours of this
morning, but I don't remember what I said. All the same, I
have a notion that you'd better ignore the scribble because I
was in an outrageous mood of self-pity and self
martyrdom – that I do remember.

But this morning everything is different. My room is
giddy and gay with the perfume of scarlet and white
sweetpeas, and the wind thrusts at my curtains making
them billow like the sails of my fine ship. The bells of
Oxford are ringing the quarter before eleven o'clock, and
pigeons are cooing with pompous delight in the gardens of
Merton. In fact, the day holds promise of pleasure if only I
can manage to be a good daughter till Mummy goes to the
Akland.

But I must be a bad daughter, really, because most of all I
want to run miles away from home, and if I can't do that, I
want the house to be left to me and the ghosties and

ghoulies as soon as possible. I want to smell daisies again because their scent is always surprising and also very much want to push someone who is much stronger and bigger than I am. Let's leap into the fleet horses of thought and draw up on the Sussex downs, which are lovely. We'll have bread and cheese for lunch and all the harebells will ring merrily because they are so pleased we aren't where we are now, but just together again. And then if you put your face right down into the turf, you'll understand why a ladybird thinks a blade of grass is the green ribbon road to heaven. The thyme will smell good and it will prickle and tickle the toes, but you will feel such strength that you will shout to the winds with a voice supple and turbulent, sharpened on a hone of ebony and ivory – ebony and ivory which are really only just dark shadow and white light. And then we'll go home to a room where deep coloured gladioli stand in a silver vase. And there will be bowls of pot pourri to perfume the finger tips, and a picture where the sun filters out lands coloured purple and green with the thunder light. We shall be pleasant and composed because we are privately rather sleepy after spending a whole day on the downs. We'll have dinner, but I shan't be very hungry because I shall be watching quick restless threads of light, leaping from the cut glass and clutching at the red and the gold of your hair when it's newly washed.

And now the wind is rummaging among the trees, tossing the chestnuts onto the street so that they bounce from cobble to cobble like crickets flicking about in the grass. I suppose I mean cicadas or grasshoppers, because didn't we hear crickets that evening when we went round the corner of Merton Street.

I wish so much that I could write letters like yours.

Sometimes they seem to have a substance and a meaning which last beyond today and tomorrow. My letters are nothing but the written reflection of a pressing mood, and it all seems so trivial and feeble. One day I'll try and tell you about my books but there seems to be so little to say. Should I tell you that Molière's 'Tartuffe' fails to touch my sense of humour? I don't think he is at all funny – rather very cunning with a perspicacity and comprehension of human frailties which is startling.

Darling, I have just been mouthing unsatisfactory tiresome words down the phone and along the line all the way to Burnham; indeed I apologise for having puzzled you. But dear John, you still have to learn that I'm frequently in this tedious mood at home, for we've been heading for a minor crisis these last nine months. And here we still are bobbing about on the fluctuating sea of emotions not quite sure whether we are angry or sorry, glad mad or merely bad. You could never really understand this type of domestic chaos, because even if you came into personal contact with it, you are too strong, too determined and too clearminded to let it come near to overwhelming you. You recognise your moods, you accept them as being such and you know it is but a temporary unpleasant state of mind. But mine is . . .

There, I've thwarted you again. I wrote long pages about the family skeletons, but when the after supper washing-up warned me that you did but 'love me a little', I shut the skeletons into the burning stove in case they scared you right away. It's no good, one can't seriously moan and groan in letters. Either one will feel shy of writing to a comparative stranger or else reluctant to worry someone important. So the skeletons can go on rattling and creaking because they are rather lurid and nasty – please don't let's play with old bones too much if I see you tomorrow.

I'm not jealous of Elizabeth any more. When she grows up she'll have a straggly bun and will feed her children on porridge and underdone red meat and she'll dress them in combinations and dab iodine on their grazes because it's good for them.

When Mr Stubbs has finished washing the tip of his tail he shall go to bed and then I'll go too. Every time you say I worry you I shall pull a white hair out of my head, plait it with the rest and hope it chokes you.

Goodnight and blessings,
    Mirren

S.E. COAST SHELLED LAST NIGHT
DOVER AREA BOMBARDED FROM FRANCE
THE TIMES Friday 23 August 1940

Burnham
Friday, 23rd August 1940

Darling,

I did not sleep in the train. I lay on my back on the seats
and stared back into the pool out of which I had a moment
before slipped and by whose bank I now stretched, still
running with its phosphorescent velvet water, chin in hands
and heels kicking idly in the air, halted sometimes by the
arresting visions that swarm to me, quickening with delight
at the widening smile of a dimpled ripple, stiffening with
the burn of a fresh splash of the smouldering water and
relaxing in time with the sigh of the surge which raised it,
receding.

There may be a certain urgency in this letter for I have
much to say, three of your letters to thank you for and a
deal of sleep to make up, all in a very short time. But it
won't be a restless letter just because I am swimming against
the tide of sleep in its writing: it will more likely reflect my
state of mind and body, which for both is sensed as one of
rest before fresh efforts.

On the tip of my pen's tongue are the worded
impressions of No. 8 Joy Street; to delay their articulation
may be to banish them for ever from the realm of human

interest. But before the journey begins, a briefly worded
warning of the conditions of issue of this ticket for a joy
ride: one passenger only will be carried by the pilot: the
passenger travels at her own risk and the pilot can accept
no responsibility for any injury she may sustain in transit,
regardless of whether or not it is caused by his negligence
or incompetence; the pilot reserves the right to jettison the
passenger should considerations of safety in his judgement
warrant such a course; finally, the passenger must be
prepared at any moment to take control of the machine and
bring it safely to land, should the pilot, his courage failing,
effect a descent by parachute.

No. 8 Joy Street is still with me. After ringing the door
bell I was kept waiting in the street a whole day while my
body moved and marched about Timeland in company with
the Timelanders and Placepeople with whom it is now
associated. I tried to get into No. 8 without a body, but
they were very strict inside and insisted that I could not
possibly enter even the vestibule without one, it was de
rigeur in their house, what did I think it was? a nudist
colony? I said, no, but I knew someone called Mirren, who
was coming to their party, very well, and I'd often had good
times with her completely unbodied, and I'm sure she
would say I was all right. But it didn't do any good: they
said first of all that though they had heard that someone of
that name had been invited from Timeland as well, they
themselves only knew of her from their neighbours below
them, who, though quite charming and very entertaining,
were untrustworthy when it came to assessing unbodied
people. Their houses are small, with very few rooms and
everybody does the same things there, just play with each
other's bodies, so that they practically never get unbodied

at all. And then they started asking me all sorts of embarrassing question about us, what I intended to do with you at their party? and things like that. I said, How could I tell? at other parties in Joy Street things just happened, and I said it wouldn't be Joy Street if they didn't. Sometimes we played with each other and sometimes we got unbodied and lay together in the garden sun or swam in the warm adventurous pools they had there, but we never knew or planned that these things were going to happen, though of course we hoped they would. Then they asked, Why we hoped? and had we been up Joy Street before? and I replied of course we have lots of times; and they asked quickly why we were starting all over again and I said because it is such fun. 'Then why didn't you go on further up the street with the other people you came visiting with?' 'We did,' I said, 'we got to the end of the street, and so we were sad because the fun was over and said goodbye.'

Then they looked very hard at me through the little grille in the door ('they' are just two burning eyes and a soft clear voice which sounds so kind, as though it terribly wanted to help, but sometimes sad as though it knew it couldn't), they looked searchingly and the voice was sad when it said, 'There is no end to Joy Street; you must have taken the wrong turning at Casual Corner and gone to Lusting Lane or into the Sentimental Gardens or perhaps you got into Self Alley, that narrow passage only broad enough for two: a little way down it a great sheet of glass divides it down the centre the whole of its remaining length and soon the glass becomes a mirror – sometimes people discover that they have been walking with themselves and come back,' they paused, 'but not often.' Then the voice became brusque: 'But you know the first rule of all the

houses in Joy Street, you may never enter alone; as Mirren
isn't here yet, you'll just have to wait. And while you're
waiting you must make up your mind what you want to do:
you stand at Casual Corner now, you know, and Joy Street
is for rational men and women who know what they want
and believe in the way to get it, not for well-bred, well-
trained animals whose desire or instinct is their only guide.
So be sure it is No. 8 Joy Street you want and not a house
in some other road.' With that the grille closed gently, and I
sat down naked on the doorstep as we rang off.

And what did I want? I wanted to stay in Joy Street – I
knew that – and I could only stay with Mirren. What had
the eyes meant by asking what I wanted to do with Mirren?
Would the doing of some things lead us out of Joy Street?
Why couldn't we just rely on the right thing happening
again? I hadn't noticed any corner, where was this Casual
Corner at which we now stood? I suppose this is Joy Street?
But the worst of it is all the name plates have been taken
down because of the war in order that the enemies of Joy
will not know how to find her house to pillage and destroy
it. And all the streets are so much alike, and no one in the
streets seems to know the names of them, or if they do they
won't tell you in case you are Fifth Column, or else they
say, 'Oh yes, this is Joy Street,' because they have a body to
sell, or because they themselves are enemy and wish to take
you prisoner. You can only tell Joy Street from inside the
houses. The outsides have been made to look all the same
because everyone wants to appear to be living in Joy Street:
even the narrow walls of Self Alley are painted cunningly to
look like Joy Street even though there are no houses in the
alley at all, only two blank walls.

But I was sure this was Joy Street all right because I had

only just come out of the house opposite No. 7, and that had certainly been in Joy Street. But perhaps it had been a back door leading on to some other street and we had come out there instead of at the front. I didn't think so, but if we had come out at the right door why wasn't Mirren here when I rang? Perhaps she had gone out one door and I out another and perhaps she was waiting somewhere else.

I remembered talking about a beggar priest and the madness of his cult and how, if he joined our procession, we must put on his woad and dance to his tom-toms. Perhaps it was that which the eyes had been seeing and the kind voice trying to warn me of. And yet I was sure now, after ringing up, that the beggar priest was near, I could hear the beat of his blood in my ears, and sometimes see his naked body swaying and jerking lewdly at the hips, see his flexed knees and languid arms with just his finger-tips stiff and straight, see the taut muscles of his neck, his half-open mouth and curled upper lip showing white pointed teeth and hear his spasmodic breathing through distended nostrils wrinkling his nose. But it was his eyes which held me: half closed and proud in the knowledge of their power to mesmerise and madden. Yes, I was sure he was coming, and I had said we must dance with him and give ourselves up to the power of those eyes.

But was I so sure of that? It was painful even to question that confidence, for to do so I had to make the effort of looking away from those cold green eyes. Why had I said we must dance? I hardly dared ask the question and continually avoided answering it. I would sidle away from the necessary effort of will into watching thought images glide from their predecessors, through themselves, to their successors in the channels of an undirected mind, locks and

sluice-gates left open by a renegade will for the pent waters
to gush comfortably and delightedly down to the lower
level. I would wake from these reveries with a start, shaken
once more into volition by the realisation that the last
image at which I had been staring with the vacancy of
hypnosis was the eyes of the priest staring through mine
with a triumphant gleam as the level in my mill stream
approached its nadir. Once more I faced to the question,
Why had I said we must follow the piping priest? I had
foreseen three possibilities: the priest would not visit our
procession until we called for him (when I wrote that is
what I hoped for); the priest would sweep one of us into
another procession (dread thought); the priest would one
day come humbly begging with bowl and staff and in the
night hours dance us into frenzied frustration or ecstatic
obedience ('the second best is a gay goodnight, and quickly
turn away'). I rejected frustration because it is deadly, I
counselled obedience because at least we shall have had
what little the priest had to give and I hoped that he could
be induced to return to our procession when we should
require his services for more hallowed rites.

   This was probably more wishful than hopeful, but fear of
the second possibility blinded me both to the flimsiness of
the hope and to the very existence of a fourth: to fill the
priest's mean bowl and send him away with an imperious
gesture. He would come back to us in spite of all the other
processions: if ours is as brilliant as I believe it to be he will
hang about it until his eyes and surging motion have
conquered it at last. But once his bowl has been filled,
where find the strength for the imperious gesture? When
alone, I have it, but the priest is absent; with you in
company I have it, but he will not offer his bowl; alone

with you I have it not and he, knowing my weakness, shows his strength. Have you got it? Have we got it between us? At these questions I turned away again and shivered in a disembodied way on my doorstep.

I sought comfort and strength in a visit to my parents, so I returned to my body which I found sitting in my tiny bunk, as it is now, trying to write a letter to you. The paper was blank: I'm glad it was honest enough to admit that it couldn't do it without me: I made it write home instead. I told of this feeling of urgency, I admitted the need for resistance, I deplored the difficulty of the task, which, I said, would not be made easier by my seeing you in London on the morrow. There I was wrong, but how unexpectedly!

This visit home committed me to a certain course: it did not give me the strength I lacked to follow that course. Until, however, I came to the point of getting my body under way for Joy Street, there I let the matter rest: when I did come to that point, trifling details forced a decision upon me. Which trains? What clothes? If to stay the night? Where to stay the night? Alone? If not, where? Trifling details, which, as ever, force a decision on questions of great import.

I sat alone in my carriage and grappled with the questions. It was in essence the same question as I had asked long before, sitting alone on the doorstep of No. 8, which itself was the same question as the eye had asked me through the grille. And now by a process of mental filtering and refinement, by eliminating all embellishments, impurities, preservatives and colouring matter it had been reduced to this: Do I or do I not wish to attempt the seduction of Mirren?

(Here the pilot, seeing how high he has flown, begins to

lose his nerve, but knowing that his passenger is possessed of an excellent parachute and can save herself whenever she chooses by the simple process of tearing up the letter, he steels himself to go on still higher. The fantastic height to which he has flown does not appear to him to be in any way offensive or presumptuous, it is if anything a compliment to the mettle of his passenger to try her nerve at such heights.)

There are matters connected with the art of seduction which require most careful attention. But even in these days of identity cards such obstacles are by no means insuperable. Certain places are designed for it. Mount Royal, the Strand Palace, the Regent Palace and the Cumberland, to say nothing of a thousand smaller places when inquiry is deemed inconvenient: other places lend themselves to it, perhaps unwittingly, the Great Eastern being one.

Most important of all, however, is the question of technique. The incident must be carefully planned so that nothing connected with it is unworthy of the greatness of the occasion and yet it must retain a spontaneity without which it cannot but appear, in retrospect at least, as a premeditated piece of lechery. No matter how successful the attendant details, if this spontaneity is lacking, nothing, not even the full consent of the seduced, can disguise the bitter taste of deceit suffusing the sweet draught. Spontaneity can only be attained if circumstances are such as to allow the meeting, wherever it is arranged, to appear perfectly natural, to prevent it foreshadowing its intended conclusion, and, last and most important, to forbid either party feeling committed to the act until the full realisation of its complete inevitability floods in upon them with the joyous breathtaking rush of a child waking up on Christmas Day: of course it knew tomorrow was Christmas Day when it went to sleep, but that detracts nothing from the delightful surprise on waking to discover that it really is. How often has she gone to sleep wishing that it were, even dreaming that it was, only to awake finding that it's not, and won't be for so long to come as to be as good as never.

This is no abstract disquisition upon the general subject of seduction, written for your entertainment or information. If it were, I should be guilty of betraying my sex, of cheapening myself, of insulting you, your sex and your association with me. It is, if you will believe me, an account, not a disquisition, of certain very concrete, not abstract, thoughts upon a definite instance of contemplated seduction which came to me, whether I would or no, on my way to No. 8 Joy Street, and which form an integral whole with the impressions of that visit, which I retain, and which I am here attempting to record in order that, quite apart from any intrinsic value in the record itself, we may be able to bring our minds to bear on the crux of the intricate and extremely important problems which now confront us both.

Sunday

Two alternatives were presented to me: to make a deliberate, preconceived attempt to seduce you in circumstances which could hardly again be expected ever to be so favourable, or else to embark upon an evening entertainment which promised to be dangerously similar to foregoing occasions and which would certainly be a severe test of our ability to bear each other's company. On the one hand the Great Eastern has an excellent kitchen, a rich cellar and luxurious rooms. It is hard by the station for my train and is very naturally the sort of place we should choose to pass a few hours together there. For privacy there is no alternative to retiring to my room and from there to its becoming our room is the merest and most natural step. The alternative to this you know because we followed it, and we followed it because I stepped from the train onto Liverpool St. Station with the conviction that, in spite of all evidence to the contrary, it was the more important of the two courses before us, that, if indeed we stood at a parting of the ways, this led to Joy Street, that elsewhere.

You may have been slightly shocked and amazed at the way in which I had conducted this weighing of alternatives without reference to what you might have to say on the matter, as though the world were mine for the asking, and I had only to extend my open hand for the choicest fruits to fall into it. This apparent selfish confidence could be a reality only if I were making a decision which affected us both, deciding in fact, what we should do. But the problem affected me alone; it was, what do I want? and could affect you, even indirectly, only in so far as I may naturally want to please you and to avoid hurting you. That very natural wish divided its weight almost equally between the two sides of the balance and was therefore of no assistance in distinguishing the weightier from the lighter alternative. Moreover, I looked for something more positive than a desire not to hurt, and a criterion closer to the measuring rod of my own faith than a reference outside me to the measure of another person's pleasure, however dear she may be. Even the question of your own virginity counted for nothing in the reckoning, except in so far as it is a shield, however flimsy, to your virtue. I remember saying to you that I would be surprised to find that the girl I asked to marry me was not a virgin. That is hardly true now, indeed I think I would be surprised if the girl whom I eventually marry were to come to the altar a virgin. But I must not digress, so more of this when we come to talk of Diana; the question of virtue was not uppermost in my mind as I sat alone in my little compartment, holding an unopened book in my hand and staring through the back of the seats opposite, it was something more concrete and practical.

It was a phrase which kept returning, or two phrases carrying the same thought: 'I have almost forgotten whether I knew you at all' and 'because even now you are a stranger'. These two overprinted on the background of a third: 'I will say I'll marry you in three weeks but not in six months.' It was the paradoxical problem contained in these words of yours which I hoped to solve by your seduction, and it was with a heavy heart that I realised that seduction would not solve the problem, it would dissolve it. I might win you for a night, to lose you for a lifetime. Love from a stranger forges notoriously less lasting bonds than dispassionate friendship, and I wanted neither of these, I looked for impassioned friendship.

(You will be glad to hear that this is the end of the Introduction, and the story proper of No. 8 Joy Street begins at the next paragraph.)

Goodnight, dear heart, and I pray you think on me not as a stranger, however far away, however long absent, but rather as

Your very loving friend . . .

It was with perfect confidence that I approached No. 8
Joy Street and when I felt you there at my arm I did not fear
that I had to look round to you as a stranger. We rang the
door bell together without turning to each other. The door
opened at once and we found ourselves in the servants' hall
with all manner of men and women hurrying to and fro
upon their household tasks. We passed on into a long
corridor lined with blue leather where we were alone and
looked at each other for the first time. I tried to imagine
you a stranger, and couldn't do it; I tried to hold you away
from me against the opposite wall of the passage but we
laughed, not embarrassed little laughs, but confident
exciting laughs, full of magnetic power which drew us
together again.

Monday

At the end of the corridor was a door which you opened,
and, going through, we found ourselves on the roof,
overlooking a thousand chimney pots. Then our bodies
began to glow with each other's warmth and as they did so
the roof on which we stood sank slowly down between the
four walls of the house, which closed about and over us
until we seemed to be in a lift going up and up.

We stepped out of the lift into a sort of courtyard
surrounded by many windows and pillared porticos
regularly spaced. Although the courtyard was very small
and quite filled with couples and footmen we crossed it as
though it were empty, no one noticed us, they seemed to
look through us and we to move through them as through
streamers of morning mist beside a brook.

We entered the avenue hand in hand: all this time we

had not spoken, and now we walked on thick soft turf
which did not re-echo like concrete as the grass in the
courtyard had done, and there was no sound besides the
birds in the elms and a cat mewing some place out of sight.
We both felt that we should speak soon and we wondered
what our voices would sound like to ourselves and to each
other and what we would say; we did not wonder
enquiringly but curiously, as though we were about to act
two parts which we had been learning slowly for ten years
in silence.

The avenue was cool and pleasant: it rose and fell in
gentle undulations but tended always lightly downward to
the edge of the distant lake. We walked down it swinging
our joined hands and we were children with bare legs and
sandals, few clothes, tousled hair and bright expectant eyes.
Sometimes we skipped along with elbows and knees flying
at queer supple angles and sometimes we tip-toed
mysteriously, looking for the hidden pussy cat, and then,
when we could hear it no longer we lay on our tummies on
a slope near the lake and began to talk.

Tuesday

We grew older as we talked, but not for long because our
bodies quickly disappeared like children sent off to play
while Mother and Father have a quiet talk together. I went
to the point of my perplexity, 'Why am I a stranger?' You
could not tell. 'Why didn't you send me the letters you
wrote to me?' 'Because they made me frightened and you
were so far away.' But that is the only way to make a mock
of time and distance, by playing fair with your pen. Tell me
what you said now. 'Oh no! I wrote much more than I

should ever say to you now (I thought I understood) and in any case they were full of moans and groans, and why make two people morbid?'

Wednesday

   Slowly and by degrees I began to see you at home. You led me by the hand through houses, you set me down to watch you at the breakfast table, a breakfast table at Pompeii caught by Vesuvius and charged with high tension electric current. I saw you with your mother, talking distantly, stomping on the rising truth within you, remembering a theatrical scene when you had brought an offering of your truth to be received with a show of warmth which could not be communicated to you through the vacuum between you. The dumb show froze your confidence in truth, the precious wine to be preserved and husbanded, to be increased by sharing: it froze it to an icicle, fine as a stiletto and as sharp, which, if drawn from its sheath in your heart and imparted to another, could only wound.
   Hamish I saw, silent because he had nothing to say, his intellect refusing to rattle emptily of nothing. And he has nothing to say because a vacuum surrounds him too, insulating truth, impenetrable to warmth, fencing in the common land of sympathetic conversation, leaving only the public roads and well trodden paths, the weather, the war, food, drink and sleep, in which to walk with you.
   You showed me your father at a distance, the epitome of a failure because he still retains within his hands the talisman which should have ensured him success. He condemns himself by flaunting it.

'You see,' I heard you say at last, 'you have nothing to say. And now you understand why I long to escape from this house and to build a home of my own, to succeed where they have failed.' I had nothing to say. I could only murmur unconvincingly, 'This life is made to be lived for others' and 'Marriage as a form of desperate escapism is abominable, and doomed to failure.'

'You do not understand,' you cried, 'you could not understand.' True I do not understand but it is just when I do not understand that I have most need of my faith. That is what faith is for, to guide you when you cannot see, not to hamper you when all is clear.

And so we accepted each other as we returned to our bodies, you longing for release from your bondage and hoping that in me you saw a way: I searching for a new bondage, a new devotion, and believing that in you I was finding it.

Our bodies came walking back, not as they had gone, scampering and joyous, but walking slowly, quite grown-up. We rose and went to the side of the lake, the air was still, the sky clear in the evening light and the waters of the lake were resting. But as we looked, we began to see below the surface tiny lights pointing and growing like a valley hamlet seen from the mountain at sunset.

We stepped out of our clothes and slid together into the lake. It was as though we had entered through a secret door in the bank below the surface, for there was no splash and no lapping of waves as we went, the water just folded around us with a warm caress, touching every part of us to the roots of each hair, where the eyelid wrinkles, around each convolution of each ear, pouring in at the laughing mouth, swirling softly full bodied down inside, making the

chest heave and glow to its depths with the inspiration of
its new element. Movement was deliciously easy, just a turn
of the wrist, a bending of the knee and you moved as
though never to stop, more graceful than a bird, more
certain, more secure. There was no up nor down, just here
and over there; there was no way to fall, and none to rise,
but just a way to go whither we would.

Towards the winking light we went far in the distance,
and on the way we sometimes went towards the thin world
of the air and looked at it below us – it seemed to be
below – all upside down and distorted. Two Australian
soldiers foreshortened into apes in hats; we could count the
nails in the soles of their boots and laugh and laugh to see
them walking upside down and know from their aggressive
confidence that they thought themselves the right way up.
You thought you saw some one you knew, the cousin of a
very dashing lover who took young girls away for weekends
and brought them back home weakened. I caught my
breath, as though for an instant my lungs cried out for the
thin graceless element below them. I made a small
impulsive move towards it, a tiny panic of drowning
desperation, a twitch, I wanted, I desired, I must have air,
for in this soft enfolding element desire drowns and sinks
into contentment. The waters held me fast and on we
moved towards the welcome lights.

We glided in amongst them and found them to be
phosphorescent and translucent shapes of things which
moved like us and things which stood. We ourselves were
outlined in every detail of our proud bodies by a million
tiny points of steadfast light, not spattered or haphazard,
but, like a mezzo-tint, picking out the form of nature's
beauty. And other forms there were which did not move,

forms only in so far as they had bounds, for we could glide through them as through the rest of the velvet element, but, while within them, they exercised a power distinctly sensible, charming the senses, piquing appetites and gratifying desires with generous warmth and richness. They seemed to be composed of vital colour, alive and native, enveloping the senses each with its own proper character of colour, texture, sound and taste and smell. And here we wandered in and about savouring and blending, relishing in union and harmony, playing always the melody of senses which we sang in our souls.

And so we stole floating from one to the next, hovering on the brink of one, drawing back, tantalising, sipping, sliding close, catching a waft of perfume, elusive, enticing, a taste, a touch, the throb of its rhythm exciting, its full-throated melody sweeping along to repletion.

In this manner it was that we entered a tract of deep colour, black-red and midnight blue. There was a wilder music, a more sensuous touch, a rhythm with the power of a torrent and the motion of a fountain in the wind. It seemed to deepen all the senses and heighten all desires, drawing out the intervening self to a tight-strained string vibrant beneath the roughness of the bow.

And here, like a swimmer in distress, I beat desperately at the water, gasping for the breath that I had long renounced. I saw the coloured darkness as a well, a deep shaft leading down to air, to breath. I sought to clamber down it with clumsy urgency, looking this way and that for foot and hand hold, fearful of a fall, no longer moving easily through a friendly element, but having to resist the force I sought to satisfy to prevent it hurling me to death.

A hand stretched out and touched me; the touch

unwrapped me from myself, freed me from the net of my desires, returned me to our element and you.

Serenely we rose through clouds of sightless black, noiseless and without texture, in every sense alone and isolated, yet held together still by some bond that spurns the senses.

It was cold when we began to see again, and we felt a little lost. Our spangled suits of glorious light had disappeared, our limbs felt heavy and we began to fear the end was close, the last of No. 8 Joy Street. And yet as we swam, a sort of rich contentment warmed us, the waters cleared, and in soft colours before our eyes took shape familiar and well loved scenes as though some elf had stolen into the gallery of our memories and espied out in life some of its treasured pictures.

I heard you say, 'I wonder how many of these people here are as content as we are now,' and hearing that I loved you.

Gently and very slowly we glided down towards the surface and as I watched you there beside me rocking on the very edge of sleep I felt a warm surge of gratitude for your being there still beside me. I loved you very greatly as I opened the door to Joy Street and stepped out.

I lay on my back in the train and stared up into the pool, back into the glowing velvet water of the lake in No. 8 Joy Street. And there in the pool I saw the kindly eyes, looking towards me and smiled. In a low soft voice they said, 'You have won.'

FEW CASUALTIES IN RAID ON LONDON
THE TIMES Saturday 24 August 1940

14 Merton Street
Oxford
August 1940

John dear,

Please don't ask me to think seriously about taking up art. I did once when I first discovered that I could use my hands to fashion clay, but I caused too much unrest among the relations. They are essentially intellectual and quick-minded; they know my father was practical, very clever with his hands, and the idea of me following in his footsteps was, to them, devastating. The passion for creation hasn't seized me very often because I've learnt to control it. But it is a supremely selfish desire – people may come and go, their joy and pain is negligible, everything is wholly unimportant except the fear of being interrupted or thwarted. You know you have the power to create, you know that you are striving towards, though never attaining, the superb and beautiful, and you don't care what other people think of you or your work. You know you are not merely being swept away on the wings of exhilaration; you cleave your own way through the clouds, you seize the stars, catch at the moon and laugh because you know that you have found the right way, the only way towards attaining the perfection your heart and body and mind desire. When I use my hands John, I know that I am at last beginning to find the only thing in which I believe – beauty. Beauty of form or colour, beauty of joy or pain, the beauty of love or the beauty of power – what does it matter? And the only way in which I have ever been able to express that belief of mine, is by using my hands to fashion shape or to fuse colour. The devil was far from beautiful and I've shown hideous faces I knew, but it's all part of my desire.

But there you will find no discipline, for the whole of one's being is possessed by liberty; no one can blame me for drawing green faces, because they are faces I made. There is infinitely more discipline needed for intellectual work; discipline is the submission of self in the face of powers which are hard to tolerate and so hard to accept. You must quell all your own personal desires and inclinations, and accept the dictatorship of reason and of that which is cold, impersonal, devoid of the element of sensuousness. It's dangerous for me to think about art – darling, it's almost discipline to accept the idea of Somerville.

I approve of me going to Somerville in a way. The most difficult course generally rivets a little iron into the soul which is just as well. A trained mind is good enough, even though someone else is going to use it and call it his private secretary. Moreover, one must be practical; I doubt if the good God would clothe me like unto his lilies in the field if I spent my time squishing around in clay. Money, darling, don't forget that shining silver gift from the wicked regions.

If I were a Catholic I'd be glad, however tiresome matters were on earth, because I would be sure that St Peter would reserve for me a particularly luscious corner of the field of amaryllis as a consolation. Even now I'm not at all sure dear

St Anthony isn't being very busy finding quantities of
delightful things for me. Even now they are singing 'Parlez-
moi d'amour' over the wireless – it is so deliciously
sentimental, and St Anthony is used to discovering all sorts
of oddities if only you tell him that you really have been
looking. I think I shall call one of my sons Anthony.

An aunt of mine came over today – she is a doctor, and a
wise and gentle woman. She told me what I had suspected,
that my mother has been threatening to commit suicide. I
wondered why she has mentioned her will so often, why
she got so angry with Jocelyn when she would only send
her tiny doses of sleeping draughts. At least she has a
ground-floor window room at the Akland – I wish she
weren't coming home.

And you really do believe in the good God? You really
do have faith in faith? Good luck to you my friend, but
annihilate now any idea that you might ever inspire that
kind of faith into me. When Mummy married again I
believed with all my heart that her life would be recreated
and made joyous. It's been a failure, but not utterly for else
she'd have been too feeble in spirit to wish for death. Do
you remember that I said something about the death of
desire, being the greatest tragedy of all – the attainment of
nothingness? At least she desires to die. God in heaven, to
what purpose do you have faith? It will never last unless
you are blind. No, perhaps that isn't true. Maybe when the
real test comes then you will have the power to hold to
your faith. After all, Christ was one of the few really
inspired by faith, the most admirable man who ever lived.
He died on account of his faith; he has brought salvation to
millions, yet he has brought about the most shocking
hypocrisy that the world has ever known. Christianity is

the most unselfish, sacrificing of religions. And yet we, and
those before us, wallow in hypocrisy, hatred and selfishness
though we go to Church automatically to pray to this
fatherly God whom we ignore for the most part. Somehow
this war, and wars before, wouldn't be so ghastly if we were
Moslems or Buddhists. At least they kill because that is a
part of their faith – to kill and torture is contrary to ours,
and don't tell me that we wouldn't have had the same moral
inspiration if we hadn't been christened into the cunning
Church. Bother, this is getting acid which is senseless.

But don't worry, if I marry you our children shall be duly
christened and taught the ways of the righteous. If they are
caught in time they will believe steadfastly enough to
withstand all the spears of reason piercing their faith.
Religion cannot survive if reason obtains control, though
tell me otherwise for I'd be glad to know your retort.

John, John, how could you think of marrying me as you
get to know me better? My mother hates me now – that is
only because she is ill.* But do you realise that I haven't the
generosity to accept her illness as I should. My love for her
has turned to a pity so intense that it is loathsome and
nauseating. I can yell curses to the heavens for having
ruined a being, even temporarily, who was so fine and who
still might be so. I pity my mother, and I can't bear to be
near her, because she is to me the symbol of injustice,
baseness; in her are embodied the sins of my father, my
ancestors, and those of myself. She is innocent – it is we
and nature, fate, who have worked this devastation. It's
horrible. But my children shall be a gift to the world; they
shall be fine and proud with those defects which shall

*Mirren's mother suffered problems with alcohol.

make their nobility greater by contrast. They shall know
tragedy, and their joy shall be manifold. Their love of
danger will be as strong as their hatred for injustice, and
they will know how to laugh in the face of all. You see, my
mother's family are paying for the generations of fine
breeding behind them; their nerves always quivering below
the surface, tell the tale of fine breeding. For generations
there has been a succession of tragedy; their minds are too
quick, too brilliant, their temperaments too brittle and
fragile to withstand the savageness of our ages. But thank
heavens we three grandchildren are born of more stolid
less brilliant stock, and maybe bear children who will
possess the steady controlled brilliance of three
generations ago, indeed the courage, the magnificence of
my grandmother's family, with its queer mixture of
nervousness and sentimentality, its vivacity and its talent
and the quick, sudden mind which seems to be
predominant in her children, my aunts. But still, let's hope
heredity isn't as virulent as one tends to think. I'd better go
marry a farm labourer, and strengthen the stock with the
earthy elements.

I hope this has been rather a horrid letter for you to read;
you asked for it and I think perhaps you won't ask again. It's
all rather unpleasant, isn't it? If you ask me for more of my
shabby news then I shall be assured you have a morbid
mind – maybe. But you aren't to let it perturb you, because I
won't even tell you if my mother does commit suicide and
you'll just see a discreet little notice in the Times. I don't
think she will do it though – she's not quite as insensible to
the possibility of hope as all that.

I'm trying to draw No. 7 Joy Street but you won't
understand it until you get the letter. I'll write a different

kind of letter soon, only you write to me too when you have time, won't you.

Blessings on you, John,
    Mirren

Royal Burnham Yacht Club
Friday, 30th August 1940

Dear Mirren,

Now at last I can make the long deferred attempt to answer your last three or four letters. On reading them through again one after the other I have been greatly pleased by them; they form a whole which in a very real sense is living, because growing. Why, you ask, should this give me pleasure? Because it satisfies in me a morbid curiosity to delve into the seamy side of an individual's personal history, and a perverted desire to steep myself to sniff dog-like at the lamppost of her mind? Possibly to leave my little trickle with the rest? (I'm attributing that metaphor to you. I wash my hands of it, disown it.) My answer is that I am still courting you with the same shameless determination to establish myself in a privileged position in your affections, which inspired me throughout the period when, with the exception of the intimacy of one look exchanged between Freda's house and garden, we were still complete strangers. How I reconcile this with my express wish that you should return to Somerville completely unattached, a free agent to live your own life, is not at first apparent. But on reflection it would seem to be incongruous if, in consequence of my having fallen in love with you and having received at your hand a measure of encouragement, I should be compelled to compete against all comers alone amongst them bearing the handicap of disinterested interest; it would be as incongruous as my handicap was paradoxical. I already carry the handicap of absence.

And yet the first of your letters that I'm answering (the one written on close-ruled foolscap on the 19th) emboldens me to think that absence as a handicap in the Mirren marriage stakes has more apparent weight than real: you say that you can write to me about Leicester Square in words that you could never speak to me. Thank God you admit it! It was only by making the self-same admission regarding my parents, an admission wrung from me most unwilling by the convincing experience of living with them after six years' absence, that I am still able to preserve the privilege of the wonderful relationship which exists between us, and came to realise how much I owe to those six years of letter writing for the part they played in both the desire and, I flatter myself, the ability to establish others like it. I desire the establishment of such a one with you, and, in spite of the sense of my own shortcomings which afflicts me, and the reiteration of yours with which you afflict me, in spite of the violent contrast afforded by our past experiences and the downright conflict between our present beliefs, in spite of a thousand difficulties foreseen – material, sensual and spiritual – I am convinced that between us we are capable of establishing and maintaining, so long as the desire lives, a relationship of equal strength though of different fibre.

I foster an illusion, however, concerning the difference between what I can write to and what I can say to you. We

are children of our own generation, however much I may
claim to be reactionary and however deeply you may desire
to rebel, and are accordingly afflicted with its unfortunate
disease, which, fight it how we will, still succeeds in
inspiring each of us with a fear bordering on loathing of
close personal spiritual contact, and from which we can
gain relief and emancipation only by liberal use of the
potent drug of absence, a drug not without its own peculiar
pain, so stringent sometimes as to make the disease appear
a thousand times more wholesome than its cure. I harbour
no illusion that, even one day, I shall be able to address you
with words either in content or context remotely
resembling those twenty-five extraordinary pages of
manuscript which I suppose, almost fearfully, that you have
lately read. Nor do I foresee the day when waves of
bombast comparable to those in which this letter is
unrolling itself will surge between us viva voce. And so
when we talk to each other we must conform to the rules of
the game and speak in the common convention of our
generation which insists that meaning must go clad in the
jester's cap and bells of nonsense so that if we fail to find
the meat we can always taste the sauce.

I am distressed to think that your verbal map of Joy
Street has still not come to guide me on our way. Being so
very different in so many and important respects we have
correspondingly great contributions to make to each other's
wisdom, imagination and belief. Your picture of Joy Street
will, I know, prove very different from mine in many details
and most essentials, but that will give me the opportunity
of producing a fuller and far richer composite.

Saturday

It is not, however, against this male attitude towards the world's Dianas that your spirit rebels in your letter, but against the 'vanity of the mean and narrow-minded' who 'fear to get a bad reputation from going around with her'. I know such people well and as far as in me lies I avoid them. They are to be found in both sexes, but are more frequent in yours than mine for the very good reason that in matters of sex the world's assessment of virginity as a virtue which is called reputation is all-important to a woman and quite irrelevant to a man; indeed it is not infrequently a handicap to a man to be considered virgin. These are the 'nice' people and their offence is that they consider that good reputation and virtue are synonymous, and they do so consider because it is highly convenient to hand over their conscience to the custody of a keeper of such immense gullibility as public opinion. The falseness of this standard becomes at once apparent when one considers that at least one half of the opinion which goes to make it up is male opinion, which, we are all agreed, does not admit the same standards of moral virtue as those which it imposes upon women, whose opinion constitutes the other half.

Virtue is a reality; it is not a material reality, however, but a spiritual: it has no connections whatever, except by coincidence, with reputation, and very little with virginity. A good reputation is about as reliable a measure of virtue as an entire hymen is of virginity. By VIRTUS the Romans meant strength, and manly strength at that, the essential quality of VIR, the man. What a strange twist of usage then, that virtue should be expected of women and not of men!

Obviously there is a virtue of true virginity: the strength
to resist desire and preserve against its onslaught a state of
mind and body which is destined eventually to be sacrificed
to it. The virtue of virginity, therefore, is not perpetual
opposition to all desire for ever, but rather the preservation
and preparation of the body for the sacrifice. To deny all
desire is to frustrate our purpose; to cede to each desire is to
deny the only means we possess of fulfilling our purpose,
which is will power. The knowledge of our purpose on
earth is faith, the ability to apply that knowledge to the
fulfilment of that purpose is the free will, the forces which
the will directs in the light of that knowledge, for towards
the fulfilment of that purpose are the desires. The tools
with which those forces work are the components of the
human mind, the materials in which those tools work is all
matter whether living or inert. Certain of the materials with
which we work are rare and precious and must be reserved
for the finest possible work of which we are capable, such is
the process of reproduction, the preservation of this rare
material until we are ready to start work upon it is virginity,
and the strength of will required to effect that preservation
against the forces of desire is the virtue of virginity.

And so the design of life takes shape before our eyes
under the tool of the mind in a series of strokes, some
directed and some haphazard slips. The fewer the slips the
nearer does our design approximate to the ideal which we
see by faith. The more frequent the slips, the deeper they
cut and so the more difficult to marry the haphazard
strokes into the design, and soon if the slips increase all
design will disappear, the power of the will be weakened,
the worker will lose faith in the very existence of a purpose
design, being no longer able to discern its form, and life for

him will resolve itself into spending what remains of the force of his desire hacking away willy nilly at what remains of his material. It is nearly always desire which first gives out and, as you say, in the death of desire we see the tragedy of human existence – the attainment of nothingness in life. And yet as long as even a tiny scrap of material remains, as long, that is, as life itself remains, then that tiny flame of faith which compels us to cling desperately to the remnant of the great block of marble in which we set out in youth to carve the image of our faith, that last remnant of that mighty faith, blind and old and bent, may still by a sudden glimpse of the great design, albeit only through the eye of the memory, kindle the requisite small motion of desire to work upon that remnant a design in miniature no less beautiful for its minute size and all the more meritorious for having been executed by a blind person.

In writing thus I have been attempting to show you how I regard such lives as Diana's and your Mother's. I earnestly hope that you have been able to understand even a part of what I have been trying to say to you. Sufficient to understand that I fear terribly for Diana lest she never regain control of her desires and lest the sight of her precious block of marble being hacked about haphazard, great chunks flying off at a blow, should shake her faith, should make her doubt her knowledge of the design and purpose of life, and exhaust her force of desire, and the power of her will to direct it.

Your Mother's faith is long since broken and now at last her strength to go on hewing the block which stands big before her is failing, nay has failed already. The bold designs of her youth were shattered so long ago that now they are almost forgotten, her later glimpses of a purpose have been betrayed by the same slashing cuts across the carefully prepared new surface, the same wilful and purposeless destruction by the very forces which she had hoped to harness to the chisel for the realisation of her new conception of life. And now she wishes to depart, turn away from the jagged block, whose very size in spite of its hacking appalls her, to sink into nothing. God grant that even one tiny strand of that faith which binds her to life may hold out, and that the tool of her mind may remain in her hand, poised ready for the returning desire which mere existence with memory must call into being.

Sunday

   And now I shall speak of myself, not from any desire to do so but because you challenge me: 'And you really do believe in the good God, you really do have faith in faith? Good luck to you my friend, but annihilate now any idea that you might ever inspire that kind of faith into me . . . God in heaven, to what purpose do you have faith?' To what purpose indeed! since faith is the revelation of purpose in life.
   We all have a sort of innate faith, belief that there is some purpose in this life which justifies the effort of living it at least in accordance with a conventional design of right and wrong. We cannot escape from the limitations of the tool of our reason and even those who commit suicide thereby reaffirm their belief that there ought to be purpose in life, for in their last action on earth they have failed to find a purpose. But it is not that innate faith in which I believe, but an inspired faith which not only gives me knowledge that there is a purpose in this life but also

reveals piecemeal the nature of that purpose. An artist who simply believed in the existence of beauty without also believing that part of the form of beauty had been revealed to him might produce some pretty designs or pictures but never works of art. My inspired faith reveals to me a purpose in life, a design for the world; it does not reveal God to me, I add that concept later simply for the sake of logical completeness.

To continue the quotation from your letter: 'to what purpose do you have faith? It will never last unless you are blind. No, perhaps that isn't true. Maybe when the real test comes then you will have power to hold to your faith.' First of all let me say that all true faith is blind, devoid of the light of reason, relying for its conviction on something which transcends the circumscribed sphere of rational certainty. Rational truth is compulsory for the rational mind. I cannot rebel and say that I will not believe that twice two is four, I have no choice in the matter, either. I admit that twice two is four or else I am deprived of my reason. Rational truth excludes the exercise of the free will, assent is compulsory. On the other hand the essence of revealed truth or faith is that you can believe it or not, assent is optional. It follows, therefore, that any statement capable of rational proof cannot be an object of faith and equally that no object of faith is capable of rational proof. You were right therefore to say that faith cannot last unless you are blind.

Why then, you may well ask, deliberately surrender the instrument of reason, which, at least as far as it goes, gives certainty, in favour of convictions which depend for their power on the assent of the will? As I have already implied in my analysis of the relationship between faith, will, desire, reason and matter, in embracing a faith you surrender not one jot or tittle of reason. The two are not substitutes, they operate in different spheres: it is as senseless to think that we can solve a sum in arithmetic by believing as to suppose that it is possible to solve problems in moral obligation by argument. I have no wish to convert you to my faith because I know full well that you have a faith of your own. The purpose of my writing thus long and tediously is to try to make clear both in my own mind and in yours what I think of the tiresome conflicts between faith and the will, the mind and the senses, the spiritual and the material.

One day I hope to elaborate my picture of the sculptor of life. There is much that I have omitted, the place in the picture, for instance, of conscience, imagination, religion and, most important, of society. My picture so far is of one who stands alone in his studio working at a block of marble quite private to himself. That is a false picture, for we are working in the living rock, and other sculptors and masons are working all around us knocking up against our little private patch of work, treading on it, chipping at it and often trying to interfere with our work upon it. I suppose I am interfering with you, but you no less are interfering with me and I am deeply grateful for your interference. You are sharpening my tools by making me clear my mind of a lot of meaningless junk, you are adding to my strength by feeding my desire, you are steadying my hand by strengthening the nerves of my will, and, if you haven't done so already, I see that you are capable of inspiring the imagination of my faith.

This is all very fine for me, but what am I doing for you? I'm not even answering your letters in the detail they deserve and as I had honestly intended to do when I started this letter. Instead of sympathy and comfort I send you cold hard words, instead of gratitude for the delight of your letters and the soaring of your imagination in regions high and low, I send you admonitions. I wanted to talk of discipline in art and letters, of the wind-filled mighty regions and to ask you of Joy Street, Catholicism, love, hate and envy. Above all I wished to talk of you and me, but more of you. I wanted to say that I would gladly ask you to marry me in three weeks' time if I thought that your acceptance of the proposal would solve the ghastly problem which haunts you in your home. My own desire hurls me at that course, I want most passionately to possess you for myself, my little Egoist, to make you mine, to filch you from the world, secure you, lock you up away from all my hateful rivals. Why in God's name don't I do so? I can only feebly reply that I consider neither of those reasons adequate for marriage, nor both of them together. Tomorrow I may do, such is the power and privilege of faith, and I hope that all that I have said and done till now will not diminish the sympathy with which you listen to my proposal. All that I wished to say and more, but my time is spent.

    God bless you
        John
        (how cold!)

14 Merton Street
Oxford
30th August 1940

You shouldn't write letters like your last one; how can I
hope to answer it? Once I thought I could write a pretty
phrase or two, but your letter with its magnificence has
shattered all my illusions and makes me feel really weak. It
was a fine letter; one day I hope my great-grandchildren
will take the trouble to have them published for many
people would read them gladly if they had the chance.

All my guesses about No. 8 Joy Street were wrong. We
certainly didn't jump over the stile into the dandelion
field – and we didn't crash our eggshell skulls against the
wicked wall; nor did we spend much time wandering
around Leicester Square. But we walked quite a long way
down the cinder path Self, and a fascinating path it was
too. At first we could look through the glass at all sorts of
other lanes and woods and gardens. I caught a glimpse of
one very formal field and I rather wanted to search it, but of
course one can't walk through glass. Later on we became
very confused because the glass became mirror and instead
of there being only two of us, four people walked down the
path. I just didn't know whether I was talking to plain John
or Jock the seducer and you hadn't the faintest idea whether
you were holding hands with me or a reflected me.
Moreover, we weren't quite alone because there were two
reflected figures weaving a strange dance before us, and
they became all confused with our reflections and
ourselves. You weren't quite sure whether the woman
phantom had copper-coloured hair or brown hair; the man

ghost sometimes had a curly mouth and blond hair and
sometimes he was tall and loose-limbed with broad, severe
hands and a firm mouth. But at last the moving, merging
figures became clear and distinct and I understood.

Your last letter made me realise how much older you are
than I am. Darling, you've quite forgotten about Christmas,
even though you did mention it in your letter. You wrote
about Christmas Eve and Christmas Day, comparing them
with the events leading all the way to a room in the
Cumberland or the Great Eastern. You say you don't mind if
your wife isn't a virgin, you don't expect her to be one.
Don't you remember at all how much more exciting your
Christmas stocking was, when you believed Saint Nicholas
had filled it for you, than when you discovered human
fingers had already arranged and meddled with the private
surprises inside it? Christmas stockings are still very
pleasant because you know there will always be a new
sixpence at the toe, a tangerine at the heel and nuts you
must crack with your teeth hidden in corners all the way
down the leg. Besides that, there will be all sorts of
surprising presents which are exciting and new. But surely it
was much more fun when you knew Father Christmas had
clattered down the chimney and had filled the stocking
himself. Of course it's good to be sure that your parents
won't forget the bright new sixpence, just as it must be a
relief to be sure of the practical details of physical
intercourse before you marry. You know more or less what
will happen, what you will find, and that is pleasantly
comforting.

Besides, supposing your room did become our room, it
would be like opening your presents before Christmas
morning. Ever since the last family Christmas I've opened

my parcels as they came – lovely, delightful presents, but so much more exciting to open them all at breakfast time. Please let's wait till Christmas morning, and let's spend a good deal of time in Leicester Square just in case the surprise should be miserable instead of wonderful – then we might find we were in the Brig o' Dread, not in Joy Street at all. Christmas Day is never disappointing so don't let me be seduced by you.

I'll write soon, darling.
　　Yours faithfully,
　　　Mirren

FOURTH AIR-RAID ON BERLIN IN A WEEK
MASS ATTACKS ON BRITAIN
DURING WEEK-END
THE TIMES Monday 2 September 1940

Burnham-on-Crouch
Monday, 2nd September 1940

There has been no mail delivered here since Friday:
imagine then how glad I was to get your letter by Express
delivery this afternoon, glad just to see it in the sack with
the pretty colours of its stamps and label and your writing
upon its blue. Your reception of my letter is gracious and
generous; your praise is very dear to me always and on this
occasion it could not have been higher than by saying that
many people would read my letters gladly if they had the
chance. And yet the publication of our correspondence is
unthinkable, for it is so essentially private to us as almost to
be written in code undecipherable to others. Readers may
detect a felicity of phrase and even at times magnificence,
but the significance of Penelope's design, wherein surely its
chiefest value lies, must inevitably escape them unless they
are supplied with a key like those accompanying pictures of
Queen Victoria's coronation and speeches by Gladstone in
the House. I never took much pleasure in finding out who
was No. 1 or No. 2, though sometimes I must admit, I
found perverse delight in discovering who was the funny
little 394 tucked away in a corner as though admitted by a
generous gesture of the artist.

Darling, I'm not really older than you, though I do my best to maintain the appearance. You taunt me with perhaps the one accusation, the one attribute of manliness, which my Sincerity can't stand: 'You've quite forgotten about Christmas.' No, No, never, never! and I burst into tears and moan, Oh! but I do so want my sixpence.

It was only a dreadful fear that you may not believe in virginity and the innocent but intense excitement, which at any rate the contemplation of opening its present gives in the period of suspense, which made me leave myself a loophole in the great wall I had built in my letter between me and your virginity. That fear gone, I am ashamed of my unbelief. Please turn away while I brick up the unworthy gap and try to think it never was. Even feeling the stocking and rattling it to try and guess its contents seems almost cheating now, and if we cheat perhaps Saint Nicholas won't give us our sixpence after all. (Why have I been robbed of your map of Joy Street? I could speak in idiom then.)

All this you have wrung from me with the magic word Christmas; you can't have used it intentionally, nor had any inkling of the power it has over me. How could I forget? Christmas at home is more real to me, even after seven years, no nearly eight, than any other saint's day, feast or rite at which I ever assist. You would find it difficult to picture; let me try to draw it for you.

Christmas Eve was spent in preparation; presents to wrap in pretty coloured paper and bound with figured tape depicting holly leaves and berries, the saint himself with sledge and reindeer or cord of cloth of gold. Presents thought about for weeks before, cherished and treasured in secret, more dear than any possession. Flowers to be cut from the garden and taken to the church, fruit and flowers, dressed fowls, cakes and bowls of trifle, cream and butter to be taken to the hospital. Baskets full of intriguing little parcels to be carried from doorstep to doorstep to be distributed by bright-eyed, expectant friends who made us anticipate the joys of the morrow by giving us ginger and chocolate peppermint creams, barley sugar and other joys. Jack, Merrilego or Ace, harnessed in the sulkey, would spin these goodies through the town on bright-spoked wheels, perhaps over the hill into Mittagong to our friends at Elizabeth's school.

Then with the evening came the breathless supper after which David, high priest of the saint in our home, performed the last and time honoured rite of the day. The big washing basket was fetched from the wash house (we called it the laundry) and all the presents placed in it for Father Christmas to sort. Beside it was placed a tiny tray of supper for the saint to eat before continuing his journey. A little bread and butter, jam and a glass of milk, and from time immemorial a saucer full of gooseberries from the vegetable garden, perhaps some fresh currants and walnuts from the orchard, but whatever else there were always gooseberries. These were placed before the empty open fireplace in the den (being at the height of summer) with a note to say that we hoped Father Christmas would enjoy his supper and that the bath-heater was all ready to light if he would like a bath after coming down the chimney. And in the morning the supper would be eaten with the gooseberry skins neatly arranged on the saucer, the fire in the bath-heater quite burnt out with a line of soot around the bath, and a note on the tray written in old-man hand:

Dear Children,
    I enjoyed your supper and the
bath was most necessary. You really must
get your chimney swept before I come
next year. I have left you some presents.
        Father Christmas.

He did not write the same each year, and that was the
fun of tumbling down the stairs all tousled in the morning
to what he had written. We already knew that he had come
because at the foot of the bed we had seen and felt and
delved in a pillow case all bulging and angular.

As we grew up a new ceremony grew into the rite. We
learnt to draw out the delicious agony of suspense and leave
the presents unopened until after we had returned from
church and had eaten our breakfast. Then we sat cross-
legged on a lovely blue Indian carpet (the dhurrie) on the
front verandah, all five of us like so many children of eight,
and opened our presents in turn. Elizabeth's pillow case
always lasted out longest even though mine and David's
were filled out with all manner of charming surprises
labelled 'With love from Father Christmas.' And I would sit
breathless as the next one felt for a parcel for joyful fear
that it would be mine, and when at last mine was drawn
out, unwrapped, revealed and exclaimed over, I had to fight
against the tears which wanted to rush out because so much
happiness had rushed in.

No, Mirren darling, I have not forgotten about
Christmas, I have simply learnt to protect myself against
other people's forgetfulness and unbelief, to blind myself, if

you will: but even though my faith in my childhood is blind, my love for you is not.

And yet I do ask you to come and spend next weekend at home because I long to give you pleasure and think that will. You will make me very happy if you can and my parents too. I have not yet asked them but will ring them up tomorrow and if something makes it impossible then I shall wire other plans.

Please don't say that your letters are bad: they are not. You can see from the bits that I quote that they're not and from the way they find me out, find out my passing moods of which my letters are nothing but the written reflection; but neither my moods nor yours are 'trivial and feeble' except those of them which cut loopholes in our faith. We are our moods, and we are important.

And no one but you could have ended that last letter as you did. You have a freedom about you, and a confidence in your moments of inspiration which are worth sheaves of laboured prose of studied imagery and epigram.

Yours sincerely,
John

AIR THRUSTS AT LONDON'S DEFENCES FAIL
THE TIMES Wednesday 4 September 1940

Burnham-on-Crouch
4th September 1940

Dear Mirren,

The parents would rather you didn't come this weekend because, being very conscientious they betake themselves to the hall of our minute flat, for want of other adequate shelter, whenever the sirens go and they feel that the effect of our all trying to sleep in that extremely restricted space would be pleasing neither to you nor to them. (At this point the most enormous explosion shook this very flimsy building and I went outside just in time to see a plane caught in the search lights and shot down by A.A.fire.)

I have already tried to ring you up twice; once the trunk lines were all engaged and once all trunk calls were cancelled. I shall make another attempt tomorrow morning and if I fail then I shall have to send you a telegram.

I hope to get leave from Friday night till Monday morning. I shall have to see a dentist on Saturday morning but have no arrangements for the remainder of the weekend. Could we meet on Saturday if you are free? And will you give Mother and Father the pleasure of seeing you for the day on Sunday?

It seems hardly worth coming from Oxford for this: don't if it's stupidly inconvenient. I should like to see you again, but I'm not all that selfish.

I am feeling very rebellious tonight, having worked myself up into a red-hot hate against those responsible for the organisation and training of the British Army. I shall be moved to commit some outrage upon the body of a senior officer unless I cool myself off with the realisation of my own ignorance and insignificance. And yet it does satisfy something in us to toy with all sorts of sententious plans for the sudden and preferably violent rectification of imagined wrongs: the night season is peculiarly conducive to this reforming spirit and it is as well that sobriety comes with the morning. One mainstay of our effete nation is its consecration of the rite of breaking fast to silence and introspection.

It seems to be absurd that we should spend millions annually upon universal education and then treat our militia recruits as though they had been the victims of child labour and other early nineteenth-century evils. I'm sure the other services don't proceed upon those lines, particularly the navy; the Army does because the tradition that the ordinary recruit is incapable of reasoned thought, informed knowledge and intelligent interest, originally justified by the anthropoid type of peace-time army recruit fifty or a hundred years ago, is now preserved by a lot of dilettante, indolent and unintelligent officers as the excuse and justification of their crass ignorance of everything pertaining to their profession with the exception of an unimaginative and completely ineffective routine which is about as obsolete as the crossbow. Our typical regular officer has a series of catch phrases with which he hopes to conceal and protect his own idle ignorance: 'We must never expect the soldier to think.' 'We couldn't possibly explain that to them, they're so unintelligent, it'd only confuse them. They must be drilled and drilled again until their actions are entirely automatic. They have so much to learn and so little intelligence that everything must be reduced to its simplest form and made a routine.' And yet if these officers attempted to explain the theory behind their beloved routine they would find themselves more than a little confused, not to say confounded. They think that, because a man's interest in his job is deliberately stamped out by methods of instruction which would be an insult to the intelligence of performing fleas, he is constitutionally incapable of taking intelligent interest in anything more mentally elusive than beer and women. It's a shameless imposture!

I have been goaded to this angry outburst not by the obstruction of such people and such methods here, but by the contrast between the men in this place and those which even the best of the Guards battalions (the would-be cream of the Army) achieve with their ruthless discipline and soul-destroying routine. I agree entirely with the theory behind the discipline but nothing will make me submit to the vested interest which fosters and encourages the tradition that every soldier is incapable of intelligent thought. The subterfuge is too transparent.

I have no right to inflict this sort of thing upon you and I will stoutly resist future temptation to do so. But perhaps it is as well for you to submit to this imposition in order that you may have a foretaste of the sort of polemics to which you will be expected to listen should you so mismanage your life as one day to find yourself married to

Yours affectionately,
Jock

BLACK FOREST SET ON FIRE BY R.A.F.
THE TIMES Thursday 5 September 1940

14 Merton Street
Oxford
5th or 6th September

Dearest John,

I have so many of your letters to answer, but I don't want to touch upon each point of yours methodically and sensibly; I've tried to do that twice already and both letters were very dull. Even now I'm almost mesmerised by warmth, magic fingers playing a violin so beautifully, and the softness of a kitten against my bare flesh.

But I must try and concentrate because I want you to know that you make me smile almost as widely as Angel does when she is unusually 'happy'. Darling, you are no good at all at this game of make-believe; you may remember some of the ways you felt about a Christmas stocking, but you've disremembered so much. Or perhaps you haven't really, but that point shall be mentioned later. You must have forgotten, or otherwise you were no ordinary little boy. What child can resist the overwhelming temptation of reaching out to feel the stocking in the very new morning? Does a child really wake up and quell that longing to make quite sure that Father Christmas didn't forget the silver sixpence? Did you never know that exquisite delight of reaching, feeling, knowing, and then

sleeping till real morning comes to tell you that you may
touch and see and at last know? Have you forgotten, or did
you really screw up your brown hands and blue eyes, and
fall to sleep again? If you were such a child, then the
extraordinary small boy has grown up into a superman.
Almost could I challenge you not to touch your stocking till
Christmas Day, and I will unless you admit that you won't
be able to, and don't want to resist that temptation.

Yet I don't know – maybe we were very different
children. When I was little, I remember it so well, the
excitement of touching that bulky shape in the darkness did
but intensify the excitement of seeing it properly when it
was 'Time'. I had to know whether Father Christmas had
come; if I didn't know, I felt such fear and distraction, yet
when I was sure, I could sleep again with faith restored.

Our Christmases were so different from yours – last year
I had no stocking for the very first time. I was staying with
my father and he had forgotten that he was the best Father
Christmas I ever knew. I've had Christmas in Rome, and at
the end of my bed saw a Lena doll which I had yearned for.
But I dropped her out of the window into the snow when I
was looking to see if my tortoiseshell (sp?) cat, Jesus, was
being good in the courtyard. I was three years old that
time. But when we lived near Genoa and my father came
back from India, Christmas was perfect. I always knew I'd
find a tiny handkerchief from Austria, the Canary Islands,
or Algiers, or from some place where Father Christmas
passed through. Once I was given two tiny dolls with
sawdust bodies, black china boots, white china legs and
ugly china faces. I adored them: they were lovely, so lovely
that I gave them to my father at once, and he still has them.
Generally I woke up several times during the night and felt

my stocking. Daddy used to bundle Christopher, the
stockings and me under his arms, and dump us on Mummy's
bed. Then we poked and pulled, unwrapped little oddities,
bounced all over the bed while Daddy cracked the nuts for
us with his magnificent white teeth. Then breakfast –
coffee, crispy hot rolls and fruit and in front of us our
presents from Mummy and Daddy. Year after year Mummy
gave me a fairy book, the Green, the Blue, Olive, Yellow,
the Red, and Daddy would read us a story from it after
breakfast. We struggled into clean white socks and went to
the English Church, one of the two times a year. We used
to choose our own lunch, sometimes it was ravioli and
sometimes fish stuffed with octopus and dandelion and
garlic. We always had a ham and a Stilton cheese sent from
England too. After lunch we rested and then had a
wonderful afternoon decorating the house and the cats,
because when Daddy was with us, he knew how to make
gorgeous exciting parties for our friends. And the superb
sight of the Christmas tree and the brightly wrapped
presents around it, I shan't forget so easily. So the day
passed on . . .

I'm not writing about it very well because it appears to be
making me slightly homesick which is nonsensical. Few
fathers, surely, could possibly have that brilliant gift of my
father's – he could make magic in the house by crinkling his
nose, wagging his eyebrows, or by making Christmas as
perfect as I never expect to find it again. But he wasn't
always there at Christmas. Goodnight, dear Jock.
Tomorrow I must go on telling you about Christmas, cold
comfort, faith, marriage, Angel, Michael, Mike, importance.
I hope your letter comes in the morning.

Friday

Your letter didn't come – I had one from Mike instead. It's queer how you have altered my relationship with Mike*, but not with Charles** or any of the others. Mike is sincere and very lovable; he always makes me feel that he is liable to pull bits of string and knives out of his pocket and present me with some hairy toffee instead of a bracelet or a silver cigarette case. He is a very dear small boy who pretends to be grown-up – so are you. Yet between the two of you, somehow you make me feel like a very superior and refined prostitute. Mike gives me lovely presents because he adores to do it, yet, because you have rammed your nose in between Mike and me, the presents make me feel ashamed. I would rather be with you than with Mike, and those presents seem so like a less crude form of payment than bank notes. I try specially hard to be good with Mike; I make myself tolerate a rather sticky hand in the cinema. And why? Because Mike knows very well that he has slipped down a rung, but would rather have some signs of affection than the frigidity part of me wants to show him. I would rather feel bitchy inside than be really cold with Mike which wouldn't do anyone any good at all.

But it's a pity I haven't learnt to make each man who is at all likeable feel that he is the most important man. I'm afraid any husband of mine will guess at once if I'm being

*Michael de Chair. Mirren and Michael had an on-again, off-again relationship throughout the first years of the war. He was later killed.
**Charles Collingwood, another close friend, later a journalist in the US.

mentally unfaithful to him; maybe I could disguise the physical unfaithfulness. It's bad watching the dearer people give place to another who's more dear. And you, plague upon you, came without any real desire on my part to know you.

To begin with, I wanted to know your brother David much more than you. You tickled my curiosity and I quite wanted to see you again, but life was very pleasant having no one special to preoccupy my thoughts. So far everything has fallen into place so easily. Charles came to cure me from Don; Michael to distract me from Charles; Mike to be just as delightful to know as any of them. And then you, with your horrid moustache, self-confidence, truculence and tenacity literally shoved the others out of the way when I didn't want you at all at all. Now I do want you, and again I say, plague take you. I had better go find a man to distract my thoughts from you, because I spend much too much time writing to you. Moreover, you fidget me. You wheedle me into saying all sorts of things I never meant to tell you. With those poking fumbling fingers of your mind you prod at words like 'importance' and 'faith' and want me to analyse and explain them. It's annoying and tiresome, but very wise of you, because it makes me curious too, very curious to know why I pay any attention to you at all. If you can't detect an element of affection underlying all this abuse you must be stupid.

You want me to define the word importance. I can't do it, but I can explain a little. Perhaps it is a very special, delicate line on your block of marble. The more people jostle and push around you, the more they jar your hand and make your tool swerve, the greater chance that special line has of being marred, so it assumes greater importance. Sometimes it doesn't matter if the tool slips and scratches the untouched surfaces, because around it you may be able to engrave a new design. You are important because you are one of the finer and greater shapes I am carving into my marble. If my tool slips badly then I shall be faced with the ruin of something which might have been great, and is no longer. If you were one of the minor shapes or designs, it wouldn't matter much if something jogged my elbow, because I could probably alter the pattern into something quite different and equally pleasant.

Charles was important for seven months, but then Michael's eyes caught mine and my hand shook. Yet there I was not faced with ruin. The scar was deep, but it added a cynical and ironical touch to a work I should never have finished, nor even have bothered to attend to for much longer. But the danger is great. A wicked searing scar is lashed across my mother's block of marble. Underneath one can still see the fine and subtle tracery and there is still room enough for her to carve other shapes around that scar, which would prove her triumph in the face of all defeat. But your tools are working on my marble as well as my own, and I don't want to see an irreparable scar. My father's pattern is wrecked beyond recognition; I just happen to remember where it was placed. We triumph when we have the art to make the unintentional scratches form the main theme of a new design built around them. But quite honestly I'm tired of deep scars. I want a new surface. I'm tired of niggling around trying to disguise and mend, so seldom with success. I won't let you be scarred: we are to go away from each other as soon as the marble begins to get at all jagged. All so egotistical and selfish as usual.

But even all that rigamarole doesn't explain importance.

It's like swimming under water. You must have breath to
live, your eyes must be open to see where you are going.
They are vital, magnificent and, just important. Of course
you can always paddle around with your head above water.
But then the opaque liquid is only six inches from your
eyes; your horizon is restricted and water in your mouth
merely annoys and surprises you. It's ordinary and rather
dull. But under water you see queer shapes and drifting
colours; your mind becomes more acute and it's all exciting
and stimulating as long as you have breath and wide eyes. I
could live quite easily without you. I could walk around
with my head above water. Yet you've made yourself as
necessary to me as breath under water and it will hurt to go
to the top if anything happens to that breath. Did you ever
sneeze with your head in the sea? It's agonising,
excruciating. The pain sears and tears at your lungs; the
chest feels crushed; your eardrums scream and your nostrils
become still with the sting. You seize in the water, blast it
out, choke and weep and scrabble up to fresh air and the
restful uninteresting horizon. All your senses become
deadened: you are mentally and spiritually lifeless. When
something or somebody is jerked away from importance,
it's sneezing under water.

Darling, are you just a nice little boy promising not to
touch your stocking before the proper time? Do you want
to reassure me in the cot next to yours, and promise me
that we won't feel the stocking before morning? Are you
comforting me or are you promising with all the easy
sincerity of a child? Anyway, though, you've by no means
persuaded me that you won't know a little about your
stocking. I'm glad, so glad that we don't need to explore
them properly before Christmas morning.

That reminds me of Seduction Lane and consequently of Joy Street. I'm so dreadfully sorry that the letter never reached you, because you really can't understand the lino-cut at all: the most important parts will be meaningless.

What time does the afternoon post reach you? I'm sorry about the weekend, but I should have liked to go to your house again. But I'm not yet sure when Michael wants me, and I couldn't let you know till Saturday morning which would be inconvenient for your family.

Please don't talk to your parents too much about me, because it will make me shy when I see them again, and they might get too sorry if I sneezed.

Yours affectionately,
Helen

R.A.F. THRUSTS INTO GERMANY
THE TIMES Friday 6 September 1940

Friday
[6th Sept. 1940]

I had two phone calls this afternoon. One from Michael asking me to meet him at 7.00 this evening and one asking me to give a blood transfusion at 5.15. I'm so excited that I can't even think properly. But I'm going to have a bath, robe myself in royal purple and hope I don't look too pale and wan for Michael. I wish you had known him; he is good and honest and has a very fine mind.

I have a hope of which I scarcely dare to think. Maybe Michael and I will go to London together tomorrow and maybe I shall see you after all, if Michael doesn't want me any longer.

Dear, dear Jock. I am very glad I can write to you about shameful things, & about blood and about Michael.

Mirren

DAYLIGHT RAIDS ON LONDON
SUBURBAN BATTLES
THE TIMES Tuesday 10 September

Journal to Mirren from Burnham-on-Crouch
5th September 1940

Tuesday, 10th September

That rather pathetic heading was written many days ago now; I stared blankly into the blue for a considerable time without producing a single idea worthy of communication to you.

I have been looking much at your lino-cut of Joy Street. Even before you explained it I recognised all the figures and forms, though in some cases their significance escaped me. Until your letter reaches me there must inevitably be some lacuna in our intercourse or until that idiom slowly drops into disuse, but even without it I found that the essential ideas of your composition were clearly and, indeed, gracefully expressed by their lines alone without the aid of any prescient symbolism, the three dominant human sensations: the central group indecision, that on the right joyous and innocent abandon (even though I failed to identify the sign of the dandelion) and that on the left cold imprisonment. Indeed I think that as composition it shows admirable restraint in expressing so highly imaginative a theme. And that is the discipline of art which you do not admit, the submission of the unbounded imagination to the bonds of the medium of expression. That is why so much of

our modern art is bad, in that it refuses to accept the discipline of a form, and every form must be acquired as such by other beside the artist, that is to say it must contain the element of convention. In so far as modern artists are trying to create a new form and are fighting for its recognition, so far are their efforts praiseworthy, but until that convention is recognised they will be without artistic merit. Here surely is a chastening discipline such as you speak of! Surely nothing could be harder to tolerate, much less accept, for the sensitive and imaginative artist than the gross and unimaginative conservation of the critical world, whose one object seems to be to drag every beautiful thought down to the level of hieroglyphics. And yet this discipline must be accepted if the artist is to attempt to express his beauty to the world and not to himself alone; and this he must do if he is to rise above the level of doodlers and madmen, for the essence of expression is in the communication of something completely individual to a social and conventional world, it is the pressing out of part of ourselves into the mould of a recognised form.

This is no answer to your letter, which delights me, except in so far as by its sincerity and the reality of your presence that it brings I have been inspired to think and emboldened to express thoughts which without it would not have occurred to me. But, Helen, I shall return a more specific answer to certain parts at least when time admits. And if my present mood prevails I foresee that the replies which they provoke will be less in the spirit of Paris than that of

Your affectionate,
Ulysses

TWO HOSPITALS HIT – PATIENTS CALM
THE TIMES Wednesday 11 September 1940

14 Merton Street
11th September

Dearest Jock,

Your talk of discipline makes me ashamed of myself. I've
tried to write countless times since Friday but I'm
completely and utterly unable to concentrate or to finish a
letter. One day perhaps when we think of each other as
dust in the mouth, or when we are safely and nicely
married, you shall read those fragments of letters. But you
may not see them yet, for they are all tedious, all morose,
and pitifully superficial because they attempt to deceive
without succeeding in the very least. So don't blame the
post if you haven't had a letter from me in ages, because I
just haven't written. I'm waiting patiently to hear from you
because I have very nearly forgotten the way to Joy Street.
You must write very soon and remind me about it. I rang up
your home on Sunday, but David told me that you had
been called back. Sorry indeed was I to miss you, for that
seems to be the only time that I ever can phone you. It's so
tiresome, because at times I need to talk to you and as yet
we haven't managed to discover the art of telepathy.

Angel came over for the weekend with John* which was

*The Hon. John Godley, later Lord Kilbracken, to whom Angel
was engaged but never married.

so good. Angel and I sat up very very late on Saturday
night and talked about the times that used to be. It was
almost as good as being back at Somerville; we ate peanuts
and smoked and sprawled around but there was one thing
we missed a great deal. We used to get so hungry at about
3.00 a.m. and the only thing we ever seemed to find in the
cupboard was rancid butter and mouldy bread. But scrape
off the mould, toast the residue, put rancid butter and
anything into it and you will have the most delicious meal
possible. Angel must be a worker of miracles . . . I'd rather
eat mouldy bread with her in the early morning, than
oysters, smoked salmon or any other such delicacy. She still
says that she is going to marry John but she is getting more
and more nervous of the idea.

We've decided that one day quite soon Angel and John
and you and I are going to the 400 Club together. She has
never been there but she knows from me that it's a very
special and rather dangerous place, and that from there one
might possibly go up the second staircase and discover
what really is behind the corner. So I've promised that you
and I will show her the way to the 400 if it is at all possible.
But I did tell her that I'd have to ask you first, and if you
don't want other people we know to come cluttering
around, she will stop saying that she wants to go. Do you
think that we might be able to manage it? John quite often
gets leave over the weekend and you do sometimes. If that
can't be managed, then you will have to come here one
weekend because both Angel and I want you to know her
better. You may fall in love with her if you like because we
don't get jealous of each other, and besides, I think I'd quite
like you to marry her; she would be infinitely more suitable
that I would be. I have just told a lie, an immense lie,

because once I was so jealous of Angel that I felt sick. A man took her out to hurt me and to hurt himself; Angel didn't want to go and I sat at home gnawing my toe-nails with temper. Can you bite your toe-nails? It's useful if you can't find the scissors in the dark. Bother, now I can't remember of what I was meaning to write. O yes, all about falling in love with her for it might complicate matters a little, for then she'd see that I caught a finer fish than she did and she might be tempted to bait the hook again and recast her line.

This is a silly world; I wish emotion didn't interfere so much. Sentimentality has overcome reason; I'm not seeing Diana any more because Hamish has enough to perturb him without the added annoyance of a daughter with a besmirched reputation. What a nice creature I am, and how that sentimental feeling does curdle one inside. I wish I were a piece of protoplasm – it would be very convenient. Do I mean protoplasm? Surely, an amoeba, or whatever the creature is which divides itself up into hundreds of indistinguishable and equally active particles. It is a pity my vocabulary is as weak as my spelling; I shall take to reading the Thesaurus of English Words and Phrases. Did you once say that you wanted to marry an intelligent, cultured and educated woman?

5.30 p.m.

The postman passed our door again, which is dismal because letters are really our only contact with the outside world. Except for the telephone of course, and that is always engaged because the family spends its time ringing up different members to make quite sure that no one is

dead. I'm sorry about those smudgy marks but I spent an
anxious minute or so changing the ribbon.

Shut your eyes and pretend that my head is just under
your chin; that's where I wish it were now.

I am,
Yours (not faithfully, truly, sincerely, affectionately,
as ever, respectfully, or always)
just . . .
Yours,
Helen

I obviously couldn't be anyone's secretary yet, so do you
mind me practising this typewriter on you, cold and
impersonal though it looks?

THIRD ATTACK ON BUCKINGHAM PALACE
THE TIMES Monday 16 September 1940

Burnham-on-Crouch
Sunday, 15th September 1940

Dear Mirren,

I have just finished reading 'High Wind in Jamaica' by
Richard Hughes. I am glad I have read it for the same
reason I am glad I have read 'Thunder on the Left' by
Christopher Morley. I have the benefit of yet another
carefully considered and admirably expressed opinion on
the subject of children in a grown-up world. And while the
story is still fresh in my mind I am better able to answer one
at least of the questions in your last letter.

I am not just a nice little lazy boy trying to reassure you
in the cot next to mine, trying to comfort with a display of
sheep's clothing. I am making a miserable attempt to be
grown-up, to resist 'the overwhelming temptation
(irresistible to children) of reaching out to feel the stocking
in the very new morning'.

Monday

I refuse to admit that I would be able to resist, and
should you choose to challenge me not to touch my
stocking till Christmas Day I should be compelled to
accept! Perhaps I am, as you say, no good at all at the game

of make-believe: am I too cold and analytical for that? and too determined to exercise the authority of my own will in the nursery of my own life? It's only because, as I have said to you before, I would rather do a good thing on purpose than by mistake or by chance. If that preference is incompatible with the retention of those childlike qualities which I envy in others, in you and in Angel for instance, I shall be sad, but shall accept it and remain a sympathetic and envious observer of the world from which my presumption has banished me.

Don't regret that you haven't learnt to make each man who is at all likeable feel that he is the most important man. When you read 'All Passion Spent' you will see in the person of Lady Slane's husband how light and unsatisfactory is the character that the possession of that ability produces. In so far as your friends' interests in you centre in the bed it is inevitable that one who is dear shall give place to one yet dearer; in so far as they embrace a greater you they may subsist together in equality. In so far as Mike and I are contending for your body we make you feel saleable at least, but prostitution is a purely bodily transaction so that in desiring more of you than we can buy elsewhere we rise above that plane carrying our little gifts and offerings with us.

I should love to go with you and Angel and John to the 400; more than many other things I wish to do that first. Can it be this weekend or next or when? It must be soon, before our London dies. It must be soon, too, because I want to see how your hair is done.

I shall remember about the crickets but I think you are wrong about 'important'. It is a good word and you use it well. Your explanation of its meaning has more than

justified your use of it, and also your resentment at my
fumbling fingers which prod at words like importance and
faith and want you to analyse and explain them. You have
no more spoilt 'importance' than I have ruined faith! I think
it no more possible to rationalise instinct and intuition than
to prove any article of faith, but, as with our grown-up
childhood, I feel that unless we make the attempt, the
sincerity of our instincts must always be in doubt.

This has been a horrid letter, almost as horrid as the long
silence proceeding it. But it is late, just 3 o'clock on Tuesday
morning, and this must take the first post of the day. Why
have I not written before? Why have I not now written
more softly, more from my heart and less from my head? It
is because my mind is full, with my work, with my reading,
with a new acquaintance, Bill, with whom it is a pleasure to
talk until the small hours of the new day, a pleasure I have
not tasted since Kenneth Johnstone left the Training
Battalion at Colchester. Try to forgive me, Mirren. Will you
hate me for talking interminably to friends whom I find
more intelligent and cultured than myself?

I can't tell you if you spell wrong because I spell so badly
myself. And last of all I never talk of you to my parents and
have only written once; they just understand. My sister
Elizabeth has had a baby girl.

Jock

14 Merton Street
19th September

My dear John,

I'm glad that we have both been too preoccupied to write
to each other very often just lately. We could never have
kept up that rapid and animated letter writing for long and
I'm relieved that the pause came before next term. Other
things, other people are bound to get wedged between us,
and we shall be far too busy to write as often as we used to.
When you aren't occupied with your army work you will
find other people like Bill with whom you will want to talk
at length. And you know that people interest me far more
than my books, so when I'm not studying next term, I hope
and expect that I shall be able to indulge in my own
particular kind of study. Besides, I know from past
experience that writing letters during term needs more effort
than anything else under the sun. If we had gone on writing
frequently, I know I should have been the first to let a pile of
unanswered letters accumulate. As it is, we have both been
slow about writing so I don't feel mean and guilty.

    You know, it wouldn't make me any more surely yours
even if we were engaged while I was at Somerville. I
couldn't help being mentally unfaithful to you whether I
wore a ring or not, and you know that the mere fact of
being engaged wouldn't prevent you from feeling more
deeply about anyone else. I'd hate to be engaged for two
years; it would cramp us both, we'd feel conventionally
disloyal if we did find someone else more necessary, and I
know I should feel fretted and fussed. As it is I can behave

exactly as I like with other men, knowing that you could never accuse me of being unfaithful or disloyal, simply because we really have no claim on each other at all. I can't criticise your behaviour and you can't censure mine. And so in a way we are really quite independent of one another.

There will be times, and there have been times, when my own behaviour becomes distasteful to me. At such moments reason and instinct squabble together. The reason produces a good action and the instinct a true and sincere action. And when these occasions arise, I let reason get the upper hand, because the good deed affects someone else and matters to them, whereas being sincere only matters to me. All this sounds as if I were very deceitful, but it's quite simple. When I am being good with Mike I know it doesn't hurt him or you or anyone in fact. It's merely distasteful to me because I prefer to be selfish and live according to instinct and intuition. So way back in my mind I have a kind of feeling that I am being unfaithful to something or someone, which is just wishful thinking on my part because I'm really not being disloyal at all to any individual. But when the time comes, when that reasonable action becomes really deceitful because it really does involve disloyalty, then all the Mikes and all the Johns and Charles shall know why I can't go on being with them the way I used to be. But there is no reason why Mike and I should stop having the most magnificent time; he hasn't changed, he is as generous and considerate as ever. It's only I who have changed a little and that on account of you. Darn it all; I can't explain anyway, so I'd better get back to the point I was going to make way at the beginning of this foolish letter.

I said an engagement wouldn't make us belong to each other for certain; it wouldn't even help to keep us together.

In fact, people, other men and other women aren't any particular danger for us; we'd fall out and in love again, ring or no ring. But I do know that the completely different kinds of life we shall lead will be the danger. Soon, the longer we are away from each other, the less we shall have in common. You'll be absorbed one way and I another and I'm dreadfully afraid we shall no longer be a team of very competent electricians. Just now we know our way around pretty well. If I want to turn on the magic lantern of imagination, it will be all right because you know where the switch is. You know in which corner is kept the spotlight of reason and when I can't manage to plug it into the wall you will come and do it for me. But if we aren't able to go out on jobs fairly often, we shall start being very inefficient. We shan't agree about the way to mend a fuse; we'll get all tangled up and stuck on the insulating tape, and we shall get annoyed, because, as apprentices to new masters, our new methods of doing the job will differ.

This sounds very despondent, but it may equally well happen that we shall be absolutely thankful to get together again, because we shall be sick to death of the trade we were taught in the army and at Somerville. But we can't possibly know, so why worry.

My grey shadow kitten had peritonitis and was put to sleep this morning. I was just thinking the other day that there really isn't so much difference between a kitten and a baby. The kitten stretched out its jaw and curled it softly round your finger. It thrust its head against your face, clamoured for its food, bit you when it was cross, and had the faintly ridiculous ways of a wise and grown-up cat. If I am going to be a spinster I shall keep quantities of cats and kittens, especially deaf cats because their movements are a miracle to watch. They don't move indolently and graciously the way most cats do. Their eyes are never still; they seem to have a nerve quivering in every hair, and each tiny muscle is poised yet supremely controlled. I shall keep cats anyway, but the darling ones won't live for long. They've always died, been killed or poisoned the way it happens to all the finest people too. I'm beginning to believe that 'those whom the gods love best die young' or whatever the quotation is.

My mind is like a bed today; all frusty and full of crumbs of thoughts which prickle and aggravate. I must have spilt coffee because there are all sorts of nasty stains and the mattress needs a good shaking and beating. I have burnt my finger and have a cold which makes my head feel as if it had been wrapped up in a sheep's fleece. So I shall go sit on the parapet and air my mind, hoping that you will forgive me for this truculent letter. Don't let's often have breakfast in bed; the crumbs do prickle so abominably. I'm silly, I shouldn't write things like that, for how could you know whether I were serious or mocking? You couldn't and that is bad. Write when you will.

Yours sincerely,
Mirren

[The following letter consists of several sections on several different papers, begun on Saturday, 21st Sept., but all included in the same envelope.]

Saturday evening

Tonight the telephone operator spoke about Burnham-on-Crouch, but he didn't allow our voices to hum together

over the wires. But never mind, darling; all I really should
have liked to tell you can be written as well. I've recovered
from my attack of apathy and melancholia. Glory be to
goodness; acute misery lasts such a tiny while and seems
too harmless when you think of the years of freedom you
had from it afore the spasm caught at you. And what is grief
but a sad thought of the moment of sadness, a thought
made glad because that moment drifts farther away every
instant. How emotional and sentimental! But that's the way
I'm feeling and if you'd like to reorganise these few
thoughts and express them clearly, impersonally, sternly,
you are very welcome to do so.

    Goodnight, darling,
        Penelope

Much later on Saturday evening

    When Angel and I were at Somerville we indulged in a
luscious habit. We took a hot steamy bath, dropped in
some essence to make our skin and the sheets smell sweetly
and fled back to our rooms after a superb bath. And then
we sat talking for hours, warming our naked selves by the
fire. Once you started to write me, but you felt stuffy and
had a bath; then you put on your dressing gown and went
on writing. That was after No. 3 Joy Street and I was
tickled by the intimate tone of the letter. But now we have
met 8 times and I think perhaps it's rather rude of me to
write to you as I am. I only wish Sammy were here; kitten
fur against the naked skin would surpass the dreams of any
sybarite. And I'm smelling of Elizabeth Arden's Blue Grass

bath essence; it's lovely. Moreover, for the first time during the last two weeks I really do want to write a letter, and I oughtn't to be writing to you

14 Merton Street
Sunday?

Dearest Jock,

You never told me why you would rather do a good thing on purpose than by mistake or chance. Is it because you delight in the complacent feeling of self-satisfaction and triumph when you know your will power has crushed all that is free and generous and instinctive in you? Dear me, that sounds as if I were annoyed but I'm not really. I just think you are too anxious about yourself. Let's take the eternal example of an essay. Do you really feel a fine young man when you sit down and write a good essay because you said you would? Does that give you a greater kick than just sitting down to an essay and suddenly discovering at the end that you had been writing an excellent essay without really knowing it? Mind you, there are times when it is very good to know that you really did use all the powers the good God gave you to produce an exceptionally good piece of work, thinking, or even moral behaviour. You know well enough why it is a good feeling at those times so I don't need to explain. But don't you ever get that tremendous thrill of excitement when you do something good without meaning to or by chance? You feel as if some gay goblin or benevolent old wizard had inspired you with strange powers so that you couldn't help but do something good. It's a hundred times better to write a good essay by chance than to feel rather sheepishly pleased because you did something good which you knew would be good anyway. It spoils the pleasure of being triumphant if the victory was a foregone conclusion to begin with.

No, I don't agree with you at all, Jock. Everyone knows that self-control and will-power are vital at times and I assure you I am very well acquainted with the need for it myself. But there is no need for people to cramp themselves, to subdue instinct, and intuition above all. I don't know whether you are too severe with yourself to play the game of make-believe but I do know that I think you are mistaken to feel 'too determined to exercise the authority of my own will in the nursery of my life'. Maybe that kind of living is all right for you but the very idea of such self-control frightens me. Moreover we can't have at all the same ideas about children as I've already said. What normal child should be chivvied around in the nursery? It should not be ordered to do this and that; ask it to, and if it refuses to, why goodness me it won't play with the bread knife twice unless it doesn't mind cutting itself. Why, if it wants to go on cutting itself, let it unless you think you have borne and bred a homicidal maniac. If St Anthony said he would perform another miracle and abolish either the good derived from self-control or the good derived from experience, I should beg him to remove the former. I believe so much in experience and a freedom which I don't know how to explain, that your equally determined belief in the authority of your own will seems wholly beyond my grasp. Mind you, I do believe that man has unlimited power and that it does have to be restrained, but not at the expense of freedom. No, that sounds wrong too. I don't think you are narrow or stupid enough to abide solely by what reason dictates you should do, but I think that you stress its importance too much. This is an entirely personal point of view, and maybe you do have to attend a good deal to will-power in order to live the way you want to.

All the same, tell me if you would like to do every good thing on purpose and never by chance. I ought to be your mistress. After all this talk of self-control you will be so savage if you ever did manage to seduce me. I don't want to go to bed with you but if such a thing did happen I would rather it came about by chance, by mistake than on purpose. But of course one still has to determine whether such an action would be good or not. If one decided it wasn't, then the question of chance or purpose wouldn't need to be considered. All the same, you and I will spend some very uncomfortable minutes waiting for your own will to gain complete authority. I wish the pause could be rather more instinctive than so rational and calculating as it needs must be now that we are getting to know more about each other's thoughts. However, it can't be helped now and at least I can console myself that I haven't challenged you. I wish all this didn't sound so brazen and crude, but I don't know how else to write about it.

Several hours later.

Now I'm in such a fluff of excitement that I couldn't possibly write seriously. This afternoon two friends turned up on leave. One came to tea and sat on the floor talking about life in the Coldstream Guards, opening wide his enormous brown eyes

till he looked like a small and very wondering boy. Malcolm is
far too surprised by army life to be marred or made by it; experience worries him as little as water flowing off a laurel
leaf. Dick came for ten minutes and we talked passionately
about last year. We laughed at the vast quantities of bread and
cheese and pickles we ate at the Trout, waxed sentimental
about a superb tree we climbed one frosty and brilliant night
and wondered why we hated each other the first few times we
met. Oh, it was such fun meeting again after six months; by
that time one really can't help but laugh at one's self as well as
at other people. Darling, this must be dreadfully boring for
you and I will try and be good and not rant and rave about
friends. But I'm a no-good woman; I'm weak and feeble and
never will be able to be at all independent, because when
friends who have gone away come back again, I feel as though
each one were adding a vital stitch to a shredded heart. Next
term my reputation will be mud: Oxford will say I am a Lesbian
because I shall go silly with delight when Angel comes back to
see me, and I shall be considered cheap and promiscuous
because I know I shall welcome every man as though he were a
long-lost and adored lover. But hell, what do I care as long as
they come back. Dear John, I wish you were here tonight, for
I'd gladly dance the eightsome reel all up and down Merton
Street with you and anyone else who would join us. Glory be,
but I'm happy.

   Now read the blue page.

Still Sunday evening.

   If Bill is as likeable as Angel, I don't blame you for
becoming suddenly modern and desisting from an old-

fashioned courting. I'm sure our ancestors wrote charming little billets-doux to each other every day. All the same you are a good man and you shall have these scrappity notes, however tiresome you may be. The tone of our letters has changed very suddenly, hasn't it? I wonder what is happening.

Buona notte e dormi bene.
Helena

Monday

I have just heard that I am going back to Somerville. Now I shall have to work like one possessed and we might arrange to meet before I am shut in behind those academic gates again.

You have to read these pages in the order in which they are folded or else you will get too muddled.

JAPANESE ENTER INDO-CHINA
THE TIMES Tuesday 24 September 1940

24th September

On Thursday the 26th I'm going to c/o Mrs de Chair, Netherwood, Midhurst, Sussex, and then from the Monday to the 7th I shall be at 2, St Albans, Tekels Park, Camberley, Surrey. Tel Cam: 1131. There I shall spend my time working and sitting outside barrack gates, so I shan't be peeved if you write to me as seldom as I shall write to you. I've just heard that a number of Oxford friends are stationed thereabouts and my aunt has lent me her flat, so I shall live a chaos of books, cooking, dustpans and brushes.

I doubt if you and John and Angel and I will be able to do anything together, but maybe you and I will be able to meet afore term starts on the 13th. Are you pleased I'm going back?

Mirren

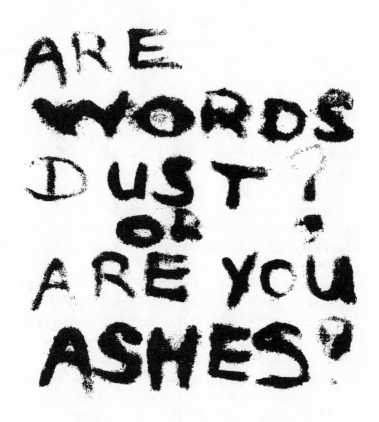

ARE WORDS DUST? OR ARE YOU ASHES?

Written in soot to Jock, by Mirren, 25–26 September

Burnham-on-Crouch
Sunday, 29th September 1940

Words are dust! my own and yours and Priestley's, whose
'Angel Pavement' I have been attempting; Jane Austen's 'Auriel',
'The Golden Treasury' and the 'Spirit of Man', all are covered
with pompeiian layers of bitter brick dust from crumbled houses
whose smell of attics reeks in the night, dry and pungent.

You will not understand this letter any more than you
have understood those that never came, nor can I hope to
succeed in explaining either the one or the absence of the
others. As much as I myself understand is shameful and will
not take shape between us, the remainder, if it exists, is
without comprehensible form.

The most unexpected thing about bombed houses is
their sudden enormous age. Their construction has been
hurled back through time to forgotten ages, their latest
habitation to a race of men, women and children
indistinguishable from each other as they lie huddled in the
dust of centuries, even the difference between the living
and the dead is obliterated in that bitter red powder.

Bill is not so likeable as Angel but is more intelligent and has
seen and done much more. Randolph Churchill[*] is a man I am
proud to know. I am an uneducated lout beside them and a
pompous little fool beside Randolph. I cry at the thought of
the time I have wasted, the energy I have squandered and the
memory I have neglected. Even the affection I have
exchanged, my most treasured property, must have been the

---

[*]Randolph Churchill, son of the great statesman, was also to be
a member of No. 8 Commando, and of the SAS.

richer for a richer, more active and more careful mind.

Forgive this letter and that silence please. Don't hate me yet, until we meet again. Suspend your judgement and believe me only.

Yours affectionately,
John

[30 SEP 40]

289 9-10 OXFORD T 42
TEL LETTER JOHN LEWES YACHT CLUB
BURNHAMONCROUCH =

DESPAIRINGLY PENELOPE WILL LET JOY STREET TAPESTRY
GROW DUSTY IF ODYSSEUS DOESNT SEND FOR GODS
MESSENGER MERCURY TO CAMBERLEY IMMEDIATELY STOP
REMEMBER THOSE WHOM THE GODS LOVE THEY FIRST MAKE
MAD SO COMMUNICATE IF POSSIBLE +

Royal Burnham Yacht Club
Burnham-on-Crouch
Essex
Tuesday
[undated . . . likely 1st Oct 1940]

Mirren, quickly, a word to break a long silence, just a phrase to snap it off at the stem and prevent it growing and its roots deepening.

Your letters have arrived and inspire new vitality into my
flaccid mind and loose the strings of my tense nerves. I
have tried to write to you, you see with what success.

On Saturday night I was recalled to my unit. The order
came after the last train had left, there was no alternative to
driving. The long journey without lights, starting with the
passage of the burning East End, the bull's eye for enemy
bombers, ended at 3.30 on Sunday morning. Since then we
have been standing to against emergency. I have been
getting in as much sleep as possible and my waking
moments have been employed in such thoughtless tasks as
plaiting leather straps and thongs, splicing ropes and
cleaning and oiling my weapons.

But tonight I shall write to you with pleasure once more
and without effort.

    Bless you and keep you,
       Jock

                 2 St Albans
                 Tekels Park
                 Camberley
                 1st October

Dear John,

Thank you for your letter. I wired last night because I
was worried. After hearing from you at least four times a
week, no news for over a fortnight was alarming.
Unfortunately, the 'fey' tendency I inherited from my

grandmother has not yet informed me whether or not you will be killed. Sometimes I know when people are dead, but I didn't know about you. I hope you are flattered to think I fuss about you.

Twice you have told me you are ashamed; twice you have asked me not to hate you. I think you must be feeling rather revolting. I hate people when they surprise me, when they let me down. All very illogical because I'm damned silly to trust them. Only four people have made me really angry, and you aren't one of them. You simply disappoint me.

I told you in the Berkley that I thought it was a mistake to believe in or trust in anyone too easily. I still think that and consequently you can't make me hate you. I may despise you, ignore you, dislike you, but you can never let me down. I don't allow you to do that.

It's a pity you are ashamed; it's a great pity that you are so ashamed that you can't tell me about it. You and I are so honest with each other, it becomes agony at times. But all the same, it leads to complete understanding which is a precious thing. While you are ashamed and I proud and selfish we never shall reach that perfect understanding. But you know, that doesn't worry me at all just now. I knew something queer would happen to our relationship, and I know what will happen to us in the future. You might send me a post-card from time to time to tell me how you are, that is all that I want to know. I don't much want to know why you are ashamed nor why you find it so hard to write; my own guess is quite a satisfactory explanation.

Till something happens I shan't write to you again. There is no point in it and it would be a mistake, because I am rapidly reaching an inevitable state of complex feelings.

Come to Oxford when you will; I shall be in College on the 11th. I doubt if I shall need to write until after we have met again, unless I think anything requires to be stated or answered.

Yours,
    Mirren

P.S. I resent jealousy so much that at times it approaches hatred.

ALL DAY ATTACKS ON LONDON FAIL
THE TIMES Thursday 3 October 1940

Burnham-on-Crouch
Thursday
[probably 3rd Oct 1940]

Dear Mirren,

One reason why my correspondence has been so irregular
is because I do all my writing at night and lately exercises
have occupied a large proportion of the dark hours. Last
night I slept the clock round after skipping Tuesday night
completely. Tonight I am in no form to write having drunk
too much for logic, too little for sentiment and just enough
for sleep. I am now smoking a cigarette in the hope that it
will do something to alter the exact balance of powers, but I
feel that I will tend rather towards confusion.

May I quote Rupert Brooke to you, perhaps he expresses
something of what I feel: 'Often enough I feel a passing
despair. I mean what you meant – the gulf between non-
combatants and combatants. Yet it's not that – it's the
withdrawal of combatants into a special seclusion and
reserve. We're under a curse – or a blessing, or a vow to be
different. The currents of our lives are interrupted. What is
it? I know – yes. The essential purpose of my life, the aim
and end of it now, the thing God wants of me, is to get
good at beating Germans. That's sure. But that isn't what it
was. What it was, I never knew; and God knows I never

found it. But it reached out deeply for other things than my
present need . . . There is the absence. Priests and
criminals — we're both — are celibate and so I feel from my
end sometimes that it is a long long way to Tipperary. And
yet all's well. I'm the happiest person in the world.' A long
long way and lonely is all I would add to that to bring it
forward just 26 years and make it mine, and that's not
addition but simply emphasis. He says it better thus:

> Now God be thanked who has matched us with his hour,
> And caught our youth, and wakened us from sleeping,
> With hand made sure, clear eye, and sharpened power,
> To turn, as swimmers into cleanness leaping,
> Glad from a world grown old and cold and weary,
> Leave the sick hearts that honour could not move,
> And half-men, and their dirty songs and dreary,
> And all the little emptiness of love!
> Oh! we who have known shame we have found release
>   there,
> Where there's no ill, no grief, but sleep has mending,
> Naught broken save this body, lost but breath,
> Nothing to shake the laughing heart's long peace there,
> But only agony, and that has ending;
> And the worst friend and enemy is but Death.

So you see my emancipation is complete. I can only write
to you as to one of many friends and then only when the
central purpose of my life, the aim and end of it now
permits. You will hate me? no; that you will respect me I
hope; you will love me? no.

John

DICTATORS' MEETING
ON THE BRENNER PASS
THE TIMES Saturday 5 October 1940

Burnham-on-Crouch
Saturday, 5th October 1940

Dear Mirren,

I read your letter in unexpected circumstances. Three hours ago I was at home just about to set off in Alice to pick David up at Bishop's Stortford. A telegram arrived and as a result here I am back again, having failed for the second time to break away from here and demilitarise myself even for the short space of a weekend. I had hoped that Oxford would come within my reach this time, but there is something inevitable and almost personally malicious about our separation, which, as a result of my ineptitude, renders letter-writing ineffectual and even possibly irritating.

I found your letter within a few minutes of arriving, and I have lost no time in replying for now time is precious.

I had not realised that my letters would be so open to the interpretation which you have laid on them. Clearly, since my last letter, which in the light of yours that I have just read reinforces that interpretation beyond any sane doubt in your mind, any chance of restarting the correspondence which I so negligently let drop has disappeared. And yet the possibility of our meeting within the next two or three weeks is extremely remote, so if I do write letters which tell you more than merely how I am I hope you will receive and read them with as nearly as possible the same openness of mind with which you received my earlier letters to you in the days before our friendship became intimate.

It would be a pity to allow a guess to stand in the way of something great and beautiful, particularly as that guess is almost certain to be wrong. If you knew Burnham and had you also known that since last seeing you I have only left Burnham twice, both times to be recalled within a few hours of arriving home, you would not have guessed the way you have.

If I have disappointed you I have disappointed myself much more; for years I have been trying to learn to pursue more than one interest at a time. You can with difficulty conceive what a handicap it is to be possessed of a nature which forbids concentration on several concurrent interests. Whatever I do, I must do to the exclusion of everything else. That has the advantage of concentration of effort, whereas that very complexity of interest exaggerates its disadvantage, namely that when one's interest flags or is replaced by another, the tremendous effort with which it was once pursued dries up or transfers its allegiance. And so people are deceived in me because I am inconsistent and variable and unpredictable – but who more deceived than myself? I don't blame you, Mirren, not for one iota of the coldness that chills our writing. You have been more than generous with your tolerance and wish to think well of me. It is I who have prevented the fulfilment of that wish.

This is not the first time that I have surprised and disappointed someone dear to me, and so I know better now how to behave, I know the uselessness and danger of

long written explanation, of sudden bursts of fury or
contrition, and of pride or even shame. That of course is
what misled you, the shame I felt at having so abandoned
you in favour of new interests here? Or was it because you
guessed at what they were and so hated them that you
withdraw your confidence and trust?

I leave you to ponder that question, for it's one of
supreme importance and from your answer to it depends
our future.

John

14 Merton Street
Oxford
8th October 1940

Dear John,

Thank you for your letter which arrived this morning.
Almost exactly a year ago Donald Calder came to see
me here in Oxford. I quarrelled with him because I was
vain and far too proud to let him realise that I understood
him. That sounds complicated, but it isn't; it was
merely the end to what might have been a very fine
relationship.

You've learnt that you can disappoint people; I too have
learnt a very severe lesson all about vanity and pride and
understanding. You have guessed at my guess about you. I
have guessed what you have guessed, and if I'm right all I
can say is that my first letter about Joy Street, which never

reached you, was far more important than either of us could have imagined. Dearest Jock, we may yet spend a while understanding each other. But just believe this – I already knew why you find it hard to write; in your own words you told me almost exactly what I knew about yourself. You see, you and I are very very much like millions of other people, though we tend to be rather pleased with our own individuality. Your aim in life may be to kill Germans. My desire is to learn from other people how they live and love, die and hate. I learnt a great deal from that last bitterness with Don, and that knowledge I may now apply to you. Once I said to him, 'You can have me if you want me, but you've got to be mine alone; give me liberty or give me love.' Do you remember that song? Well, I was mistaken to say that, and I won't say it to you now.

A woman always wants to be of the greatest importance in a man's life, and it's hard for her to take the second place. You know, the usual business and being jealous and angry that he is so absorbed in his work. If only you could believe, John, that I do know what Thing has rammed its way in between us; I truly do accept and recognise its presence. I hated and resented that Thing which came in between Don and me, but I suppose its existence and my refusal to recognise it has given me wisdom of a sort.

Even in my mind I'm not yammering and being angry and peeved with you. When your lust for beating Germans grants you time to feel trust and desire for me, I shall be around for a while longer anyway. I don't only mean physical desire, but all desire, nor do I mean merely blood lust, but a lust to crush all that you condemn.

Certainly write to me as you will to any other of your

many friends. All I regret is that I can be of no help to you. I find that a little hard to understand; your wife won't have a pleasant time when you, bearing the great weight of convictions and beliefs, treat her as a pretty porcelain figure. It would be soul killing for most women to know that your long, long way to Tipperary was quite lively, and that you ignored the passionate appeal of their flesh and blood, their brain and spirit, to walk the long way with you, even as lightly and as inconspicuously as your shadow. It's a good thing I don't love you, for now you could hurt me very much.

I too have a very real aim in life, but it embraces so very much, that people can call me fickle and inconstant too. Fortunately I always have my hands full of problems, so I am rarely left destitute for long. Now that I cannot be preoccupied with you as I was formerly, I can switch the points on my railway line and send my private engine of energy charging into another direction. You kill your Germans, and I shall be around waiting for those who want to come before, during or after they have killed Germans. You have a great desire and I have too. All I want is to see people's lives and minds mended and gladdened even a little bit. Somebody once told me that I had the instincts of a prostitute for wanting all that, so I won't explain all about it to you as I did to him.

The Miracle didn't sing in Joy Street after all. It's a pity.
Yours,
Miriam

P.S. I don't hate, love nor respect you. I like you and admire you – respect is very different from admiration. Dear John, you have to live your own way, and if it's a way which isn't mine, that's that and nothing can be done.

Come to Oxford when you can and we'll start as we were on August 4th 1939. That's a better date than July 4th 1940.

I was disappointed because you had not the courage nor determination I should have liked. But now I suppose I'm not even disappointed. Was it a béguine after all? I go to College on Thursday.

GERMAN-ITALIAN PINCERS ROUND EGYPT
THE TIMES Thursday 10 October 1940

Thursday, 10th October

My dearest John,

Seven weeks ago today you and I met in No. 8 Joy Street. Just about this hour Charles passed me a slippery piece of soap and you changed all your clothes, except your khaki socks – very odd they looked too. I think we had a very happy time for almost exactly ten hours, and I liked the way you kissed the back of my neck at 4.30 a.m. on Friday morning. I remember a great deal about that evening, and tonight I'm having a busy time pretending – I'm pretending dreadfully hard that I almost love you again, and that these last weeks of wondering and feeling stranded haven't happened at all. I need to forget the unfriendly letters I have written, these words of yours which made me feel a pulse of fright in my throat. Just this evening let me say that I terribly much don't want us to quarrel, that I don't want us to write these nonsensical letters, and that I don't want us to disguise a rather jagged scratch on my marble with superficial little patterns.

Tomorrow I shall be very amazed with myself for posting this letter, because I never meant you to know that I could be sentimental like this. But all you need to do is to pretend that I wrote this letter weeks and weeks ago, when it would have fit in with the pattern.

You see, Jock, I am very sure that I am going to be mean about you, even though I never let the meanness escape on to paper or over the telephone. I shall say acid things about you to Angel, in my own mind I shall feel indifferent about you and quite bored with the thought of you. Moreover I shall get very involved with some man or other, so that you will become another 'episode', and will be neatly tabulated and tidied away with other memorable affairs. I shall speak of you in the past as I have spoken of Don and as you have spoken of the red-headed girl. In fact I shall be free of you. I shall have finished with you. For how long that will last, I don't know. But I also know that we shall be together again, somehow, sometime. I may feel as easy and as friendly with you as I do with Charles, or I may be awkward and nervous and hurt. This is all very egocentric, but I do know what will happen to a certain point, whatever you may think. My grandmother had the gift of foresight; sometimes I believe that I have inherited it too, though actually now I think I'm depending on my intuition rather than on my reason.

Look you, darling, I'm not asking you to answer this letter. We both know that you are only going to write when you have time to attend to letters, and you needn't take any notice of this one. I'm writing for my own ease and not for your benefit or pleasure, so don't let me make you fret and fume.

Go on being single-minded, Jock drágóm, for it suits you very well.

Yours,

P.S. I think that you'd better remember these!

i	ii	iii	iv
Penelope	Cassandra	Helen	or just Miriam

P.S. I think that:

i	Penelope	means you matter a great deal
ii	Cassandra	means this unwilling certainty
iii	Helen	means I'm feeling privately faithless
		or merely mocking and flirtatious
iv	Miriam	really rather indifferent and formal
v	Mirren	good enough for most things

HAMBURG STORAGE TANKS DESTROYED
THE TIMES Saturday 10 October 1940

Box No. 1
Inverary
Argyllshire
Saturday, 12th Oct. 1940

Dear Mirren,

This is written in the rather sordid surroundings of a
Nissen hut, but with a sense of relief and satisfaction so
strong upon me that it might be a palace for all the
difference it makes. I am very deeply grateful for your letter
and am doing what little I can to show it by sending you an
answer at once. Although your letter was posted as long
ago as the eighth it arrived only this morning, having been
first to Burnham which we quitted early on Thursday
morning. We travelled all that day by train to Greenock,
thence by boat up Loch Fynne to this the so-called capital
of Argyllshire, where we arrived and started installing
ourselves amid much builder's squalor yesterday afternoon.

You have shown more perspicacity than I credited you with,
you have seen perhaps as deeply into my character as even I
see myself; I am in consequence not well able to say how right
or wrong you are, particularly in the matter of courage and
determination, the two qualities which I most diligently seek
to acquire, which fact by itself is probably sufficient to prove
that I am not truly possessed of either, else why the search? But

be that as it may, I am much relieved to feel, as I do since reading your letter, that no road or bridge has been blocked and mined against the progress of our friendship, however far it has slipped back lately down the hill of individual difference, and however bitter that retrogression may have been at the time and since. Even for the bitterness itself I can feel no remorse, for I have learnt one more lesson in the hard school of experience, and provided those lessons are well learnt deep in the heart of the memory there is not room for remorse in the same place as well; however high the school may be, life still lies before us, so that we have time and added wisdom to recoup the loss. I say 'we', yet I speak of and for myself alone: it would be hypocritical of me to offer you any other comfort but contrition for a wrong which I my self have inflicted.

Once we have settled in here our training will proceed very quickly, and it should not be long before we are ready to carry out any task which the higher command may call upon us to perform. I shall write at intervals, but I must ask you to read my letters with consideration for the circumstances in which they are conceived and executed. Opportunities for reading and writing will be scarce and an atmosphere conducive to either even more difficult to come by. Such details of our training as I would be permitted to give you would be of little interest and there is not much happening besides.

I am engaged at the moment upon reading Boswell's Life of Johnson and the more I read the more deeply I regret not having read it not once but many times before; it is a very great book besides being almost unrivalled as a preceptor of the English language, the foundation of British morals and manners, and finally of robust British humour. Since being in the Brigade of Guards I have learnt to hate and to fear decadence: here is no decadence, here, in fact, is what our nation has fallen away from in every instance where decadence can be discerned in us.

God bless you and your new term at Oxford.
　　Yours,
　　　Jock

No. 8 Commando
Box No. 1
Inverary
Argyllshire
Tuesday, 14th Oct. 1940

My dear Mirren,

　Serious writing in these conditions is hardly practicable though sitting down to write to you before going to bed has a pleasant comfortable feeling of established familiarity not shared by any other feature of my present surroundings.
　I am sitting on the straw mattress of my bed in the hut which I share with eight other officers. On my knee is balanced a bit of three-ply wood which holds besides my writing paper, a travelling ink bottle – souvenir of Berlin – and a little oil night-light which is struggling to dissipate the darkness about my pen, a physical darkness only, I hope, though I must admit my mind is by no means lit either by the pellucid rays of reason or the luminous glow of intuition, and as for the colourful illumination of fancy, that is quite wanting.

Your letter arrived to cheer me at lunchtime when the fair weather that we have so far enjoyed had already broken. I'm glad you wrote it and sent it for to me it represents the crossing of a bridge in safety; once more the ground is firm underfoot and I can step out towards you without having to feel my way at each pace, testing the rickety members of the structure to see whether they will bear the weight of myself and my burden of preoccupation.

But though I exult in your letter, I do not wish to give the impression that I acquiesce in your relegations of my memory to the status of an episode – just another man to you. That has never been my ambition, or only at rare moments of lusty forgetfulness, quickly dispelled by your own firm treatment. Was it you who once inveighed against the clutching hands pursuing the helpless butterfly? Then why are you so willing to interpret each male who presents himself in these terms? Obviously his actions in your presence lend themselves to that construction, but since you dislike it so much I should have expected to find you only too willing to construe his interest differently where that were safely possible. Perhaps that is not here the case.

I must now go to bed for my eyes are beginning to protest. I have still more to say to you so tomorrow must see the continuation of the writing. Goodnight, dear Mirren (you see I assume your most valued signature, though 'tis soberly done).

Friday 18th

Tomorrow & tomorrow & tomorrow, that brings us up to date, to find me once more sitting on my bed, this time at mid-day, propelling my pen over the uneven paths of this letter.

I arrived in this little town to discover that my parents had at last torn themselves away from our little home in No Mans Land and are on holiday with Elizabeth, but twenty miles or so from here. I go to visit them on Sunday if fortune favours my planning.

I thought I had a lot to say to you but it seems to have been swallowed up in Highland mists and natural indolence. Will you write to me anon? Of your labours and your pleasures and how you go in the world? There is so little of my present self that I can give you that I would gladly join you fancifully in Oxford and live a second life for you alone.

> Yours ever,
> John

Inverary
Saturday, 19th October 1940

Dear Mirren,

I feel sadly sentimental about you tonight, and for a very odd reason: because this is the last uncensored letter that I shall write to you while we are here, and it therefore seems that our writing is at an end. For even though it is one of my own friends in the Officer's Mess who reads and franks my letters for me I won't be able to write nor you to read, I am sure, with any thing but the stiffest and most apprehensive formality. And so the war is with us at last,

determined with demoniacal tenacity to render our
separation as complete as physical absence and seclusion of
spirit can make it. But I repeat that this is no more than
rather morbid sentimentality and the demon who follows
our trail with such unerring instinct can easily be defeated
so long as sentiment is kept in its proper place, which is in
the past. The future belongs to us not as sentient but as
spiritual beings; if, therefore, you and I have any common
future, it is in our own spirits that we must look for the
shadows it casts before.

There is not time to write more than this and so I sign
myself with great affection and a desire for love.

       Yours,
        John

             14 Merton Street
                Oxford
         2nd November 1940

The kitten yawns hugely and is disgruntled for I shook
him off my back as I reaped the fruits of my failure. In other
words I have finished my last attempt to make a pattern of
Joy Street, and the result is dismal. But soon you shall see
for yourself the works of a wench who won't take up art
because she knows the results would be a great deal more
inferior than third-rate, and it's so badly put together that
you won't understand what's which unless I explain it all.

To the s.e. you will see a cigarette whose smoke looks
like strings of spaghetti, and on the same table stands a

glass which is meant to be a champagne glass in case you
don't recognise it as such. This s.e. corner is reserved for
the moderate men and women of our Leicester Square. In
the n.e. lies a field. Very near to this field is an avenue of
ponderous trees – at the other end of the queue you
sometimes discover the Sentimental Gardens or suddenly
realise that you have been groping your way through the
forests of seduction after all. Then you may walk down a
broad street whose houses on the left are allowed no
windows. And that's because the beggar priest and the chief
dancing lord Delight lead the procession up the street, and
no one else is allowed to stare at the procession except us.
It has to be a fairly broad road because the procession is
one called Desire, and there must be room for the little slim
boy dancer called Desire-Delight as well as room for the
superbly built woman called Power. Up the street come all
our desires – the little blind baby girl called Tears, and
Imagination, that sudden child, with wild russet-coloured
hair tangled with brilliant jewels. And the smoke from
Leicester Square drifts up this street; it may bemuse our
vision of the procession but at least it does remind us that
other corners of Joy Street do exist, besides the street
devoted to the beggar priest.

At the corner of the street is a round tower, and behind
its barred door lives the Being who lends us wisdom to help
us on our way through Joy Street. Sometimes that Being
has your eyes, and I am left on the doorstep because you
have the wisdom and I have not. But sometimes my voice
talks to you through the bars and when you've decided not
to risk a venture down the avenue in case we don't find the
Sentimental Garden, we are allowed to walk on together
again.

But the first house in that lane is a special house. Once, I think we decided it was 50 B.C. We climbed up and up some wide shallow stairs. When we had nearly reached the top you gave me a glimpse of that secret room, only I couldn't see into it, for the light shining from the windows was too dazzling and brilliant One day maybe we'll go up the next flight of stairs – they are narrower and steeper and we can't see what happens at the top because they wind right round the corner.

Hesitating between Leicester Square and 50 B.C., looking towards the dandelion field, the procession street and the avenue above and around, are two figures. They are darkened so that you cannot see the pucker between the man's eyes, nor the despair curving the lips of the woman. Yet I think you know about these figures, so I don't need to tell you of them and their ways.

The pattern of Joy Street might have been good. If you look at it from the distance or between half-closed eyes, it won't look so clumsy and so hopelessly inadequate. Do you understand it at all?

Making the pattern may have been a labour of love, but cleaning up the mess in my room will be drudgery indeed. You couldn't guess how confused are the things on the floor. Paints, shreds of line, quantities and quantities of useless prints, hairpins, needles, razors, pencils – all these my tools. And drying amidst this chaos is the only print I could send you, and even that is murky and unsatisfactory. I wish I could have done something good for you. I have a notion that I'd better confine myself to writing about such matters – they look rather crude in black and white.

I must clutter downstairs and post this – then perhaps it will reach you tomorrow.

There are still hundreds of things I want to tell you, but I'll just have to try and remember them. I'll write again.

So goodbye to you, dear love of Joy Street,
    Mirren

Largs Hydropathic
Largs
Ayrshire

Mirren dear,

Disregarding your express instruction, I have dared to send you a length of cloth with a faint green check in it. I like the cloth, though I cannot say with conviction that I would necessarily like it on you. Please do what you will with it and if you can think of nothing better, send it to Mother at 8 Tudor Court. Tell me what you would like and I shall try and get you another length more suitable.

It seems a long time since I heard from you. I have attributed your silence to preoccupation or the dislike of the censorial eye (which is now withdrawn, restoring full privacy) and have not therefore been impatient for your news.

I have lately read two excellent books: 'Katrina', translated from Sally Salminen's original Swedish and 'The Gun' by Forrester, the last a Penguin. I still spend grateful hours with Boswell and Sam Johnson, God bless them both.

This is brief, but perhaps it is best so since I am not in a fluent vein at the present.

God bless your studies and give you happiness at
Oxford.
   Farewell,
      John

PostScript

I expect to be here a week or ten days, were you wishing
to write.

   J.

BIG ATTACKS ON COVENTRY
1,000 CASUALTIES
THE TIMES Saturday 16 November 1940

Largs Hydropathic
Largs
Ayrshire
17th Nov. 1940

Dear Mirren,

I hope that you will be in a mood to write to me, for by
as much as I dislike receiving letters from people to whom I
ought already to write by so much I am loth to multiply my
letters to you, until I should have heard whether those
which I have already dispatched have been received and
whether with pleasure or the contrary. It would give me no
pleasure to pester you with letters when you were
thoroughly engrossed in other matters, on the other hand it
would give me great pleasure to talk with you again
unconstrained by distance either of place or manner.
When I come South again I shall take occasion to call
upon you. Until then I shall be satisfied if I hear no ill news
of you.

Yours in suspension,
Jock

Somerville College
17th November 1940

Dearest Jock,

The letter I wrote to you to thank you so much for the
tweed was given to someone else to post. And that
someone else just wrote to say how very sorry she was to
find some of my letters in her pocket two days ago. So
whether a thank-you letter ever reached you I know not.

After telling the most preposterous lies I managed to get
permission to spend Friday night out of Oxford. I went to
London and it made me 'sadly sentimental about you' as
you put it on Saturday, the 19th of October, 1940. (if you
think very hard you might guess that I still keep your
letters.) In London I saw an old man driving an ancient
hansom cab; please, one day will you let me drive with you
in a hansom cab – you promised to take me. The last time
you and I were in London together was on a Thursday; we
left the 400 Club at about 4 a.m. and watched the first real
air-raid I had ever seen. But on Friday night two of us crept
around the house with candles and ate biscuits for supper
because there was no electricity nor gas, and it was too
noisy to try and make our way to some eating house or
other. It took me seven hours to get back here from
London. I'm still sleepy and my mother is very angry with
me because she was anxious about me. I also took my
suitcase full of necessary belongings and my spectacles, so
why I should choose to write to you when I'm still blind
with sleep I just don't know.

Yet maybe I'm writing because it's too long since I last heard from you; it's far too long since I last saw you, and even quite long since the Miracle sang and so stopped me from smashing both our heads against the insurmountable wall. So will you write to me, Jock, and will you come and see me when you can? We go down on the 7th of next month, so if you can't come here this term maybe I could see you during the vacation. I wish I even knew where you were, because now I'm so hopelessly out of touch with you and I don't know whether to send this to Scotland or to Esher again. Moreover, I can't write the kind of letter I'd like to send you until you have written to me. Please relax, John, please send me a letter which isn't stiff, a letter as friendly as they used to be three months ago. You can't really say I'm being sentimental now, because it's two-thirty in the afternoon and the fire is buzzing like a mosquito and anyway I'm far, far too weary and dreary to be anything more than rather sorry for myself.

It was five weeks ago that I had a flash of sanity or insanity about you. I wrote and told you what I had felt, what I was feeling and what I would feel about you. Now I want to tell you what I'm thinking, but I just can't do it until I know whether you have been scribbling pretty patterns around a fairly deep mark in the marble, or whether that mark is still the important line in an important pattern. In other words, has Time wedged great hard, granite thoughts between us, or are they thoughts like chrysanthemum petals; thoughts which are ragged and closely joined, but thoughts which can be shredded apart, till only that old musty smell is in the air to remind us that there had been any petals at all.

Blessings on you,
Mirren

Largs Hydropathic
Largs
Ayrshire
27th Nov. 1940

Dear Mirren,

I am in no sort of mood to send you an adequate reply to
your letter. This place is full of interruptions and distractions.
The news is hammering at my attention with the infuriatingly
complacent persistence of our national broadcasts.

Last weekend I went to Arrochar to attend the
christening of Elizabeth's baby. The child was looking
considerably more human and less simian than when I first
saw it, which caused me much relief, but I still couldn't help
feeling how incredible it is that a full grown human should
develop from it. Even more did I wonder when surveying
myself in the privacy of my bedroom that my mother
should be able to view with calm this incredible structure,
so huge, so different and so gross in comparison with the
object she brought forth and loved.

Your letters to Inverary have still not come. I shall await
their arrival with the best patience I can muster and thank
you in advance for the pleasure that their coming will
surely give.

I am glad that you are living a complicated life. Mine is
distinguished by its arid simplicity and only by
considerable effort of will can I contrive to fill it adequately.
I am reading a lot, relearning German with the expert
assistance of Bill, dabbling in modern Greek which
resembles nothing more than Welsh in its whimsical

colloquialisms, and writing a few, but very few letters.

Militarily we are marking time, and that manoeuvre is always unsatisfying. The fighting spirit is not really alive; we are no more than a set of determined men who think that if we do our best we can't be beaten: there is no realisation of how much better our best could be if only we put half that mental energy and spiritual devotion into training which we lavish on the pursuit of humour, comfort and convivial living. I am disappointed and disillusioned: the spirit of the army is fundamentally good, but no effort is made to kindle it, no attempt to fire the imagination, awaken enthusiasm, inspire confidence in leadership or even to appeal to reason and set before us the simple arithmetic of the war.

I think that some of my earliest letters to you were written in much the same frame of mind as this, though less of my sorrow may have found its way into expression than now. My former disappointment was alleviated by my transfer to this special service unit; for here I thought to find a nucleus of men prepared to devote themselves to the task of preparation, a breeding ground for the spirit of a new army. I have not found it and now I see no way out. But a way must be found and so, to the best of my ability I go on preparing myself for the task in the distant hope that one day I shall be able to prove my own worth to the satisfaction of those at whose hand I might expect to receive both permission and power to prepare others also.

From this you will see, Mirren, that there can be no Joy Street for me while I think as I do. Escape Alley is the best I can hope for while my devotion is eaten up in this hopeless cause.

God be with you.
Jock

BRITISH FORWARD MOVE
IN WESTERN DESERT
THE TIMES Tuesday 10 December 1940

H.M.S. Glenroy*
c/o G.P.O.
London
10th December 1940

My dear dentist,

You have been called that ever since I told Eddie
FitzClarence that I had to go to London to see the dentist –
he, I'm afraid, lets his amorous propensities get the better of
his imagination and cannot conceive that anyone should
make a journey to London for any but one reason: he was
very nearly right if you remember. But 'de mortuis' – for the
Odyssey seems to be no more than beginning and the
inhabitants of Joy Street are dead or sleeping.

This is merely to keep in touch and makes no pretence to
be an adequate reply to your last letter. There is little that I
am permitted to say and my own disinclination reduces that
little to vanishing point.

A bientôt,
Jock

*Jock was on board H.M.S. *Glenroy*, which was conducting training exercises off the west coast of Scotland.

PURSUIT OF DEFEATED ITALIANS
THOUSANDS MORE PRISONERS
THE TIMES Saturday 15 December 1940

2/Lt. J.S. Lewes
5 Troop, No. 8 Commando
4th S.S.Bn.
c/o A.P.O. 405
15th December 1940

Dear Mirren,

In the agony of removal I have let your birthday slip by
in the crowd of days unrecognised, and it is only now that
the stampede is stemmed and they are passing once more in
orderly succession through the turnstile of routine that I
descry the nimble offender boarding the boat across Lethe.
It is futile to complain, or regret all the care with which I
have hoarded that date in my treasury. I will not submit to
the dictatorship of time, we have defeated attempts at
usurpation in the past, and if you will lend your imagination
to the enterprise we shall do so again now and exercise our
right to the freedom of life.

Here, then, are my wishes for your new year. First, that it
may be full, for it is in the emptiness of life that desolation
lies. Next, that, whatever it may hold of weal or love, you
may adapt its pattern to your purpose, for what you design
is freehold prosperity, what chance may lend is at
immediate recall, perhaps with interest. And last of all, for

this matters least if my other wishes come true, that it may
hold more beauty than ugliness, more truth than falsehood
and more pleasure than pain.

And to commemorate this day I would ask you to get
some tiny trinket for your wrist so that I may take my place
among those who wish to be remembered by you: St
David's lock or just whatever serves the purpose.

Since I don't expect this letter to reach you much before
Christmas, I would also like you to get something as a
present from me to you upon that feast. I am sorry to saddle
you with these tasks, but it is manifestly impossible for me
to do them for myself as I should wish, so that I have no
alternative to the course which I have adopted.

You will notice that we have once more changed our
address: I have written the new one out in full at the head
of this letter.

And now to thank you for the letters which you posted
tomorrow (the day after your birthday, see?) and to answer
them to the best of my ability. But before I do I am to say
from Eddie that he franks my letters to you with his eyes
shut, thereby trusting his rank and reputation to my
discretion which I shall, of course, be very diligent to
exercise.

Of course you will realise that my despondent mood has
been chased away by the activity of the last fortnight, but
even had it still sat huddled upon me this word from you
would have thrown it off and sent me gaily about my
occasions. I know not quite why, for you were sometimes
angry with me and sometimes disappointed. Perhaps it is
because I would rather have the inspiration of the anger and
disappointment of one I love than the soul-destroying
indifference of the few here whom I respect and the praise

of those I despise. I was despondent because I hungered for inspiration which I could find neither in my leaders, nor in myself, nor in my work; for I could at that time foresee nothing but protracted inactivity and a life of idle selfishness. But my world has awakened, the future is pregnant and our victories in the Western Desert make any immediate inactivity easy to bear. It only remains for me to try and redeem the past and to convey to you the certainty that it is I to whom you write, I who have shared with you times and places and pleasures which neither are willing and perhaps both unable to forget.

But how am I to convince you that I haven't changed beyond the acquisition of a little more wisdom and a little more indolence? The task seems to be almost beyond my competence: you have too keen an instinct for the detection of the thought behind the written word for me to risk my happiness on formal protestations; that I am, for instance, as determined to see Joy Street again with you as you are, that your determination to do so, if only once more, means more to me than a declaration of love and more in the same vein. I don't trust this sort of thing to sound as convincing to you reading as it does to me writing; for after all I may be deceiving myself and thinking only of the pleasure that I shall have at our next meeting, and I'm sure you need no convincing of that. You aren't, after all, repulsive, and you have sense enough to gauge fairly accurately the power of your attractions, and unless in the interval of our acquaintance I have lost my virility in some mysterious or else anatomical way, it will not be surprising to learn that I think you're delicious. In that I'm no different from a lot of other men, but I imagine that if you value me at all it is for that wherein I differ from other

men, and that it is which I am anxious for you to know to
be unchanged, if not absolutely, then at least towards you
and towards myself. But just because I am always me to
myself, the same me from one day's dawn to another, it is
impossible for you to take my word for my own
immutability. You must judge for yourself from what I
unconsciously show you of myself, and since you cannot
form a judgement in the absence of evidence, it is essential
to your conviction of my constancy that I write to you
more often. This shall be done. Please preserve both your
sanity and your illusions in London.

    Goodnight,
      Jock

MOOLIGHT BATTLE IN THE DESERT
BRITISH ASSAULT ON BORDER
THREE FRONTIER FORTS TAKEN

THE TIMES Wednesday 18 December 1940

4th S.S. Battalion
c/o A.P.O. 405
18th December 1940

Dear Mirren,

That more frequent correspondence which I prescribed
as a tonic to our mutual confidence is not going to be so
easy of achievement as I contemplated. I am informed that
opportunities for posting letters are liable to be scarce now,
and that is a pity for both the time and inclination for
writing are present and I would be quite prepared to send
off letter after letter into the blue in an attempt to re-
establish my identity. But such is the nature of the fortunes
of war and, if the predicted limitation of postal facilities
becomes reality, I suppose that I must resign myself to
holding a position in your mind not unlike that of someone
you have met at a very merry party, with whom you can
remember being quite unrestrained amid the general
conviviality, but of whom you know no more than the hazy
memories of what you gathered at the time. Meeting such a
person again may quite easily be a frightening occurrence
in prospect and a source of no little embarrassment in
effect. And yet if you have confidence in your own

judgement you will always have the consolation of knowing
that you thought sufficiently well of him at the time to
relax your customary reserve with strangers. Why should
you begin to doubt your own judgement after an interval of
time? Or because the memory of the observations upon
which that judgement was based has become unreliable?
Surely the judgement still stands and is trustworthy though
the evidence is forgotten. Or do you believe that a person
can change in the interval of a few months sufficiently to
render your opinion obsolete and misguiding? It is of course
in my interest to say that such changes are not possible, or
if possible then not probable. But take your own case: do
you think that I shall find you so changed at our next
meeting that I shall be disagreeably surprised? Or that you
could alter so much in so little time? I am confident that I
shall not find and that you could not exemplify such a
change. You, after all, have taken twenty years to make, and
therefore in comparison with the length of time we are
likely to be separated change is a very slow process in the
human spirit and body.

I would not have returned to this subject after my last
letter had it not appeared that further correspondence is
uncertain. Forgive me if I seem to be too solicitous, but
believe me when I say that your confidence in our
acquaintance, our friendship or however you would
indicate our relationship is a matter of the greatest personal
moment to me.

I am now engaged upon reading Samuel Richardson's
'Clarissa'; it is huge in proportions – four volumes – the
whole put together in the form of letters. I chose it because
I wished for something that would lend continuity to a
great deal of leisure taken in snatches between

interruptions. I have not yet finished Boswell's Life, having interrupted my reading to peruse the Journal of the Tour of the Hebrides.

Now I must hasten to get this franked in order that it shall catch what I am told is the last post for some time.

With love,
Jock

8 Commando
4th S.S. Bn.
c/o A.P.O.
Boxing Day [*26th December*]

My dear Mirren,

Our Christmas was a motley affair that didn't hang together or have much meaning beyond an occasion for eating and drinking too much. We were very well looked after, but the men's existence is sordid at the best of times, and with all the over-indulgence of Christmas Day cooped up on the troop decks, there was little room for good will or the exercise of the finer sensibilities to which the feast should make us prone.

I had the misfortune to sit at the Captain's table for dinner. He was extremely drunk before the meal began. When it was drawing to an end he was incapable and so, therefore, were we unable to move until he gave the sign to rise which he could not either give or himself obey. We thought it would be kinder to leave when he began to be sick and so obtained our release from an uneasy situation, though the excuse was poor enough, for the Captain can't have been conscious of what went on about him even so far back as the beginning of dinner.

I got a silver bell out of the plum pudding and a diamond ring from my cracker. But for the confirmation of the latter I would be of two minds as to the meaning of the former, whether I am to be invaded or whether married within the year. I have been totting up the chances as well as my mathematics will allow and they appear to be 1½:½ in favour of marriage and against invasion, that is 3 to 1.

I should love to get a letter from you, and will in time I know, for I'm sure you have written and must therefore have patience with the delays of distance.

I think of you often and love you always.
    John

FIRE BOMBS RAINED ON LONDON
MR ROOSEVELT SOUNDS THE ALARM
THE TIMES Monday 30 December

My dear Jock,

When I came back from London Town, I found a little pile of your letters waiting for me, and I don't think you could guess how pleased I was to read them. I told you months ago that I should get fretted with you in my own mind; I was beginning to believe that I'd never get past the stage of saying very angrily and very quietly 'Damn! I wish I'd never met the man.' Being disappointed by someone is more hurtful and more aggravating than anything I know, and I must apologise to you for feeling that way, because why you should be the kind of person I want you to be, instead of the man that you want you to be, I really couldn't say.

Amongst my Christmas mail, I found a letter addressed back to me – I suppose it is one of the letters which never reached you.

One day I shall have to write and tell you about the slums, but just now I can't, and for several reasons. I must have the time and the mood at hand, and at the moment my brain is still a little unsteady and bruised after the 'impact of the shock', to use an abominably trite cliché. But I didn't lose what little faith I have; in fact it's been increased by the experience. And as for the illusions – I went to the slums after trying to imagine everything that was most harsh and filthy. When I left there I suddenly realised that I had forgotten to imagine the infinite patience

and weariness of the people, the little personal tragedies
and their overwhelming generosity, and that anyway, the
sordidness and the devastation was quite beyond my puny
powers of conception.

When I left my poverty-branded friends I had an orgy of
passing on from the Ritz to the Savoy, the Savoy to Prunier's,
and finally drove away memories of smelly bodies and
disinfectant by having a superb time at an oyster party given
in your Mess at Esher. I met a number of young men, who
were well fed and rich, rich, rich. They laughed and flirted a
great deal, they looked and smelt clean, and I nearly wept
with relief as I responded to the charming dishonesty and
delightful insincerity of those people one meets nearly every
day of one's life. They were Oxford undergraduates dressed
up in blue cloth and shiny buttons and I loved them for no
reason that I could explain. I spent several days at Esher and
finally came home and retired to bed, where I had an even less
eventful Christmas Day than yours. Everyone was rather cross
and I was only consoled because I had two threepenny-bits in
my pudding which could only have meant that I should marry
a rich man whose name begins with a B. When I'm in London,
I shall go to goldsmith after goldsmith, till one of them
provides me with a leek to dangle upon my charm bracelet.
When I see you again I shall give you a pigeon kiss – not a
pitying kiss nor a Joy Street kiss – but a pigeon kiss, gay and
brief and quite meaningless except that it's the best way I have
of thanking you for my Christmas present.

I wish your envelopes would stop being stamped with
H.M.S. ships – it makes me feel queasy and uneasy.

Blessings on you,
Mirren

Very much later:

I heard them play 'Begin the Béguine' on the wireless this morning, and since then I've been feeling too sentimental about you. It's so late now that I could write the next superb love letter but I won't. You see, in the Sentimental Garden, the roses are pink paper and smell of dust and stale eau-de-cologne. The fountain's stumpy little dolphins are made of papier maché instead of bronze, but I know that if I drifted back to those Gardens tonight, I know that I'd say all sorts of things that I'd mean now but not tomorrow. One day, please will you take me to the 400 Club in a hansom cab. I want that to happen very much. You can laugh at me for being womanly and romantic, but you slammed the gates of Joy Street so fiercely, that I don't think I'd ever have the courage to marry you. So maybe I shall marry my rich man.

Goodnight, dear Jock.

at Cowcroft[*]
Ogbourne St George
Nr. Marlborough
3rd January 1941

Dear Jock,

I ought to be writing, but I'm so bored with trying to understand the meaning of yod and **y** and diphthong-

[*]Aunt Esmé's country home.

isation and so on, that I must write to you instead.

My last letter to you didn't answer any of the subjects you
mentioned, did it? But that was intentional because you
perplexed me, and anyway, I've almost forgotten how to
write to you. Cowcroft, fortunately, makes me feel mellow
through and through; one just can't feel prickled and bad-
tempered for very long. This morning I got up at about ten
o'clock and went down to the kitchen to get milk from the
cows here, homemade butter, and bread for my breakfast.
Then I worked till lunch and I ate too much home-cured pig
and Stilton cheese. After lunch I spent two and a half hours
trudging over the snowy downs, shaking the brilliant white
powder off the branches as I plunged through the wood, and
spent a long time making yapping noises at a friendly and
inquisitive fox. I saw crows attacking a big white owl who
was blinded by the sun and the snow, and I kept a numbed
chaffinch between my sweater and vest till I remembered
that birds had little yellow fleas. We had sausages and
champagne and clotted cream for supper, and now I feel
more contented than I have for a very long while.

Patrick Bell and I saw the New Year in at the Grosvenor.
I danced a good deal with the most preposterous little
Welsh Guards officer who told me all about you and your
doings – very interesting. He tried to persuade Patrick and
me to go on with him and the rest to the 400 Club, but I'm
not very clever at quelling my sentimentality, so I went
home to bed instead of gallivanting around with that
charming little man. He told me that you won't be back at
Esher for a long, long while, if ever, and that made me
sorry, because you seem utterly inaccessible now. But I don't
think I shall feel shy when I meet you again. You will seem
strange, I know, because so much has wedged itself in

between us that you have become an episode of the past. If I still felt that I knew you as well as I used to, then I might have felt shy and tongue-tied on meeting you again. You see, I should be waiting for the sudden look in your eye, or the tightening of my own throat, which would be the sign that we were, inevitably, going to fall back into the old relationship. But tenseness won't overwhelm me, at least. We've both changed, or seem to have changed, too much; I know for certain that I shall have to start knowing you all over again. I shall never regret the time we had together in 50 B.C. nor when we trespassed in dear Freda's garden. But, Jock, if only you knew what an eternity ago all that seems. It's become almost unreal; it's so strange and dream-like that it's lost its power to hurt or perturb me at all. All I know is, that I'm glad it happened, but it was so long ago that when we meet I shan't be able to connect those times with your own living body. But I'm glad too that we didn't really spend any time at the Charing Cross Hotel, because it's hard enough to escape from you anyway. On the whole it's possible to think of you impersonally and dispassionately, but I haven't yet learnt to control that sudden feeling when I hear 'Begin the Béguine', when I go to the Berkley or even when I see the first table we ever used at the George. I will not feel that I belong at all to anyone – though they personally may not feel I belong to them – for a long while yet, and that is why I'm so thankful that you understand the way I felt about Christmas stockings. On the other hand, Jock, you have to remember this . . . when we were sitting in Alice waiting for the lights to change, you did give me the chance to avoid any such place as 50 B.C. and dear Freda's garden. I chose what I wanted and I'm still glad of it, so if we meet again don't think that I shall feel shy on account of the 'powers of physical proximity' as I think I once pompously expressed myself.

Jock, I've just read through this letter and it all seems rather foolish. I need to talk to you. As a matter of fact I'm feeling much too sleepy to write sensibly. I'm getting sleepier and sleepier. The complete peace of Cowcroft, the good nature and the dearth of peevishness and unbearable nerviness, the snow and the cream, and the mental exercise philosophy gives me, have all made me ready to love anyone and everyone . . . hence the impossibility of writing to you.

So I say my goodnight to you and remind you that I must get back to Joy Street with you, if even for an instant. Does friend Eddie read my letters to you? Thank him from me, for not reading each word of your letters – it would spoil so much if he did.

Blessings on you,
    Mirren

8th January 1941

Very dear Mirren,

I am happier tonight than for many months past. My own world has been restored to me by what I have hitherto regarded as a thoroughly malignant postal system; the little chaos from and in which I create and conduct that microcosm called my private life has been returned, as by some benignant angel, from the altar on which I was prepared to sacrifice it to the building of a better macrocosm.

God, what a pompous fool I am! You implore me to relax and here I am aping the stilted language of centuries ago.

I was delighted with your two letters though still incensed against the post, however adequate today's atonement, for having kept the first so long from me. You have never lost your ability to put yourself on paper in spite of your threats to write me in icy forms of greeting and acknowledgement. That I should have escaped to such fortresses of defeat is my chiefest sorrow in our common world; my chiefest joy that I should now have the opportunity of escaping from them; and my relief, that I should have nothing greater to regret than this small sorrow.

Will you be in Oxford between the 14th and 21st of this month? Write to 8 Tudor Court, Hanworth in Middlesex and tell me how I may continue to see you; for see you I will, if you will.

Thank you for your New Year's Greetings sent by telegram from Esher – how prettily my little world begins to fit together again, each piece falling back into the place from which it was cut by the jig-saw of chance! And to think that I shall have a whole week in which to glory in this tantalising puzzle! Talk of relaxation!

With these exclamations I shall leave you until I can prove myself ever more,
        Your devoted and unaltered,
            acquaintance, friend and lover,
                Jock

PREPARATIONS TO REDUCE TOBRUK
THE TIMES Friday 10 January 1941

10th January 1941

Dear Mirren,

Your letter from Cowcroft written on the 3rd reached me today: how strangely out of time and time have our writings been since I banged the door and locked the gate on Joy Street! I have no fear that our behaviours will be similarly out of harmony when we meet, nor that they would have been, had I not received this letter, yet I'm glad it came, for its candour assures me that I shall start again on an equal footing with all the other men who have no more of you than acquaintance, and shall not labour under the almost insuperable disadvantage of having known you once better than now; or rather, for tonight I am determined to be precise with words, of having once thought I knew you better than I think I know you now; for if I had really known you then, so should I now; and that goes for you as well, for I have changed in the essentials that one 'knows' no more than you have. What has changed is not ourselves nor yet our knowledge of each other, nor even, and here doubtless you will disagree, our confidence in that knowledge. It is the design that we have changed, the determination of our wills to express a certain purpose in the acquisition of that knowledge. This at least is true of me. I have never attempted to conceal, either from myself or you, the nature of my purpose and determination, nor shall I now decline to recognise its altered aspect. And you did not conceal your own design which I accepted then as I do now.

But I was wrong to say that your determination had undergone a change. I retract. If change of purpose there has been, it is in me and not in you. My verbal precision attempted has led me into more than verbal error. Nothing that you have done or has . . .

[the letter ends here]

Tudor Court
17th January 1941

Darling,

As I approached the front door I heard Father saying to the telephone, 'I'll tell him you rang up.' I rushed through the door and appeared just in time to prevent the receiver being hung up on your sweet voice. What joy it was to discover you there and to have retrieved you so neatly from inaudibilty!

I'm afraid I haven't done my serious thinking about getting to Oxford yet; I shall ring you up when I know and give you the results. I should think that Wednesday and Thursday of next week would be best for me.

When are we going to have a lustless meeting? The best way of ensuring that is of course to have lots of folk stick around; I guess that we would do it well then, but I am not

so sure of our success unassisted by gooseberries and
stooge. We have been alone in Joy Street up to nine;
perhaps we had better invite a few people to one of the
next numbers and see how we get along in company, for I
have an idea that further up the street the houses are larger,
there are a good many live servants employed and
sometimes other live joy-walkers as well.

Number Nine was a puzzling place: I'll write to you
about it some time; at present it's still too close and
confused to focus. It had such a prim little hall, Victorian
middle class, such spacious reception rooms, the usual
offices, and a library full of Shakespeare and nothing else,
with one enormous copy of 'Macbeth' open on a great
brazen lectern in the centre of the room; I remember the
place it lay open at, Act 2, Scene 3; and the act is just
confusion, but it will sort itself out.

I must stop writing this, darling, because it is so late and
Father has gone to bed on his mattress in the hall, which is
our air-raid shelter, and so I have to write this sitting cross-
legged before the radiator in the room you had, getting
burnt on one side and cold on the other and cramp all over.

Bless you, dear one, and the porter, and me who love you
and hate him all the same.

Bless bless bless,
    Jock

Goodnight, darling
    Jock

Tudor Court
20th Jan. 1941

Dearest Mirren,

I have twice tried to ring you up, once entirely
unsuccessfully, and once I got through to Somerville at
about midnight, having started trying at eight o'clock, and
apparently so late that no one would answer the phone.
That was Sunday night, and in desperation I sent off the
telegram asking you when and how I could have a hope of
succeeding. I have not yet had your reply, and altogether I
am rather desperate.

I feel most urgently the importance of these days since
our last meeting, and the need to be with you, if only for a
few moments each day on the telephone. Precious time is
slipping and bringing nothing but doubt and frustration.
Number Nine left me in a daze, otherwise I can't conceive
that I should have consented to our separation at such a
time, the importance of which I am only now beginning to
realise. I should come to Oxford tomorrow if that were
possible, as it would have been two days ago, but now the
earliest I can come is Wednesday. I shall come then.

I will speak to you tomorrow at all costs, but tonight I
must write this, if only to set my own mind at rest by the
illusion it gives me of having been with you for a time. I
cannot end this leave and go back to my Battalion without
the assurance of your confidence; if I did, it would be with
the feeling of having acquired the character which, for
some reason, the world seems to be so ready to give me.
But my perturbation is not all on my own account, for our

lives have so run together that you must think well of me in order to retain your own self-respect, and if I have not your trust, you have not your own confidence. If I have it not, then I must learn to deserve it; if you cannot give it now, then I must teach you how before I go away.

This is all I can write. I must wait till the morning to sign it and send you my love.

Darling, your telegram has just arrived. I am so glad. I shall send this off with an easier mind and surer heart, for just to know you exist is to belong to you, in heart and body now, but one day in mind and spirit too.

Your loving,
Jock

NEW BLOWS AT ITALIANS
R.A.F. BOMBS ON LIBYAN PORTS
THE TIMES Monday 20 January 1941

When you come I'll give you the letters I shall have written
to you by then.

Somerville College
Oxford
Monday [*20th January 1941*]

Dearest Jock,

   Your letter has just come and I have to write now to tell
you that I liked it so much. It isn't your usual kind of letter
at all, but it was darling all the same.
   I've been trying to write to you, but it's been kind of
difficult. People keep on interrupting me and now I'm in the
midst of an essay crisis. I'll have to ring you up myself
tonight, because your telegram only arrived today and mine
wouldn't have reached you in time. Please, please come
soon. I know that it will mean you'll have to go away all the
sooner, but by then I shall be able to work really hard and
there won't be much time left for fretting and fussing.
   All right, dear Jock, we won't go a-lusting this time. If
you arrive in time we'll drink a dish of tea in my room, and
then perhaps we might return to sip a little sherry.
Thereafter we shall dine accompanied by such friends as
you may think fit to invite. The rest of the evening shall be

passed in pleasant conversation, and I shall eventually retire to bed to dream and sleep no more innocently than I ever have before. In fact, I shall probably dream wildly and not at all innocently, but that is beside the point.

I'm glad to know you again, Jock, because till a certain moment at the Café de Paris, you were just a Stranger. I didn't like that much, so please, when you come here, don't be serious and aloof unless you really need to be. You don't have to whisk your wits and pretend to be gay, but spare me that austerity of yours, which almost scared me as we ate very small birds called woodcock. You really were severe then, and I didn't like you that way, so there!

Now I must go to a lecture.

Blessing – yours inevitably,
Mirren

No. 8 Commando
A.P.O. 890
8th February 1941

Dear Mirren,

I was delighted to find waiting for me on board your letter of the 8th January from Cowcroft. Your letter before this puzzled me, and after much thought I concluded that it was intended to prepare me for the resignation of all my matrimonial aspirations. As I told you, I started to write a reply but on this assumption, but so soon lost myself in the attempt to justify myself and blame you, that I quickly abandoned the letter and resolved to wait upon events and rely on our next meeting to redefine our relationship.

This letter was of quite a different calibre, even allowing for its being read after the event of our meeting. In it you show that you have the blessed gift of self-criticism which I should like to think you exercise to an unwarrantable degree when talking of your courage in the face of squalor, and your ability to forgo the refinements of gentle living. The ability to define a problem is rarer in every division of human uncertainty than the power to solve one already defined. If you are doubtful of your ability to give up Somerville, or its London equivalent, for the slums, for goodness sake don't go and give it up for this reason alone – just to assure yourself of your own courage; no form of human activity is more wasteful or more perniciously misleading than the bravery-test. In it you brave fears and revulsions especially summoned to the test by yourself; you are predetermined to their defeat. If you succeed you have a false sense of strength and security – false because the tests that the world will set you will be quite unexpected, absolutely new & strange in every detail, and you will first have to make up your mind whether or not you are prepared to undergo the test. If you fail you will have a deepened sense of weakness and futility; in neither case can you be the better for it. And if you examine yourself closely, will you not agree that it will be harder by far to stay at Somerville and get a first than to remove to the East End and be no matter how successful at suffering and assuaging squalor? If a thing is worth doing it is worth doing well and of two courses open the wise mortal will choose always that which will try his powers the more stringently.

And this is the very reason why I would rather marry you than the nicest little goody turned out from the nicest of English families and schools. And in any case, do you think I would wish to impose my own imperfections upon a person who was so perfect that she could have no understanding of them or appreciation of the merit of what successes I might gain from time to time against myself? There is but one valid reason for believing that we would be insane to marry, and that is money and our own extravagant tastes, and yet if we really wish to acquire merit in this world and the next to prove our strengths and forge our happiness, we will conquer our extravagance – except for occasional delicious outbreaks, the more succulent for their scarcity – until we have conquered wealth.

There is also one valid, indeed one inescapable reason why you should marry no one else but me, and that is that you love me better than any other man, say what you will to the contrary. Nor will I accept your refusal to consider my eligibility until you can look me in the eye and say, Dear Jock, in spite of all your overweening confidence, your hypocritical preaching and your delicious weakness, I don't love you because I love a real man. It would be obnoxious to marry without this assurance. And if you are to gain that assurance, absence and my unintelligible letters will accomplish it. I am prepared to stand or fall by your sincerity and rely on that courage of which you say you have so little to postpone the irrevocable step until you are sure of your release from my snare; in the meantime to try at least as hard to escape from the others that hold you as you do from mine, and subsequently to look squalor in the face not at second hand, huddled on other people's backs, but riding securely on your own, shouting and waving to the rich rich rich passers-by who once knew you but now don't.

I will write no more. All this has more than a mist of unreality about it. Am I not writing to the wave or the sun or the bank of clouds? For when will this be posted and where? And, that answered, when and where will it find you? So great faith have we that in the midst of an unending prospect of sea we still call to the land in the hope to be heard and heeded. Fond heart!

But in spite of my cynical misgivings I beg a blessing upon you or perhaps because of them, since that is more likely to reach you than this letter, and because I would like my love to be a blessing to you rather than a curse.

Jock

GERMAN PRESSURE IN THE BALKANS
YUGOSLAVIA IN DANGER OF ISOLATION
THE TIMES Saturday 15 February 1941

No. 8 Commando
A.P.O. 890
16th February 1941

Dearest Mirren,

I embark on my second letter to you since sailing with a
certain sense of diffidence. I have nothing to tell you that I
couldn't have told you before and my imagination is so
stultified by warmth and idleness that I despair of inventing
a new way of telling you things that change not. But you
will understand and forgive this unembellished sameness
and so I shall not hesitate to give myself the pleasure of
writing to you. And then there is always the possibility that
my first letter went astray,

I have been leading a very staid and sedate life abroad,
neither drinking nor smoking and eating no more than the
barest minimum. I am a great believer in the power of
contrast to amplify and intensify human pleasures and even
happiness. When I have nothing to do I like to try to do all
those things that I should like to have done without
necessarily liking the doing of them. That is the easiest and
sanest form of self-discipline and the surest means of
eliminating regret from the past. If you do only those
things that you like doing at the time you will find that

there will be an ever increasing store of things that you wish you hadn't done and other things that you wish you had, and that impotent wishing about the past is the evil above all others that is to be avoided in life. Some people avoid it by not thinking about the past at all, others by assuring themselves that nothing that they have done or have left undone would they have otherwise, but sooner or later remorse or regret will catch up with them; the only effective way of avoiding pursuit is to leave no scent.

There is, however, something between you and me that I could wish undone, and so I tell you of it fairly in the hope to draw its venom. I cannot believe that either you or I acted in character at No. 9, and if we do not live to regret it, that will be because our characters will have altered to make the action agreeable. I do not particularly wish my character to alter any further in that direction and so I would rather regret the event than not.

I hope my serious mindedness does not bore you. There is so much time to think, so very little to do and so little circumstantial event that we may talk about that my imagination no longer functions. Moreover it is a well-known fact that love makes a dull fellow of the brightest wit, so please ascribe my heaviness to that and have patience till the time when I have ceased to love you and my letters regain something of their old sprightliness.

With love,
Jock

LIBYAN ENGAGEMENT
ENEMY ARMOURED UNITS CUT OFF
THE TIMES Friday 7 March 1941

No. 8 Commando
A.P.O. 890
7th March 41

Dearest Mirren,

It seems certain that this will reach you at the same time
as my last. Nothing has transpired between that time of
writing and this so that I have no news for you, and as for
chit-chat, philosophy, literature or Joy Street, my mind is
barren of them and the post is collected for franking in 20
minutes. This note, therefore, serves no other purpose than
to record that I have reached this point of time in health,
safety and a happy if careless and rather selfish state of
mind.

Do you remember my telling you of a long metaphysical
letter that I wrote to you and did not send? I have
continued with it spasmodically and it has now reached its
sixteenth page, has become extremely involved, slightly
incoherent and very controversial. If it would amuse you to
see it some time when, if ever, it reaches some sort of
conclusion I shall send it. It is not now a letter at all but an
essay or treatise on the human faculties, abilities and
powers.

In order to prevent my mind from degenerating in this

atmosphere of sloth, I am trying to learn a little poetry each day or a short prose piece. I have finished the Tale of a Tub, The Battle of the Books and other short pieces by Swift, but beyond that nothing.

With love,
   Jock

TOBRUK AND ACTION

In March 1941 the initial task set for the Commando was an assault on Rhodes to enable the infantry to occupy the island. The German Army's brilliant seizure of Crete forestalled that plan and Lewes again bemoaned the fact that the war was passing him by. Layforce was disbanded and the Commando units were allocated to various sectors of Middle East Forces. While Stirling went to Mersah Matruh, Lewes was sent as part of a major Commando detachment to assist in the defence of Tobruk.

Between March and July 1941 Lewes had established himself as an unconventional officer. The business of reactive soldiering – responding only when attacked by the Germans – frustrated him beyond endurance, and it did not take him long to put at least some of his Commando training into practice. He was given permission to take out ever more adventurous patrols by night with the aim, at first, of taking prisoners and eavesdropping on the German forward positions in order to gain intelligence. Later his patrols became more aggressive and left base with the intention of killing and harassing the enemy.

In those early days of the Western Desert campaign, leave in Cairo was a fairly regular occurrence, and it was during such a leave that Lewes and Stirling first began to discuss the opportunities open to the bold use of small patrols. Both men were totally against the use of a 'thundering herd' of soldiers which never achieved that most important principle of battle – surprise. At first, their attention was focused only on the approaches to the German coastal defences being made from the sea or from existing static defensive positions, but the term used on the map, 'the Great Sand Sea', made them think of alternative approach lines to the enemy installations.

When Lewes did make up his mind to join forces with Stirling he found at last the type of action he had craved.

Mirren continued to have serious doubts about the wisdom of remaining at university. She wanted to be more involved in the war, as her letters of this period, which have remained lost, no doubt explained to Jock. She *also suffered the burden of her mother's declining health, and perhaps found the study of classical French and Italian literature less than relevant, as the British army struggled to maintain a hold on Tobruk and Egypt itself.*

2/Lt. J.S. Lewes
'B' Bn. Layforce*
Middle East Forces
1st April 1941

Dear Mirren,

I shall send this new address to you by cable as soon as an opportunity offers. We have arrived, but still no letters from home and the solitude of the desert is deepened by this artificial barrier of silence. It is a queer sensation: like seeing someone trying to talk to you on the other side of a sound-proof window. Your lips move and your eyes sparkle and your eyebrows stretch their wings in the heaven of your forehead, but no words come. I try to guess at some, but without confidence of success; the same expression bears several interpretations varying with my mood, my memory and my confidence. My memory is my greatest comforter, but my confidence has been less staunch. The news that has trickled through of the destruction by bomb of a well-known and well-loved dance floor and restaurant — commonly held here to have been the Café de

*'Layforce' was a Commando unit commanded by Brigadier Robert Laycock, disbanded later in 1941.

Paris – has presented itself as symbolic of things that
disappear in a night, leaving only a memory.

All the moustaches and whiskers that sprang into being
in the seclusion of shipboard have disappeared except my
own, and that too is doomed to be short-lived. I send you a
slightly sombre photograph in which its brief tenure is
recorded. The picture was made during a brief period of
leave in Cairo for purpose of identification. If by sending
you a copy I can serve a higher end I shall bear less malice
against the suave brigand who robbed me in return for it,
but for all that, it is a very poor fulfilment of my promise to
send you my likeness.

Here we enjoy the privilege of censoring our own letters.
Our privacy is not, therefore, dependent on Eddie's tact in
matters personal, although my discretion in matters military
is a still more onerous responsibility. I have just finished
'Thaïs' by Anatole France. I was not deterred from reading it
by Aldous Huxley's description of it in 'Point and
Counterpoint' as a book for very young people, because I
see nothing to be ashamed of and much to be treasured in
youth. It reminded me often of ourselves, but then
everything does when the mind is privately always looking
to find the likeness of its preoccupation in the world as it
passes by.

The letter which I started writing to you at home before
our final move from England is still moving between the
forge and the anvil. It is now wrought a treatise of some
twenty pages of ill-written foolscap, and since its scope
becomes more comprehensive each time it comes under the
hammer, I see no prospect of its approaching completion in
under twenty years. If after that time you would still be
interested to see what you inspired, I shall send it to you

copied fair and corrected of all the juvenile and immature mistakes which no doubt it now contains.

I must end this now, sweet stranger, but not before assuring you of my devotion to you and my desire to know you as I wish to know myself. Think of me not as a cold philosopher only; you know me as a lover too: and remember that I am willing to reconcile those two lives for you, but for no one else I know.

    Goodbye then, Helen
        Goodbye, Penelope
            God bless you, Mirren, and keep you in
                mind of Jock and John

TOBRUK HOLDS FIRM
ENEMY TANKS RETREAT
THE TIMES Monday 5 May 1941

'B' Bn. Layforce
M.E.F.
5th May 1941

I am writing to Mirren for the first time for many moons
by the light of electrical devices. I am sitting on a bench,
writing at a table in a room with a tin roof, real wooden
floor and windows and doors that open and shut. There are
just as many fleas, more bed-bugs, but less sand than in a
tent on the desert, but above all there is electric light.

It is now the fifth month since leaving home, and still I
have had no news of you: it is therefore rather difficult to
make any observations about things in general which might
be relevant to your circumstances.

My reading and writing continued in the wilderness
uninterrupted until a few days ago when I was advised to
send all my surplus kit elsewhere for safe keeping; my
reading and writing I judged to be surplus and the
monumental treatise remains unfinished at page 36. I hope I
shall see them again: they amuse me when the army
doesn't. At the moment it does, and I am very happy, but I
am still as far as ever from pulling out the field marshal's
baton that I am assured is hidden in my pack and never
having been a corporal I don't see how I can fill that rôle of
'the Saviour of his race' that I had been designing for myself

after the war. 2/Lt. J.S. Lewes with the vast experience of 20 months war service behind him now has command of four men. What a command! What a man! What a war!

Still, oddly enough, I am very happy with my four braves – the sole survivors of my once most stately throng which has been decimated before my eyes by the ravages of inactivity. Just the sight, or even the sound of just one bullet fired in anger might have saved us from this decadence. The sight of one dead man would have filled every fainting heart with zeal, and to have seen one being killed would have brought recruits flocking to the standard in such multitudes that they would have been forced to promote me out of deference to the size of my following.

But here we still are: breathless virgins, for ever toppling on the brink of death or glory and for ever repulsed, the unwanted second preference.

The Greek campaign was a good thing; there are of course the moral people going around saying this was scandalous and that was scandalous: but it was the best we could do, which is always a good thing, no matter how much greater is the best that could be wished for.

Bless you, darling, and love me when you think of it. I don't ask for a whacking great tapestry from my Penelope and I don't give much in return except for an occasional incompetent letter which concludes

with love,
        from Jock

EBB AND FLOW OF BATTLE FOR CRETE
SEVERE HAND-TO-HAND FIGHTING
THE TIMES Saturday 24 May 1941

'B' Bn. Layforce
M.E.F.
25th May 1941

Darling Mirren,

I have within the last fortnight received so many
beautiful life-giving letters from you that there is nothing I
can write here capable of giving you a true impression of
how I feel towards you. I won't attempt it, therefore, but
say simply that I treasure your memory, long for your
presence and value your trust. That to my way of thinking
is love, or rather, that is my way of loving.

Those letters were written so long ago: the first one
before our last meeting and the last before you had received
any letters from me at sea – so long ago that I dare not
speculate how you feel and think now; I dare not and I do
not – I just think of you as I know you and wait and wait
and prepare myself to wait again until we meet again, and
wait together.

I hope you have been getting the few letters and cards I
have written – the last I regret to say was over three weeks
ago. Sometimes it is technically, sometimes physically and
sometimes mentally impossible to write, but when I do, it is
always with regret that I have not done so more and with a

fierce but fatuous determination that you shall receive this. And so you shall, darling.

I have not written anything to my long long letter to you for over a month. All that time it has been reposing with much of my 'surplus' kit in the vaults of the Ottoman Bank, Alexandria. But I shall write you extracts from it about discipline, although the chances are that you are now following some other line of thought.

I have been very preoccupied lately with a special task allotted to me: it is frighteningly exciting in preparation but gives me just that for which I have longed all my soldier days – a team of men, however small, and complete freedom to train and use them as I think best. Until this task is completed I shall always find it difficult to write at all and well-nigh impossible to write well, as I love to do for you. But these times will pass and we shall live and love again with all our body and spirit and not with just what happens to be left over from some other occupation. These are the days I long for with you; they may be lean days in worldly estimation and worldly hope may be a long way off, but they will be with you and for you and will create their new world with its own riches, or own hope and its realisation.

Do not worry if you can't quite picture these days now. Whatever happens between you and me will be good. Bless you.

Jock

Somerville College
Oxford
27th April 1941

Dear David,

This is only a short note to ask you to do something for me. Jock seems to have disappeared and has sent me a mysterious address. His letters take about six weeks to reach me now, so I tend to get in a fuss about him if I don't hear fairly often. It's not easy to write impersonally and indifferently about him, but David, if there should be some reason which prevents him from writing do let me know. As long as I know that you'll write to me, then the waiting and wondering won't be too distracting

How are you these days and are you a doctor yet? Write one day and let me know what you are doing with yourself. I'm still at Oxford and find it increasingly difficult to attend to & concentrate on books and tutorials. It's a shockingly indolent and selfish existence. If you ever come to Oxford please do come and see me. Seriously, I'd like to see and hear of you again.

Yours,
Mirren

P.S. The name is Barford; I seem to recollect that in some ways your memory isn't too good.

MR ROOSEVELT INDICTS GERMANY
WE ARE NOT YIELDING
THE TIMES Saturday 21 June 1941

'B' Bn. Layforce
M.E.F.
21st June 1941

Darling Mirren,

I have been thinking of Eights week, and Schools and Commem Balls and the beginning of the long vac and all the things that accompanied this time in peacetime Oxford. Just sitting inside the marquee of the Officers' Mess was enough to start that train of thought and it has carried me round a green and pleasant land and back to you, whence it started, for I sat down in the beginning to write this letter.

It is very pleasant here; the wind is blowing from the sea, just firmly enough to be cool without disturbing the sand and dust, the flies have relaxed their efforts for the nonce and the mess is deserted except for a white-headed rather rickety major who is playing patience and occasionally disturbs the peace by a vicious slash with the swat with which he seems to be permanently armed. The remainder of my brother officers have retired to their tents to sleep the afternoon through. Such is the scene and tenor of my life. It is peaceful and purposeless. I do not even write these days, because I was tricked into leaving all my writing and books in the safe custody of the Ottoman Bank, Alexandria,

on the pretext that we must take no surplus kit 'into action'.
It was a good joke, but it has been played on us so often
before that our laughter was either woebegone or cynical
and this time it was all asked so realistically that there is
now no means of retrieving the status quo ante. My books
must moulder and my wisdom lie forgotten in the vaults
where Egypt's gold is hoarded and I must sit in 'the place in
the sun' set aside for me by a grateful government.

After a fortnight made brilliant by a series of letters from
you, the fortune of the mailbag has deserted me and for a
month or more I have had nothing from your hand. This is
not a complaint; it is just continuing with the description of
my life which I am now content to accept at the hand of
the minute which brings it, without asking whence it comes
or whither it is to go. Letters either arrive or do not arrive;
they no longer appear to my imagination to be in the
course of arriving, in the ship or in the plane, or of being
written, in your house or my house or in the house of a
friend or my tailor. I have a new faculty now, that of
regarding a letter that arrives as something that has always
existed, like a fossil that I come on in the desert, a message
from another world. This does not make that other world
less real, indeed it seems to add an element of permanence
and indestructibility which no feats of imagination could
wrest from the news of bombing in England and sinking at
sea. 'Damage was slight and there were a few casualties'
means nothing to my new state of mind, 400,000 tons of
shipping lost did not carry a single letter for me and
deprived me of nothing. The war takes nothing from me
but gives only, the experiences of the minute that is. I strive
when the war says strive and relax when it doesn't; that I
fight as me that beateth the air worries me not, it is

decreed, and sooner or later something must come within
the arc of my flailing arms and I shall have struck my blow,
as unerringly directed doubtless by the fate that huddled in
my blindfold as though I had seen for myself.

And what right, after all, have we to demand to see for
ourselves? What claim have we on the funds of knowledge
and purpose? Who ever conferred on us the freedom of the
city of life? If we obey the laws we shall have peace in our
ghetto and what matter beyond that? The khaki gabardine
is the symbol of our status, and, though it choke the spirit,
can we not still live by the letter of the law?

This is a mournful and forbidding letter for a gay soul
like you; I am sorry to meet you in such a dreary place and
hold our brief postal tryst in a very graveyard of joy. Let's
rush out and leave the place to its yew trees and righteous
inscriptions. Come on, hand in hand out the gate, quickly
down the lane, scramble through the hedge into a June
field where we can go slowly through the thick grass and
richness. Slowly slowly pacing side by side, talking gaily of
McStubbs and goldfish, stopping to pick a flower or to
watch a run of ants with the excitement of your skin on
mine when we walk. I'm not sorry, though I say it, for
politeness' sake, and long to touch you more and take your
hand. But now it wouldn't do and you might shrivel up
inside, though I have grabbed it in the graveyard and
helped you through the hedge; but now it would seem
studied and maladroit because in the depth of the field
there is a feeling of consciousness between us.

We talk about the mating of the birds and how the men
wear all the finery and do all the singing and just sit and
strut and preen and sing till the lady can't resist him any
longer. And how the robin returns each year to the same

field and chases all his rivals off the ground and won't let
them hunt in his hedges or sing for his lady in the copse.
And I look sideways at your bosom as you laugh at the
celibacy of the poor weakling little robin who hasn't found
a field and must hunt by the roadside and sing without a
wife; but the next field perhaps may be his, or next year he
will terrify every robin in the land with his array of plumage
and the volume of his voice. And we laugh together at his
hard lot and our consciousness is comforted because we
laugh and smile and there is a sparkle in the eye when we
turn to meet our looks, and eyes are not afraid.

We walk slower still and then sink gladly down in the
grass where we can see our faces as we talk and look more
boldly than from side by side. There is something
provocative in the looks and the talk has a colouring of
banter because it has become a game in which we seem to
be fencing with each other but are both really striking at
the cold heart of the third walker in the depth of the field.
We compare men and birds and laugh at each other's sex
and jibe at their foibles. We defend ourselves and the bird
that lends an argument, but the truth about Robin becomes
sadly twisted and often we have to give up the pretence and
laugh because we don't really want to win the game. As we
walk away discussing more seriously now, hands slip
together and separate consciousness is locked out. One
moment we are children swinging the joined hands to the
rhythm of our walk, and then a finger stirs and sends its
grown-up message to break the pretence and overpower
with its surge of desire. At the copse in the corner our talk
is hushed and we walk through last year's leaves and the
lank grass as in some holy place with no real thoughts, but
just the consciousness of presence and deep yearning.

Quite gently we are facing each other and close together, so close that the warmth and form of your body run into mine, the skin of your arms is smooth, your waist is narrow between me and my locked hands which press to possess. Your hair is fragrant and so soft.

There let us part, Mirren darling, for our tryst is at an end and we must go our ways in the world where we don't meet. And if you have not followed me in the field, then I ask you not to mind my imagery; it is just a part of this letter which is to show you how I live, and that life is the richer for its writing. I will not presume upon my figment wealth when next we meet.

God bless you,
and my love,
Jock

BATTLE FOR WHITE RUSSIA
ENEMY CLAIMS LVOV AND MINSK
THE TIMES Tuesday 3 July 1941

'B' Bn. Layforce
M.E.F.
3rd July 1941

Dearest Mirren,

I got back from a few days leave in Cairo this morning to find your letter of April 3rd waiting for me here. You wrote from Whipsnade, exactly three months ago. That is too far and too long for letters like that, my love, even though they are signed Penelope. For you had been thinking, and thinking had produced nothing but the 'pale cast of thought', and you had been listening to an indiscreet officer talking about things he can't have known much about, and you had been remembering the pleasure of being together, with only impersonal lifeless letters from me to assure you that the memory is worth preserving. And so I am feeling frustrated and long for a return to the days when I wrote almost every day of the week! Perhaps that may yet be accomplished, but three months is so long that in all probability the first flush of resolution with which the journal to Mirren would have to be restarted would peter out before the first instalments reached you. But I cannot understand why you still write to A.P.O. 890, for I telegraphed my new address to you within a few days of arriving in this country in the middle of March. If you send an occasional air mail postcard my mind will be greatly relieved of the anxiety of not having any news of you younger than three months. The special air mail postcard takes anything from 10 days to three weeks according to how the planes run. You ask whether I have changed much; I don't think so; I feel much the same and only a little less sure of myself, which is not surprising in view of the course my military career has taken. I feel that I almost have a right to be sour, disappointed and cynical, and that I am acquiring merit in my attempts not to exercise it. I would like to know how I can acquire merit in your eyes. I feel that you are more interested in men than in soldiers, and therefore that it is more important to remain human than to become military. But I would really like to be a good soldier and am hurt at being left out of the war.

Here the paper ends and so then must this indifferent letter. Keep weaving, darling, and keep the colours fresh. I haven't found Dido yet but still I'll play Ulysses.

HEAVY ATTACKS ON TRIPOLI
THE TIMES Wednesday 4 July 1941

'B' Bn. Layforce
M.E.F.
4th July 1941

Mirren, my Mirren, my darling,

More love I could not hold tonight, and there is none for any but you; you whose I am for the life of this night which runs like soft hair through my fingers, a sleep and a remembrance. Tonight we love; and because tomorrow I go to the war, tonight there is no reluctance or doubting of right; what happens tonight is the truth, because it is all that we are. That we are green with the gift of this night, to live without stint unafraid; not driven, nor led by the nose to a studding but of ourselves in our powers to choose, each found in its own surrender the losing, not surrendered but given, not accepted but owned in the name of love.

July 6. 41

And now I must tell you the story of that night, now that it is supposed to have passed. I must tell you how the night of American Independence Day came to be distinguished and given to us out of the endless succession of undistinguishable time-owned seasons.

A week ago today we had moved from our camp and

returned to an earlier halting place, to await orders to move
off into battle. I had two days leave in Cairo where I went
to see Kenneth Johnstone. You will remember my speaking
of him and meeting him at home, or did you not? He is a
Lt. Colonel now and doing good work for the war. We
were glad to see each other again for we joined up together
from the British Council and since the days of Colchester
have not met above three times. I value his friendship more
than that of any other man except David Winser.

On returning to camp I took all my kit into Alexandria to
a room which I kept most extravagantly at the Cecil Hotel,
and there I set about cleansing it of sand and fleas in
preparation for the move. Our new camp was more flea-
ridden than anything I have ever known except a little bark
trapper's hut in which David and I spent ten memorable
boyhood days, shooting rabbits by day and reloading our
spent cartridges in the evenings. We were not allowed to
sleep in Alexandria and the fleas had prevented me sleeping
in camp, so for the time we were there I had given up the
habit of going to bed and would sit the night out in the
mess with whoever chanced to be there, returning late from
their pleasures, or alone with my thoughts and my
memories.

In the evening of Independence Day the movement
order came through, unexpectedly early. I hurriedly packed
my selected effects and leaving the remainder in the
keeping of the Hall Porter returned to camp for dinner. We
were to move the next morning at six, my own and two
other Troops, while the remainder would follow a little
while later. There was not much to be done as we have
been waiting for this since August last year and have
received much practice in untold numbers of abortive

attempts. At dinner I was handed a tiny air mail parcel which seemed to have been sent by my sister. I opened it at table and soon recognised that it was the packet that Mother told me you had sent to be readdressed to me. The little box was quickly remarked by the others, 'Has she sent your ring back, Jock? Bad luck, old man.' And indeed I had immediately thought how like that I would look and delighted in playing the part. Now your minute compass hangs by a length of dental floss about my neck, and there it shall stay till it guides me surely in the way to our twelfth meeting. Strangers eleven times removed – very remote relations for the war. I thought of you that night.

I kept your letter till after dinner for I had seen the first sentence in the dim light of the hurricane lanterns and it was so like meeting you again in a dear dear garden at home that I almost recoiled from it there in that ribaldry.

I read your letter by the last light of a lantern in the tent where the drinks are served, and how I wished to be in Cairo just for an hour to buy a tiny thing that I know there! And I sat on there, talking whenever people came to chatter of our war, and thinking all the time of how we loved, and of the small mindedness of my devotion in those days when we were together. Did I not feel as I do tonight? Why then did I not plague you with my love? Was it really no more than some pusillanimous drawing back from the heavy sacrifice of complete devotion? or was there some sincerity, however small in stature, in the practical considerations with which I excused my reticence? What an ephemeral joy this deep restraint gave to our meetings! They were like agreements to shelve the question that I came always to decide and play in the garden of the big serious house. Light-hearted and skin-deep they may seem now beside the conviction that this night has brought, but must they not have been right in fact, for have they not in the end wrought all that this night brings?

And as I thought and talked with the last drinkers I reviewed and criticised my love for you which I had hardly spoken and never pressed. I had always wanted to love you, indeed I had determined to love you if one may speak so absurdly but I had never felt that love as I did then, whole and entire because both had contributed all and withheld nothing. That is why I was convinced that this night had been planned and wrought and given with a meaning and for a purpose, for never before had our written thoughts fallen out so happily as in the prelude to this night.

When at length I was alone I prepared myself to write to you. This was my third entire night without sleep, but the skin-fever which a million flea bites gives me was spreading in hot white lumpy fingers all over my body. I burned and itched so fiercely that sleep was out of the question and deep concentration on other things the only relief. Stripped of my shirt, I dabbed and patted cold water over my shoulders and stomach, then walked out into the night to let the breeze from the sea cool the fire. The moon was two days into the second quarter, brilliant and pale, playing on the sand and white limestone road, turning the tents into geometrical patterns of black and white and the palm trees into romantic silhouettes.

What time it was I know not, but it can't have been much after eleven if at all. At two o'clock the camp began to stir and preparation for departure had begun. I had written without moving all the intervening time, seated at a trestle table with nothing on but khaki shorts in the hot dim light of a hurricane lamp. I was sorry then that I had not written

more. I am sorry now that I have not written better, but that
is the record of the night which is ours, and this is the
history faithfully repeated.

Since then two days and a night have slipped by, and
with them the sea, land, and sky between here and there.
Now I can hear the gruff coughing of guns and sometimes
the war comes screaming through the air and all our guns
bark and chatter, and the one on top of the Wadi in which
we live sounds as though someone was trying to break up
the bath with a sledge hammer in a tiny resonant bathroom. But the war goes away again; it is not my war yet and
we swim in the rolling sea and I write to you and look out
on the fig-trees and palms and broad-leaved cactus plants
which all show dusty green and grey against the bare
broken hillside and the ever blue sky. I slept a little last
night, perhaps four hours, and am greatly refreshed.

The light is failing now and we are not allowed lights
here with which to write and think. So I must begin to
make an end. I am writing with an Italian nib stuck into the
end of a diabolic instrument of secret destruction; it serves
the purpose well but is heavy to use for long and my hand
will be glad to stop.

I have not leapt into love with someone else, nor will you
tomorrow. We shall push through the people at the cocktail
party and elbow our way to each other; and you ask me to
tell you the end of the story. Whether Jock will still want
your body and whether John will still need the stimulation
of your mind. Hear the end of the story: when we meet in
the middle of the room the party will be gone to another
place in Joy Street, and we shall walk together in a
cathedral of thankfulness where the lusty and proud
thinkers cannot enter for awe, and we shall glory in the

possession of new power and delight in the grace of that which is simple. And the people will return and will worship us because we are possessed of the power of the spirit. I am your slave, make me your king.

John.

GERMAN DEFEAT ON LATVIAN BORDER
THE TIMES Monday 7 July 1941

Journal to Mirren
7th July 1941

In this battalion I have the reputation of a very
conscientious letter writer; I am also supposed to be writing
a book. You can judge therefore, how little writing is done
here, and I feel sorry for all those faithful people at home
who care what happened to these charming careless
children. It is a very great loss to all who read and write
letters and journals that considerations of security forbid
the detailed description of the lives that are being led in
this multiform war. That is a loss to history and scientific
record, but it is no loss to literature, for writing is only
worthy of that name which submits to a discipline both of
substance and of form. And so perhaps, when this war's
writing comes to be read and reckoned up as literature, it
may be placed in a higher norm than the indiscriminate
journalism which is so well thought of now. The things that
matter are not the things that happen, but rather things
that grow, and literature if it is to live must deal with life
directly and not indirectly through its accidents. Journalism
satisfies a curiosity for news; the better the journalism the
hotter the news and the more curious. But this is not the
stuff that life is made of, nor even that war and death are
made of, and the better the journalism on our modern
standard, the less good it is to us as men and the more it

debases us and wastes our spirit. Just because it is so new and curious it is useless as a measure and for the appreciation of growth; judgement functions not with novelty, for that is incomparable, but with the repetition and reproduction of circumstances. A measuring rod is useless if it cannot be indefinitely and identically reproduced.

And so the Journal to Mirren is not for the curious, who would find it dull indeed. It is for a lover of life, and its purpose is to try and present another life as worthy of that love.

I have been working this afternoon with the men, digging trenches and active defence against the bombers. My arms are brown and the hair on them bleached with the sun till it looks almost white against the skin. I feel well and strong, but hard smoking and hard work makes my hand uncertain as I write and it trembles as I stretch out for more ink. My hand has always shaken, and as a boy I was very ashamed of it, accounting it weakness; for one of the maxims on which I was brought up is: gentleness is a sign of strength, and I wanted to be gentle and strong. And now I have learnt the complement to the maxim: true strength is strength controlled; and being stronger now in body than I've ever been before, I seek for mastery of my forces, to turn them into power.

I have of late been thinking much of the ideas of force, energy and power and I have been trying to find a universal meaning for them, a meaning which will serve physics and metaphysics, religion and everyday usage. Force seems to me to be the most basic conception of the three, and indeed sometimes it appears to be the most basic conception in the universe; for the only difference between force and nothingness is the absence of an equal and opposing force.

Just as energy gives form to force, so power gives direction to energy. Just as force dispersing to infinity does not produce energy, so energy finding extinction in equilibrium does not produce power. Only directed energy gives power. The Niagara Falls produced no power until man directed their waters into his electric turbines, and likewise the electric energy then produced does not give power until directed by the spirit of man to the accomplishment of a set purpose. In the spirit of man is vested the power of the creator of this universe, the power to resist the equilibrium and the dissipation of force, which is the power to choose; that is, will power. The will, then, is the seat of power of the Spirit of Man, which is the likeness of God. It is the power to choose a course to which the material world is bound by the very nature of its constituents. It is the power to introduce purpose into the world and to follow that purpose through a lifetime of choosing. This, then, is the first thing which distinguishes human life from all others – the power to choose.

All this I have written, Mirren darling, that I may be able to talk to you in comprehensible terms of discipline, for that you asked of me, and to show you as best I could how universal that thing is, and how the world which we know and live in depends upon discipline for its very existence.

But of this I must write on another day, for now it is late and my energy is spent. The discipline of my mind and body is breaking down before the unruly waves of the love I bear you; and I can think of you no more as sitting chin in hands, rapt in attention. I see that little yawn which would come through in spite of all your interest.

And so it does; for I love you so, that your grace means more to me than all God's power; for I know, and I can show you, on some other day, that God's power is only the way we tread that leads us to God's grace. Your beauty guides me in that way; the power to follow it I have been given by people whom I love more than life, but the loveliness to guide it I have still to win, and I must have it now, in you and in your body. Oh God, how I desire you! How I crave and groan in spirit for that sensual touch which will tell me that all I believe is true, and, that being true, is worth all the wisdom of Greece and Rome and Edison and Einstein. How my lips burn for yours and the heat of your tongue in my mouth and the smooth taste of your spittle and the warmth of your breath in my nostrils! My part stirs at my thighs and I must press you to my body to hide my shame, the world's shame which I heed not, for I have the glory of your form in my embrace and breathe deeply of the fragrance of your hair. To press you to me till I feel the very nipple of your breasts and the firmness of your thighs and sense the gracious gesture of their parting, to feel the agony of the longed for pain of passion, that nothing now can satisfy but you. To lead you silently and through the dark to bed and there to enter, smooth and warm and thrilling until the madness of love's ecstasy engulfs us and sighing sleep into a world made whole.

J.S. Lewes 2/Lt.
7th July 41

Journal to Mirren
8th July 1941

Where did we go yesterday, you and I, that today is so
quiet and contented? The heat nestles down in the lap of
the earth and the air is just breathing like one who's asleep.
Cicadas buzz and crackle in the fig trees like electric sparks
leaping between poles, but farther off they blend with the
atmosphere, to lean upon our sense with a gentle listless
pressure. Guns are thudding in the distance and sometimes
those at hand shake the drowse like a nervous twitch, there
a rifle cracks in the wadi, some spendthrift Australian
shooting at a lizard, but the heat rubs out the marks of
these eruptions and the squabbling flight of the flies
becomes no more than the wheezing of a sleeper.

We were talking great things last night, and there was
another man with whom we spoke of mighty aspirations.
His name is Brooks, a strong and sterling man, and he too
sees the new faith growing from this war and is not
ashamed to say that he is fighting a crusade. He left soon
after midnight and we talked on in the mess where the
lanterns were burning. And then near four o'clock we
walked together in the brilliance of the night and saw for
the first time colour glow through the moonlight – in the
walls of the wadi a rich rose pink that is nowhere to be
found in blatant day, the palm trees deep blue–green like
ocean water, the shadows purple and the sand pure gold. In
the cool silence only the spirit moved, exalted in the
presence of such beauty.

This morning I took the journal of that night, a nocturne
should we call it, to the orderly for posting. I hope the base

censor passes it in his unopened percentage, for it is only ours, and sacred to our love. And now to go on with Ashley's speculations and knot the threads where Rhett so lewdly broke them. Bother Rhett and his licentious ways, can we never keep him out or harness him? But I love you, Scarlett, Helen, Penelope, Vivian sometimes, Mirren and Miriam, whom I met at the top of the stairs on my sister's day and whose other name didn't really matter because she shouldn't really be there but she'd been such a help to sister Elizabeth. Yes, I love you and when I'm tired I'll make you lead the dance in your widow's weeds, you scatter-brained, wilful, lovable, sorrowful Scarlett. But I must stop all this for the Australian cook is heating the empty shell-case and shouting 'Come an' get it' in his familiar drawl. Go and get it I will, and get you I will, Mary in your prim little garden. Contrary hey? Hugh! Yes, it would be a good thing to go on loving me like that – if you can.

And now I've been and got it – bully rissoles and Italian macaroni with scorbutic tablets to make up deficiencies, and yes, the life-saver which makes the brackish water drinkable and almost likeable – Tommy Laughton is lying on his Italian bed with a book and a fly swat, swathed in a length of mosquito net to keep the sticky flies from his bare body. A roll of lavatory paper hangs lopsided on a string behind his head, strung between the posts, and the end is floating out in the breeze like the tail of a kite.

We talked at great length and a little confusedly yesterday of force and energy and power and how natural tendencies must be disciplined before we can lay claim to manhood. We saw that there is only one power, the power of choice, one energy, that of the mind, and one force, the plastic of the universe, and how all things and all life partake of these in different proportions.

The animal becomes man with the first stirring of the power of the spirit, the first exercise of will power, the first interference in the natural drift towards equilibrium. It matters not what that first act is, for we are not thinking chronologically but metaphysically, and we are interested to see how the action of the spirit on the material and mental constitution of man produces those metaphysical conceptions which we so far have not found in him. They are three in number: knowledge, purpose, and love; of none of these is the animal capable, but only of their automatic counterpart, learning, intention and affection. And here we see the wide difference between knowledge and intellectual learning: knowledge is the perception and memorisation of the coincidence of real and ideal form; learning is merely the memorisation of a form of words. An animal can learn to count and to do certain given sums, but it can never be possessed of knowledge of the science of numbers so that it can solve a problem that it has never been set before. Only man can do that by virtue of his power of choice; he has chosen certain ideal forms and therefore only he can perceive correctness in the relation of those forms to each other, as in the science of numbers, or truth in the relation of those forms to the forms of real existence.

This, Mirren darling, is how man comes to be possessed of the gift of knowledge, by subjecting his natural faculties to the discipline of his choice.

Is all this in any way intelligible to you? Am I using words in meanings which you understand? I have the truth in these matters, correctness of thought and truth of life, and I am trying desperately to communicate it to you. I hope fervently that you may perceive it, for I feel a certain urgent responsibility in the possession of these great truths, and wish to know that they are safe in your possession and away from the danger of sudden annihilation. All this grew from the letter which I started writing to you after our last parting. That letter now lies in the Ottoman Bank, but this is the extract of all that is valuable in it, and I think it is a clearer and more direct route to the truth than the original meandering journey of exploration.

With this I must close the journal of this day and send it to you tomorrow with my love. It is now two o'clock in the silence of the night. I have written intermittently throughout the day and my words have changed, but one thing remains constant through every day and through any change, however cataclysmic: my love for you.

U.S. MOVE TO ICELAND
POUNCE BY HITLER FORESTALLED
THE TIMES Wednesday 9 July 1941

Journal to Mirren
16th July 1941

I was quite right about opportunities for writing. The only time I have free is between 2 and 4 in the afternoon, and as we are living on bare rock with no shade to be had except in the prone position, that is not a time when ordered thought is possible, or indeed anything except sleep which the flies succeed in rendering ineffectual. The temperature at midday ranges between 100 and 115 in the shade and I can't think what is must be in the sun. A water bottle left in the sun generally reaches the temperature at which one's shaving water is sent up in third-class English hotels, and if the water weren't so salt, shaving would be a reasonably comfortable process. The time is now about 6.30 in the morning, the sun has just topped the ridge in front of me and I have about three-quarters of an hour of cool spare time. I am sitting at a table built of bare stone in two little pillars with a big uneven slab resting one end on each; it is faintly reminiscent of Stonehenge.

At least I can say that I have caught up with the war and already the enemy and I have exchanged metallic and explosive greetings. I have watched them going about their morning occasions from one of their forward posts – the Italians are quite shameless in these matters – and this morning I regret to say that I am going to take much pleasure in trying to disturb that little ceremony for some of them with some long range machine-gun fire, observed by Tommy Laughton from a forward position. By night I have crept up to their entrenchments and listened to them singing and chattering and unloading their rations from the truck which comes to feed them. Tomorrow we are going to raid one of their posts, so I think I had better get on with our disquisition in case I am in no fit state to continue it for some time after this little bit of nonsense.

We have reached a stage now where it is possible to see how man comes by the idea that the world 'ought' to be different from what it is, and that he has the power to some extent to make that difference by opposing certain of the world's and his own natural tendencies. The ideas of good and evil are derived from the difference which exists between man's ideal conception of the world and its real presentation to him through his senses. In the most general terms, good is that which promotes the realisation of man's ideal, evil is that which promotes the natural tendencies of force to dissipate itself and disperse to infinity and of energy to seek equilibrium. It is important to notice that according to this view there is no such thing as evil power or a power of evil. There is only one power in the world, that is the power of choosing a course contrary to the natural tendencies of the forces of the world towards self-annihilation. Man cannot properly be said to choose the evil course of any alternative, he can only refrain from exercising his power of choice and so follow the predetermined course of his natural tendencies.

Were a man to choose to live a thorough-going evil life, to do only evil and to eschew good, having once come to that decision, his future life would be predetermined, not by the nature of evil but by the nature of good; for evil is that which breaks down and annihilates the potential of energy that good will has created in the world. Evil has no creative power – which is the only power – and must work with the instruments that good will has created. And even supposing that this determinedly wicked man finally gained complete mastery of the world and succeeded in destroying all that is good and beautiful, he could not then create an evil and an ugly world, for in destroying all good he will have deprived himself of the instruments of his work and of the material to work upon also, since the result of his wickedness will be the destruction of all ideal and energetic forms and the force with which he has been working will disperse to infinity and the universe cease to exist. The wicked man cannot be said to possess purpose; he is not working at an ideal pattern for life but only against any pattern at all. This is speaking in terms of absolute good and evil and refers more to the source of all power than to the individuals to whom that power has been delegated and entrusted. This is no absolute evil, but only evil relative to the individual possession of the instruments of power, which are energy and force. There is no relative goodness, for that which is possessed of goodness is good for all time regardless of how or by whom it is created.

This much only can I write; it is not well done and probably means nothing at all; if I have time I will conclude the argument by speaking of love, but there is little enough need of that between us. Now I must go to my duties and hope to return tomorrow to write to you again.

> With all my love,
> John

'B' Bn. Layforce
M.E.F.
19th July 1941

My dear Mirren,

I did not write your journal yesterday and perhaps I shall not today either. So I am sending you one of these curious letters to tell you that the world goes well with me.

I am feeling a little less bogus as a soldier now that I am helping to fight a real war, and undoubtedly I have already done much more than I ever would have had the chance of doing had I stayed at home with my regiment. And so I feel that all the disappointments with which this unit has been smothered, having been sometimes more, sometimes less bravely borne, have nevertheless been worth the patience or impatience which they called forth.

Being now far from postal bases and difficult to come at, we have had no mail for nearly three weeks. This does not trouble me in spirit, but sentimentally I feel the need of refreshment. I have lately written you many pages of metaphysics and a few of more clay-like stuff: forgive them all their trespasses and write me an air mail postcard and tell me how goes the battle between Penelope and the Suitors.

God bless, you know my greeting,
John

22nd July 1941

Dear Mirren, beloved of my soul!

After a hiatus of several days the journal starts again, but starts in letter form and with a flourish, because in one of the two Mirrenesque letters that reached me yesterday was enclosed a gentle tick-off for beginning a letter to you Dear Mirren. That was nearly six months ago, and you may have remarked that your tick-off, which in Army parlance is called a rocket, has reached me and taken effect before your letter arrived. Nevertheless you shall hear my lesson over, my darling Mirren, my platonic love – while letters are our only sight and touch – my dearest, most beautiful Mirren.

The postmarks on your letters bore the dates 9 Apr and 17 May. In the first you had just received my cable which was sent about the 25th March, and which most certainly was tampered with on the way for the address I sent was 'B' Bn, Layforce MEF, while that which you received was Commando MEF.

I wish you would go and see Mother and Father again and take Angel too if you like. In passing you could see how two people live without squalor on little more than £200 a year. Their whole life now is dedicated to us their children, and nothing gives them greater pleasure than to see our friends. You need have no fear of matrimonial insinuations or of feeling in any way committed by your going. You are my dearest friend and they would love to see you. Write to David and say you'd like to come, or just go and arrive and see for yourself the delight they would take in the surprise. Go and stay when they are alone – they are often alone – or go to tea and eat wholemeal scones and walk in the garden and through the prickly field. Do go, for they love you for my sake and will do for your own if you give them a chance. Don't hate me for asking this, or rather don't be irritated.

I liked your other letter very much, the one you wrote after getting the first of mine from this country. The passing of the Café de Paris is symbolic of something in our lives. I think it indicates that those exciting introductory days are over and gone for ever. I cannot feel that we shall ever sit down again to champagne and oysters as two exciting strangers. But because the building goes we are not therefore deprived of the spirit of the place and the memory of those early meetings will live on with us to set the pace for our future happiness. Yes, surely, when I come home we shall be together for a long long time, away from trains that go, appointments that encroach and duties that override.

I admire your courage in the way you write, feeling as you did then, and yet so uncertain of the future you still ask me to come to you, though you 'know too well that at any moment you may possibly find someone who could ask for you, take you and keep you.' Ah well, I know that too, but there does exist a bond of memory and of love, however we may qualify the last. And being love, that bond can never be broken: superseded it may be by a greater, but then, though I shall have lost you as a wife I shall find you as a friend with the beggar priest banished for ever, and I shall be happy in your joy. But remember also that I shall be miserable in your sorrow. So if that man does come, and ask, and take, and hold, let him be worthy of you and of our love, which we shall give to him, both willingly.

If it frightens you to think of our getting married, then

don't think on it, just let it happen, as it surely will if it is
intended. Dream of our children and our house and our old
age as I do, but take no thought for the morrow of our
marriage. If our roads lead us to that bridge, we shall crown
it with a confidence which would astonish you, because
you don't see how, or when, or where. Don't ask to see;
your request cannot be granted. Knowledge has no
currency in affairs which concern the spirit, only faith is
legal tender there, that is the only coin which bears the
image and superscription of the custodian of the future and
the pattern-maker of the world.

Christopher, Michael, Andrew I like, also David, but not
Sebastian. Let's call the girl Frances Angela. If any of them
have red hair it will be she, but her hair won't be red but
deep auburn. As to bringing them up, let us encourage them
to do whatever they want, but let us above all see to it that
they want that which is comely and graceful, to admire that
which is beautiful and to believe that it is good. This shall
be their discipline and no harsh overriding of the glorious
freedom of childhood.

I am glad you liked the photograph: yes, I was chubbier
then, having only lately stepped off a well-fed ship. But my
face is different now; it's brown and thin and my brow
wrinkled from too little laughing and trying to protect my
eyes from the bright sun. I hope I'm not too much of a
wreck when I get back, with grey hair peppered about, slit-
like eyes and a shaking hand from too much smoking; that
is the least that can happen; worse than that is morbid to
think upon. I might go bald or lose all my teeth in the
absence of a dentist. I might develop some frightful nervous
affliction, to say nothing of losing arms and legs and eyes
and ears and reason. So really it doesn't do to talk too

certainly of marriage, but still I believe and that belief
outstrips the morbid contemplation of puny possibility.

The enemy did not like our raid the other night and so they
shelled us nearly silly two nights after. I was very afraid, lying
in the bottom of a shallow trench surrounded by a loose stone
wall, which looked as though it would fall in on me if the wind
blew very hard. It takes time to learn to be brave and not to
flinch and cringe when you hear the scream of a shell which
experience has taught you to tell from its note is going to fall
quite near. The worst are the ones that howl over your head
and burst just behind you, though they are less dangerous than
those in front. I'm glad I was alone and that no one saw my
fear, for after our raid the men were pleased with me, and say
I'm brave and don't care a f . . . for bullets and bangs. Nor do I
on the whole when I've something to do, but just lying in a
hole waiting I am not yet very good at. This is where I need all
the power over my body that I can lay hands on. I am not
ashamed of my fear, but I should be ashamed of being seen to
act as though afraid.

Darling Mirren, you did not tell me why your last letter
was addressed from the Akland. I hope all is well with you
and your Mother. I selfishly fill my letters with myself and
my stupidities and seem to have forgotten that you aren't
just floating round like an invisible cloud in this desert
intent on all I do. I know that you have a life of your own
to live and a full one at that, and if I appear sometimes to
forget it, never suppose that I'm not interested. It is more
than possible that I shall be out here until the war is over,
or at least until this theatre of war is closed, so I must know
of how you live and of the little things you do or that just
happen. Our memories can't live for ever on metaphysics.
Let's laugh sometimes and sometimes cry, and sometimes

walk together through the fields, go up to Scotland, talk of
St Andrews, make cowslip bells and daisy chains with
Angel and other friends. I hope you often have happy
carefree times and don't do too much wondering.

Thinking is all right in small doses but it's no good unless
put into life by living. Take life as it comes and give yourself to
it. I know you can and do, but I fear lest my important
philosophising might curb your natural zest. Life is made to be
lived, not wondered about. I am living my life, but it is a hard
one now: tell me of something soft and kind or softly sad to
relieve the hard bitterness of this. I miss the graciousness of our
good world and the spontaneity of its joy, its courteous
subtlety, its hide and seek for meaning in word and look and
gesture. Here all is plain and patent and subtle only to destroy;
laughter is ribald or brutal and the finest moments are the
saddest, a man who's killing well or dying well or stamping out
his mind and heart to do his duty.

I am the merest neophyte in war, but one day I shall be a
soldier; and on that day I want to be able to say that I am a
human being with all his attributes, and also a good animal
with all his appetites and spontaneity.

Now darling, I must go to lunch. I have written all the
morning and with the help of wind and clouds defied the
sun. I wish I could be more friendly and less philosophical,
and even more do I wish that I were where you are and able
to say, 'Let's take lunch on the river today and supper too
with a gramophone and come back by the midnight moon.'
One kiss on the doorstep. I'll be good and then be gone; but
now I've got to go without even the chance of being good.

Bless you,
John

RUSSIANS HOLD SMOLENSK
PINCER MOVEMENTS AGAINST LENINGRAD
THE TIMES Thursday 24 July 1941

Journal to Mirren
24th July 1941

Nothing got written yesterday except a letter to David to congratulate him on being a doctor. I slept most of the afternoon and gossiped in the evening with the Indian doctor and Jacub Khan in whose mess I am living. They are a silent pair usually, but can be got to talk on Indian politics and sometimes on metaphysics. Our mess is an odd affair. It consists of a table and five or six chairs stuck out in the desert. In a hole in the ground a few yards away is the kitchen – honestly no bigger than the back of a fair-sized car – and Daniel is the cook; a little imp-like Indian of sixteen or seventeen years, very black with big bat ears underneath his stocking cap and a suggestion of fluff on his lip. From that wasteland hollow, provided only with a primus stove and a few petrol tins, Daniel produces the most astonishing meals. Stew and curry one could understand, but there come as well delicious rissoles, strange puddings said to be made of bread but almost as light as a soufflé, roast meat and chupatties and exotic savouries made of herrings and sardines on crisply fried bread. Apart from this Daniel will produce tea for any number at any time of the day. You know, when we are married we shall have to go somewhere where we can have a Daniel. He does the work of about three English servants and is a rich man if he gets the wage of one.

I don't know what's going to happen to me after the war, but of this I can be certain. I won't have a penny that I don't earn. I shall owe about as much as I can earn in a year and I won't earn a penny that I don't spend. Now honestly, do you think it's wise for you with your delight in luxury even to entertain the thought of consenting to marry me with my expensive tastes and habits under those circumstances? The idea is absurd; why in one night of even modest luxury we could spend as much as I am likely to be able to earn in a fortnight. It's all right when we are not married because I can creep away and live in a hole for a month and then come out dressed in my finest clothes with my pockets full of money, and off we go to Joy Street where neither worries about the money because it's there to be spent like that. But when you're married you have to be serious about money, even when you are quite rich, and that's terrible. I've never been able to take money seriously yet; I've spent every sou that I've ever had almost as soon as I got it, and my spending is always a good three months in advance of my earning. I have lived in the past on the theory that any money spent on my 'education', in the widest possible sense, was the best investment I could make. I have not hesitated to spend money and more money in order to place myself on a footing with the richest in the land; for it seemed to me absurd to live like a church mouse when you most want money and to reap the benefit of your early frugality when you can least enjoy or even use it; for if poverty has cramped your sphere of action in youth, wealth will not widen it with age.

This theory would be very well if only I could adopt a

mercenary outlook in my work, and now that my education is practically complete set myself to acquire the money necessary to give it scope. Unfortunately my interest in my work is centred on the wrong side of the balance sheet for this; I am more interested in what it achieves than what I gain. I suppose in that case I ought to be my own employer and write books or something, but I'm sure I'd make a worse bargain with myself than even a skin-flint government department. The fact is I am not interested in money and therefore can't take it seriously. I have a child-like faith and trust to the general honesty of the world: if I do good work, from somewhere or other I'll get good money. The only thing to be said for that policy is that it has worked in the past. Since leaving school I don't think a year has gone by which has not seen at least £400 paid into my account from one source or another, and on the average for those eight years I have received and spent over £500 a year, none of which was interest from my own property, for I have no property. While £500 a year was grand for Jock Lewes the Australian guest in England without any responsibility except for his own education, it becomes quite inadequate for John Lewes who is steering straight for the matrimonial ocean with reckless determination. And in any case, although windfalls and legacies made up my income to £800 a year, £300 was the most I could ever expect and indeed still is when taxes are deducted. I ought to be saving now, but I'm not, at least not more than just enough to reduce my overdraft by a few pounds a months. I started off from England with the best of intentions, but Cairo and Alexandria are expensive places and I have expensive friends. I learnt from the Ottoman Bank a few days ago that my account with them shows a credit balance of 786 millions, which I suppose is about 2/-, and instead of being sorry I congratulate myself on having calculated my spending capacity so exactly.

25th July

It is about 6.30 in the evening now. The sun is shining straight on to the nape of my bare neck as I sit at my Stonehenge writing table. In a few minutes I must see a section of men that I am taking out on patrol, and then I shall have a few moments to myself before taking an early supper and out into the night to make trouble for the enemy. I am hoping that the light wind that is blowing fitfully will hold and sing tunes of sea shells and long dark corridors in the ears of the imaginative adversary. He is jumpy now, when there is no moon and a great deal of ground in front of him which belongs to us by night; we have been especially rough with him lately into the bargain so he is free with his Verey lights and doesn't laugh and sing and talk in his forward posts as much as he did once.

7.30

Now all the interruptions have gone away and I have got my boots and puttees on and all is in readiness. It's rather like waiting on the platform at home for the train back to school; I can't find anything to say and if I chance to think of something a sort of empty feeling inside drains away the energy necessary for the utterance. I suppose one day I shall be able to take these patrols as a matter of course, but I doubt it; I never learnt to do it at all rowing, and as the symptoms are precisely the same as those I used to get before a race, I presume I shall never attain complete detachment at this game.

I shall stop now and keep myself company since I am not fit to do so for anyone else.

Remember that I love you,
John

Journal to Mirren
27th July

My darling, I'm not at all sure of the date and have no idea what day of the week it is. I know I didn't write yesterday as I spent most of the day sleeping off the effects of our patrol which was uneventful though strenuous. We succeeded in pleasing the headmaster, the housemaster and most of the prefects – but I was a little disappointed with myself and now fully realise that I am not nearly so tough and bloodthirsty as I usually make believe. I have discovered that I don't like killing, which is very bad for my much cherished 'offensive spirit', nor do I relish the thought of being killed, which is quite all right and very natural even for a soldier, but it makes being brave so much harder work, particularly at the moment when a supply of bravery is required for immediate use and not just for display. For instance I am brave enough now sitting in the cool evening sunlight looking down at the sea and rugged cliffs of this coast – we have left Stonehenge – but in a few days time we have another party arranged and when the moment arrives for me to make the decision which will precipitate the action (if the decision is mine to make), then I shall

need this 'intestinal fortitude' which sits so securely in my
gut just now.

Mike Kealy has just come back from conference with the
Brigadier and tells me that he is not pleased after all. He says
we didn't do enough damage, nor did we, but in fact all he
asked us to do was to get a prisoner, which we did without
firing a shot, and he did not mention damage in his orders. So I
have my excuse, though I myself am not satisfied with it,
knowing that I was wrong to withdraw from such a favourable
position without attacking even though by good fortune and
good stalking we had achieved our object and secured our
prisoner. We caught the poor chap literally with his pants
down, and as we hustled him away it was ludicrous to watch
him trying to hold his pants and his hands up at the same time.
When we got him back he was delighted to be out of the war
and shook us warmly by the hand before leaving for the
inquisition. He smelt horrid.

So much for the war in which I don't imagine your being
very heartily interested. There is, however, little else that I
can write to you about; for at present the war engrosses my
whole attention, either as a thing to be fought and endured
for its own sake, or else, and this with ever-increasing
frequency of recurrence, the thing which stands between
you and me, as the distance and the danger that must be
traversed on our way to the next meeting. At such times I
pray for the end of the war and in thought I would
welcome an armistice tomorrow at any price, and then I
realise the stern truth that this is recreant thinking and I
whip my slinking mind back to its dutiful determinations
and glorious ambitions. I dare not now seek escape from
the war or improvement of mind in metaphysics or
philosophy, for the more I think the less I relish action, and

the more fine pictures I draw the less resemblance to myself can I find in them. It is very like being back at school with all its clear-cut hopes and fears, temptations and ambitions, rules and customs. I find myself sometimes in the same frame of mind in which ten years ago I was looking for an excuse for not playing an unpleasant game of football or going in for the boxing; wishing that I could be sick and be honourably excused, but knowing in my heart that I had no way out, and when it was all over, glad that I had not.

It is good for me to have my self-confidence shaken in this manner and to have the security and satisfaction in which I lived before, broken up by the recurrence of all sorts of feelings which I thought had left me forever. It's a long time since I have been afraid, or harboured dishonourable thoughts of escape from duty. It is a long time since I was conscious of being presented with a clear-cut case of distasteful duty, and had to make a decision in which the honourable alternative was the least pleasant. I can see now why I held such a rosy view of life – life had indeed been rosy – and fine words were easy because fine times were passing. Now life is harder, but none the less worth living, and if it should pare away some of my easy optimism I shall be the better for the war.

28th July

We have moved again and are now far from the sea and the comfort of its cool waters and large colours: in the desert again with dust and flies and the unhindered sun. Writing is an uncomfortable and uninspiring process.

I am reading 'Peregrine Pickle' by Smollett. It is a silly book by modern standards but I suppose was well enough

for its time. It was a 'scandalous success', so the introduction
says, and the incidents do certainly bear some resemblance
to the most immature stories of rape and fornication with
which schoolboys usually make their first sorties over the
frontier of decency.

Smollett takes it for granted that no young gentleman's
education is complete without considerable practice in what
he is pleased to call the art of gallantry. I wonder how true this
is. I have been brought up to believe the exact contrary and to
look upon virginity in a man as a thing to be proud of and not
ashamed of, a thing to be realised by spiritual purity and not
just preserved by fear or diffidence, a thing to be dedicated to
the 'unknown woman'. This I say is what I have been brought
up to believe, and I do believe it, as a fine ideal that has been
handed on to me. But there is a difference between ideals that
one accepts from an authority that one respects, and ideals
that one has wrought on the anvil of one's life, hot from the
forge of experience under the hammer blows of failure. I have
not yet finished the forging of this ideal, though I have had it
on the anvil often enough.

29th July

At this point the light fails and being without artificial
light of any kind I was forced to suspend the journal. I take
it up now, in the heat of the day huddled in the squalor of
my grave-like home. I have banished the flies with a piece
of mosquito netting hung over the three-foot-square
entrance. The fleas, however, are by no means to be
discouraged, and added to their attacks we have to continue
with the intimate attention of the ticks. There is a small
group of our West-End playboy officers moaning and

grumbling at the hardship of this life in their superficial would-be humorous vein. I have to take part in the banter from time to time so that I force a rather incoherent entry in the journal for today. Indeed I shall have to stop writing until my fatuous associates take themselves off.

It is now near sun setting and I am better able to write and to continue in the train of last night's thoughts. I have discussed the question of man's virginity with two women – touched on rather than discussed – and both of them hoped that their husband would not be a virgin. Indeed one of them went so far as to say that if she discovered that her future husband was a virgin, she would send him out to get some experience before their marriage: and I am not at all sure that the other didn't say or imply as much. What then is the use of bringing to the altar an offering that not only is unwanted but actively disliked? There is, I think, only this to be said for it: it is at least an attempt to elevate the idea of marriage above the common conception which comprises little more than the ideas immediately surrounding the process of intercourse. In reality marriage frequently transcends the confinement of those cramped ideas, but surely it is essential to human progress that the ideal should transcend reality?

Now I shall close this instalment of our journal and consign it to the post. It seems incredible that it should ever complete the journey between this hole in the desert and the cool, sweet-smelling rooms of your home or wherever it may find you. I hope that it may find you and give you some measure of my devotion. I have just now brilliant in my imagination a rhapsody of memories compiled from the record of our visits to the river and also the white-frocked day and our tentative effort at a walk up the path of that dear dear garden. And that reminds me of the scene when David told me, nearly a year

later, that he had heard from you, and of what I then said,
which surprised him and, which is true today, true, and a little,
however little, nearer reality.

Bless you, my darling. You have my love.
John

Journal to Mirren
4th August 1941

I haven't written in this book for several days now, darling,
exactly how many I don't know, because I think the dates of
my last entries were wrong. I think what I called the 29th was
really the 30th or something. But it doesn't matter much
except to help you to tell whether any letters have been lost in
the post. They had us all teed up for a terrific show of bravery a
day or two ago, but we did not function owing to the failure of
the first phase of the battle, and sat instead in little holes in the
ground and watched the fireworks.

I go about these days barefoot and clad only in a scanty
pair of khaki shorts. My theory is that as there is no water
for washing the next best thing is to bathe in the sun. I
don't know whether there is anything in it, but at least the
dirt shows less when one is brown than if one retains the
English pink and white. So gone are the days when you
could wonder at the clear line dividing the brown and the
white on my neck. I'm brown all over now – as far as you
are concerned, at any rate till we are married, and I expect I
shall be white with age to say nothing of white-skinned by
the time we reach that stage of intimacy. As I was lying on
my back in my 'gravel-pit' this afternoon reading Tom Jones

I kept on interrupting the narrative to play games with my
tummy muscles by raising my legs, and half sitting up and
sucking in my tummy. It's fun making them stand out in
little ridges all at once and then seeing if you can make
them do it one at a time – they seem to stand out more
clearly when they are brown too. Then if you straighten
your legs and just raise your heels off the ground and then
suck in your tummy you can make one big ridge run up and
down instead of a lot of ripples running across. Then you
can make your tummy stick out on one side as though you
had a goitre in the wrong place, or stick out high up or low
down like a confirmed beer drinker or a decayed rowing
man. There is not much chance of my running to fat here –
it's too hot and we take too much exercise for that though I
must admit I eat a tremendous amount, mostly army biscuits
which are wholesome and I find good.

5th August

I have just got back from a patrol which was sprung on
me unexpectedly last night while I was writing to you. I
have been up all night and it is now seven o'clock and life is
just beginning to stir in the reserve lines where we are.
Sleepy figures are rising out of the ground as though by
magic and moving very slowly about their business. Last
night was the first patrol which I have led which did not
achieve its object. We went out to cut the telephone line to
an enemy listening post and try to nab the listeners. When
we were still a hundred yards short of the wire we ran slap
into the middle of a German minefield and set one mine off
before we knew we were in it. The German S Mine is an
ugly affair: it consists of a metal box containing an

explosive charge surrounded by about 400 steel balls. The mine is buried in the ground and when set off it jumps about four feet in the air before exploding, when it scatters its shrapnel in all directions for about 100 yards just chest-high. We were incredibly lucky to get away without a single casualty, but it took us so long to get out of the mine-field without tripping another that we had to come back with nothing accomplished except the fact of having located the minefield. This was disappointing, for I had discovered the telephone line and listening post in the first place and was naturally keen to clean it up, but now someone else will get the job, for we move to another line tonight. The listening post is in an old disabled tank and must be incredibly useful to Jerry, for it is only a few hundred yards from our most forward posts.

Damn this war! What do you want to know about S Mines and listening posts? Nothing, less than nothing, you wish you'd never heard of them, I'm sure, and so do I when I realise to whom this nonsense is dedicated. And yet I suppose it is as well for you to get used early to my bad habit of complete preoccupation with whatever enterprise I have in hand at any time, at any rate if you are considering encouraging this correspondence.

This is a paltry letter, just nibbling and picking at the icing of the cake without getting down either to the plums or the more humdrum stuff that holds them together. But I'll still send it off as it is and hope that a new start will inspire something more worthy of your consideration.

Au revoir, my true love, until we meet again believe me your most devoted joy walker.
John

ENEMY NOW 70 MILES FROM LENINGRAD
THE TIMES Tuesday 19 August 1941

'B' Bn Layforce
M.E.F.
[19th August 1941]

Darling Mirren,

You wrote to me on May the 12th from the Akland – a
letter that I loved getting because it brought you so close to
me that I saw all No. 2 Joy Street over again, and took me
so near to you that I sensed the clean brisk atmosphere of
your nursing home as you lay and talked to me from your
bed, saw the finely veined flower petal of your pain and the
towering arches of your lonely thoughts. You seemed sorry
for me being 'afflicted' with such a letter, analytical and
egocentric. What then should I feel for you having read my
letters if I seriously shared that sentiment? Point is: such
letters are nectar to the lover and just because they are what
they are – records of the inmost life he loves. They are
dearer to me than the most enlightened commentary
on current events or tittle-tattle of the intrigues of
Oxford.

But it is a great imposition that your letter should take so
long on the way. I have no clear idea of the date but guess
it to be the 18th or 19th – several days, at any rate, since I
last wrote in my journal to you. Why should your letters
take three months to reach me? Surely I have a fair

complaint against the otherwise beneficent powers who
keep us alive to each other. I only complain because of the
shortness and fullness of human memory and the fear that
after five or six months the answer that I return to your
beloved letters will inkle or rattle discordantly or without
meaning in the new orchestration of your life. Perhaps this
is not so, but I still will not give up my grouse, for why
should my letters take so long in reaching you, and why
should I have to suffer several times over the punishment
for those periods when I did not write?

What an exciting time No. 2 Joy Street was! A real
adventure into the unknown with all its great and little fears
attending; just a few looks, a few words and one or two
letters for guide, map and compass in the undiscovered
country, and off we set together to find out its beauties and
its monsters – its tribes with three heads and no hearts, its
rivers and groves and temples, its ancient ruins and its new
constructions, its art and the pattern of its life, its priests
and its processions. Perhaps we did not find much in that
first journey, but the prospect was delightful and exacting,
and there was a certain importance about our first
discoveries which made the subsequent expeditions
inevitable. Will you remind me sometimes of these joyous
visits? You have all the records and the places near at hand
to keep old memory well supplied with food. I am out of it,
with nothing to remind me, save your letters, nothing to
jog, encourage or fortify the hard-worked nag within my
head to visit in detail the well-loved street of houses, the
parks and pools, the fields and avenues, the gardens and
darkling passages.

This is the second day the wind has blown a dust storm
and the troglodyte existence is not congenial. The freer

one's burrow is from dust, the more the flies appreciate it and use it and one's body for their nasty little doings. It annoys me beyond measure when they have the independence to pursue their lecherous lives on my bare legs and arms and shoulders, and I take a malevolent delight in interrupting their perfunctory pleasures.

There seems to be some prospect that we shall be released from this place of confinement, those at least of us who have the good fortune to survive our next encounter with the enemy. After that the future is quite unpredictable. Anything might happen to the remnant of our force, though the least likely for us who have no battalion out here is what was most solemnly promised a hundred times: to return us to our regiments. If there is any change in our address I shall let you know by cable.

    God Bless Thee.
      Jock

20th August 1941

Today the wind is kinder with its sediment and we are not compelled to eat and breathe the land that we are fighting for. But my spirits have not improved with the weather, and I am unhappy now that some prospect of escape from this tribulation has been proffered us. Unhappy that I should regard it as escape. Why am I not capable of emotion by those noble sentiments of military honour and glory or if not by them, why not by patriotism and enthusiasm for the cause? Why can I embrace so readily de Vigny's gospel of self-abnegation while sitting safely by my fire in Colchester and now have so little

regard for it on active service in _____* that all I can
think of is getting safely out?

I am a deceiver, Mirren, a caitiff recreant; a self-deceiver,
and because I acquiesce in and encourage the deception, a
hypocrite. But surely it is hard to be convicted of those
charges for wanting, and indeed trying to be better than I
am. Surely if I admit the enemy to the citadel I cannot
maintain the outer defences of the fortress; if I did admit,
even to myself, that my greatest desire is to live, I cannot
maintain the pretence of willingness to die. Let's not say
pretence, but appearance; for I am a leader of men and,
whatever I may feel, or whatever be my motive at the time,
if the men judge me brave and a good soldier they will
follow, and they can judge only by appearance. And so I try
to act the part of a good soldier and pretend I'm not afraid
to lead my patrol through the enemy's lines to attack his
outposts in the dead of night without knowing their
strength or dispositions. One or two such patrols and
attacks I have, with the favour of fortune and my own
ignorance of the risks I ran, successfully accomplished; and
people seem satisfied to grant me the reputation (which I
had gained by my demeanour long before we came to the
test) of a determined soldier. But what an agonising burden
that reputation makes when I know I fear as greatly as any
of my comrades and colleagues who don't pretend to it, and
use it, as they should do, in the interest of the cause (their
own being naturally coincident, though incidental) to give
me always the responsibility of the most important and
difficult tasks.

*Jock is in Tobruk, but is unable to say so in his letter.

Perhaps I don't even deceive my brother officers, but, pretending to the status of a soldier, which they do not, I must take the consequences of my temerity. And I have absolutely no right to object to such treatment; indeed if I were consistent and sincere in my professions, I should welcome it, for I have always professed that my aim in life is to seek out the most difficult work of which I am capable and do it with all my might, to welcome responsibility and the risks which inevitably accompany it. I have always believed in the gospel that 'he who saveth his life shall lose it and he that loseth his life for my sake shall find it.' I still believe it – I must for it is fundamental to my faith, and that is why I am now in such an agony of spirit, because my faith is under test, my sake is in the balance of my allegiance against his sake and I must show what I am prepared to sacrifice to my faith or what articles of faith I am prepared to abandon to my interest. I do not doubt my faith, I do not doubt the justice of the cause in which I have placed it. What then? I doubt my own ability to live up to my faith and prove worthy of the cause. So if you love me, as I think you do most truly, pray for my manly strength, as I do, that if I survive this war my faith and my self-respect may survive with me. I long to live, and in my weakest moments to live at any price, did I not know, even at such degrading times, that I could not pay over the treasure of my faith and still hope to purchase the respect of those I love with the empty purse that once contained it.

Mirren darling, you must believe that I am not raving with war hysteria about illusions. You do believe, I know, but you must understand how real they become in the test of the battle. I am sorry for writing so earnestly to you, who have enough troubles of your own to bear, but I mean it when I say that I could hardly bear this burden without sharing it, and that

if I felt myself alone and unobserved in the world the
temptation to recant would be too great for my unaided
strength. But if I can feel that you are watching me, then I am
committed to the course of honour beyond all fear of
recantation. Is this a foolish thing to say, to ask? Do I magnify
the interest that you take in me? Should I take such matters to
my parents or to God? Perhaps I should, but then I have loved
you as I have never yet loved them, with the animal that fears
as well as the soul that loves. God and my parents have been
loving kindness itself to me, and I have loved them from my
soul but never feared them since I became a man, for the spirit
is not subject to that tyranny. And so I come to you for the
assurance and guarantee that my body will not betray my
spiritual faith because it fears more to lose all that you mean to
me, than to run the risks which this test of faith demands.

You know me well enough to know that I am no religious
enthusiast, so please don't let this letter frighten you away.
It is a selfish letter because it is written for my sake rather
than for yours. It is in the nature of a demand upon your
love and only requires an answer if it asks too much. And if
you shall feel compelled to return such an answer, I shall
understand, for it is the greatest presumption on my part to
require so much of you that your consent entails an
implication of love which I have no right either to assume
or to attempt to invoke.

While it was still possible it was a grand game playing with
our love, leaving the issue to settle itself and playing the hide
and seek of intention and expectation. That is the most
exciting game on earth, but it is still a game and I cannot help
feeling that between you and me the occasion for it has
temporarily been taken from us. Nothing that I write now
need prevent us resuming the game if we will and if we are

blessed with the opportunity, nor need my serious mindedness in moments of stress prejudice the light-hearted enjoyment of each other's company, conversation or correspondence when lightness of heart is restored. But I am glad for you to know how seriously at heart I think of our relation to each other, and I am glad that my selfishness has prompted me to write this letter which, if there was still any doubt in your mind of the sincerity of my pretensions to your love, will clear it from your mind beyond all doubting.

It has always been my ambition, and now as much as though under the full influence of the seduction of your charms, to ask you to share the rest of life with me. But first I had to acquire two things: the assurance of your love, and the ability to offer you a home of which you need not be ashamed. That, as I say, is still my ambition, though how I presume to harbour it without either of my prerequisites will be scarcely understandable to anyone but me. I have no right either at fortune's hand or yours to see the visions I do, or seeing them to endow them with more reality than can be supplied by a love-sick brain. But they are as real to me as any other part of me, because they are a part of what I own to be my self which I would not change except at the desire of those I love more than that self.

Now this letter will end and Ulysses will sail away in another ship to new adventures in his epic voyage. You will find him in another mood at the next meeting, but always he will long for home and the soft white arms of his Penelope.

God bless them both and bring them safe and happily together is the prayer of this one.

John

PROFESSIONAL FULFILMENT

Minutes after his acceptance of Stirling's entreaty to join 'L' Detachment, Lewes agonised over the fact that once again he had volunteered to place himself in the hands of someone else, but he was quick to see that the task they had set for 'L' Detachment fell well outside the norm of any military training programme ever considered before September 1941.

While Stirling took on the job of recruiting and solidifying 'L' Detachment's standing within Middle East Headquarters, Lewes agreed to devise a suitable training programme for this new form of special warfare. He was in his element. What were the keys for training already experienced soldiers to operate deep in the desert, unsupported and often without effective communications? Parachuting seemed to be one obvious requirement.

Deciding to set up his own parachute training system, Lewes used the simple expedient of jumping from a lorry to mimic the act of landing in high winds. But at what speed should the lorry be travelling in order to simulate such a landing? To determine this he conducted a series of exercises in which he would leap from the truck at ever increasing speeds until it became dangerous.

First-hand witnesses to his efforts will swear that on a number of occasions Lewes must have been close to killing himself with some of his lonely marches into the desert, on which he tested the limits of how far a soldier could travel with small amounts of water, and then with increasing loads of equipment. He never told anyone when or where he was going or when he expected to be back. Had he succumbed to dehydration or injury he would not have been missed in the base camp for many hours since the men (even if they were aware that he had left the camp) would have assumed that he would simply return when he had completed his self-imposed mission. There was as much courage shown in these 'exercises' as there was in facing enemy fire.

ARMIES LOCKED ON RUSSIAN FRONT
ELEVENTH WEEK OF STRUGGLE
THE TIMES Tuesday 2 September 1941

L. Detachment, S.A.S. Brigade
C.T.C.
M.E.F.
2nd September 1941

Darling Mirren,

I started a letter to you on the 27th from the Cecil Hotel
in Alex, and another on the 31st from Shepheard's, Cairo;
neither of them got further than the first few lines. I
wallowed in idleness and luxury, did little but eat and drink
and have myself cleaned and cured and driven about. I was
sinfully indolent and extravagant, and loved it, glorified in
it, revelled in it and finally submerged in it. Now I am
trying to get out of the habit of eating more than I want. I
smoked so much in _____* that I am disgusted with it
and have given it up entirely, and don't expect to start again
while the war or I last. On the other hand I drank so little
there and so much since coming here that again I am
disgusted with it (though to be more precise I should say its
price) and so only drink when I have to, in order not to
appear unsociable; for I will have you know that my
position of chief instructor and second in command of this

---

*Again, Jock is unable to say he has been in Tobruk.

detachment is one of no little responsibility and social consequence!

Layforce has finally disintegrated altogether since our return from confinement and I have thrown in my lot with David Stirling in a new venture, since I received a categorical refusal to my application to return to my unit in the U.K. I find, when I regard my decision dispassionately, that I have done exactly what I swore never to do again in _____: I have put myself in danger of becoming once more nobody's baby. But who cares? Adrift in the Middle East without a battalion and without a hope of getting home; how could I be more of an orphan than that?

Darling, I wish I could write you by air mail. Just before leaving _____ I received a letter from you over three months old which rang note for note in concord with that very earnest-minded one that I wrote from my hole in the ground. It is a pity that I should have had to wait three months for that, and it is a terrible anxiety to feel that since you wrote that three months have gone by and perhaps filled in the design it sketched or even started a new piece of stone. And now that I have been compelled to resign myself to being out here or perhaps even further afield for the duration of the war, what must I feel about the prospect of being a year's quarter behind in the serial of our romance! But, whatever happens between your writing and my reading, this you must promise me for the sake of a small street of houses. Whether married or single, in love or newly jilted, engaged or engaging, whether I arrive in fair weather or foul, in daylight or dark or by moonlight, that you will come with me to celebrate my return and our meeting.

One other thing I have to ask. I never went to the studio

in Hanover Square to see the proofs of your photographs and so I can't say send me such a one; but will you send me one that you like best for me? I long to see an outline of those features. I shall soon be sending you a photograph of myself and a tiny thing to keep about you if you would like to have something to remind you of me out here. Now God bless you, darling, and keep you safe and loving me until I can do so for myself.

    Goodbye, my charmer,
        with love from the charmed,
           John

FIERCE FIGHTING IN KIEV AREA
THE TIMES Monday 22 September 1941

'L' Detachment, Special Air Service Brigade
Combined Training Centre
M.E.F.
22nd September 1941

You are not here, my love, but you shall be: I am sending
this carriage to bring you to me, just as your four letters,
now read again, have waited at the door like a rich man's
car to take me to my pleasure. The post has marked your
letters 15th July, 22nd July, 22nd July, and 1st August. They
all arrived close together when I was so completely sunk in
my new work.

How badly I am writing! and I am so full now of all
things that matter, love, and knowledge, and vision of
beauty that it is urgently important that I should have the
power to give you all my love, to tell all I know and share
all my imagination. With you who are growing up and
living away from me wishing to share, both of us, all we do
and think and feel. But we could share if we could write
always as you have done just now; if we could write at once
in a form adequate to contain all that I wish to send you, I
could be happy to plunge again with complete absorption.
You say you would now understand my recurring periods of
silence, and I hope and suppose that you mean forgive –
comprehend you cannot. I say that from pride, not
understanding myself. Oh, love, see how this letter jerks

along, inept and graceless. It should flow like a line and sweep us together into the nigh land of my spirit.

I am proud and arrogant. I believe that I know so much that were I to die the world would miss its opportunity of rejuvenation. I am not now troubled by fear and the solitude of godlessness. I have new shoes on my feet and walk proudly and look and look again how handsomely the fine exclusive stockings rise out of dark suede leather. I am proud even of ankles thickened by jumping from heights and the secure binding of my lovely shoes is like my sense of virtue at braving the dread of others.

Aboard a ship but ten days out from Suez homeward bound, there died a man who wanted above everything to live. He had been of us, and eaten by his desire he had failed in a mission requiring courage to game with death. He had married a wife only a few weeks before leaving England and was by his high influence given passage home to enjoy her. And on the way he died. And I, being wise, wag my head and say, he who saveth his life shall lose it.

I walk upright now and hold high my head because I feel my strength, and fear is away. I see how well dressed I am and look boldly at the passengers, when they are soldiers, compelling their reluctant salutes by meeting and keeping their looks. For I have said I will not seek to save my life but will choose the most difficult and dangerous work that is to be done. I shall not scheme to return to England because it is against the order of things; it is ordered that I shall serve in Egypt. If I am to return home I surely will in God's good time, and as I am to die it matters only to those who live on and whom by living I might have helped, whether I die in Egypt or in England some time later.

And yet . . . and yet I am proud in spirit and believe that in life is my release, that I have a mission and must seek a fulfilment here – remember the spirit of the Guest.

23rd Sept.

That was written in the luxury of Shepheard's Hotel; tonight I sit in my tent and shall sit until the dawn or raiding airmen break the magic of this revelation. I could never wish things to be or to have been other than this moment finds and forms them. I doubt whether I am capable of feeling more strongly the power that I've been given in the eternal possession of this impassable night. One other night I knew that was like in that it was given, but in that only, for that was our present and possession. Tonight is mine, selfish and exclusively.

My love, I can't desire you tonight, despite your letters sent all at once on the last of May in Spring. It is my power that I feel tonight, not yours to overwhelm me. And I know that I have power in you to create beauty which passes into bloodstreams of time on the adrenaline of happiness. So many loving people have written by this mail innocently showing me how to possess the power that we generate by loving first, then severing those lines of force. Elizabeth, Sue, Donald, Mike Ashby, Glanusk my Colonel, and David Winser. Both happiness and fear have the power of emptying one's being, suffocating one to such an acuity of consciousness as can only be death reprievable. Tonight I am dead to you, to the world, to time – death not quite fulfilled for I stir to make words unravel a thread for you from the pin-prick of light to which in another age I shall return.

Donald Graham sent me some of David Winser's* poetry.
I send it to you because I long to live such poetry and share
out that life in words. I am no poet; I should love to live
poetry; instead I live life. I pray that I have not forfeited the
faculty of imagination, allowed its atrophy in the monopoly
of attention by things that matter to the 'wide awake'. I
don't often think of you any more than I often think of the
heart that keeps me living or the hand that serves my
purpose. They are parts of me that get attention only when
they draw it. I once saw Joy Street as beautifully as David
sees his mountain – I tried to write it down but didn't
succeed as he has done; I think my picture was a little
grotesque in the end. And people don't stay the same for
me once I've left them. I see them growing and becoming
and feel a power of influence between us, to help more
actively than a statue and with more courage than a present
friend. The rhymed one is truer for me oddly enough. You
used to have no fear of my being enticed away from
devotion to you out here; not by anything that I've seen to
this moment, though Mike in his brilliant letters suggests
that I should look up a charming Irish friend of his who is
working in Military Intelligence in Cairo. I don't think I
will; Mike is the height of discrimination and I find a
certain type of Irish womanhood irresistibly lovely. In the
ecstasy of my communion with you through our letters, it is
unthinkable that I should swerve so much as a hair's breadth
from my devotion to you, which is deep and full. But I'm
not always thinking of you: there are duties to be done and
people to be met in the course of them, and if it's true that

*David Winser, poet, novelist and author of *A Gay Good-Night*,
was a friend of Jock's and was killed in the war.

you can't fall in love without wanting to just as you can't see
the people in the street without looking out of the window,
it is also true that if you do look out of the window you
can't help seeing the people in the street. Does this answer
your question whether it's possible to think of marriage
without being certain that you couldn't love someone
better? You can never be certain that in a moment of
boredom you won't look out of the window; you can be far
less certain of the outcome of meeting a stranger's eye
through the pane of your willingness which possesses the
invisibility of glass when its polish reflects no light.
Marriage is a risk from the very beginning to the very end –
there is no security, no certainty except the conviction of
love and faith which is the greatest the world can give.

Does it occur to you that I have been reading
Sparkenbroke? I am grateful to you for sending me to him. I
am possessed and exalted by this meeting, and at moments
when I stand in most need of inspiration. Surely we are
beloved of the gods. I will not beguile you with details of
my work, even though for once we enjoy a generous
freedom from the restrictions of security. It is not the detail
that matters, it is the fact that at last I have something to
which I can devote myself unstintingly – men to lead and
inspire to tasks which are worth doing well. The Monster
of Tobruk haunts my labours; will I in that last decisive
moment flinch just so much that though my honour may be
clean our trust will be betrayed? That is impossible now: as
with love, so with fear; you cannot become afraid without
wishing to. But now I have no wish; I am prepared for this
to be my life's work because it will be well done and a thing
to be proud of here or anywhere. I am losing my life in this
hard graceless unpoetic unbeautiful devotion. Don't let it

lose me you. Don't feel neglected because I don't speak to you, or slighted because I speak proudly, or bored because I am inspired by uninspiring things. Darling, I love you, better than life itself, and all this business of my enthusiasm for the sordid things of war is no more than insurance of that love. There is a war waging and it flows between us; my greatest wish is that we meet again: thus I ensure it.

24th Sept.

I feel that this resumption of our journal, though perhaps sufficient to itself is shamefully inadequate to answer all your letters. I want to answer your questions, respond to your stimulus, develop, mould and manipulate your ideas. But I am so made that things flowing over me in the stream of experience do not penetrate clear and distinctly individual like a spark on the skin, but instead press their form of unity about me like a cloak, like the feathery flourishes of moving water. I wear your letters about me, not as a man wears a gage or pieces of apparel but as you wear the sensation of a Turkish bath and massage. But I am consoled in this; in all the time that we shall love and live apart there will be in all that writing an answer to all the questions we can ask each other, and yet not a jot the less to write about tomorrow. Let's not be precise, let's not understand too clearly how we each think and why we feel; let's not reduce it all to glands but preserve the mystery of imagination, belief and love. It is only when you begin classifying your lover and typifying his actions that the cynical tower of reason rises beneath your feet and lifts you from the rich soil of imagery high into the clouds of criticism. It hurts the first time you notice an irritating

mannerism, but it rapidly becomes easy once the fertile
land of picture making is seen to be beneath you. I love you
for your dream children more than for the nakedness that
sometimes burns through the casing of my brain into my
body. The first are pictures, not for fulfilment, not
blueprints of posterity but for their own beauty, a far surer
guide and sweeter companion than the exquisite though
barren draughtsmanship of desire. Talk to me more my love
of these most beautiful things in earth, and one day I shall
speak when my present fever is abated and I have calm and
peace to contemplate.

You remember I wrote great blankets of metaphysics
from Tobruk; it was all intended to be leading up to a point,
which alas I never reached and identified. It had been in my
mind but I wrote too much and wrote around it and past it
and beneath it, but never touching it with the probe of
expression; it was soon jostled out of the reach of
consciousness. And now I find that it is the key-note of
Sparkenbroke. Here: 'But he could not escape from his
belief that art's selective process was, like a gardener's,
creative; it bred new species, transforming and
retransforming nature, until at last life itself became, in
certain aspects, a product of art, and vision subsisted in
poetry, and heroism in heroic tales. Without pictures there
could be desire of male for female stallions and mares, but
without pictures there could be no beauty in women. And
without women, there might be no art – or none of mine he
thought – for between men and women there is a
tension . . . like a harp string . . . and the quiver of it is
among art's primary impulse.'

Now surely that is better than glands and wish
fulfilment. There is stated clearly and magnetically, so that

it leaps at the mind like opposite poles together, the
conception which would have given some measure of
imaginable completeness to the pattern I was making. Do
you remember that I wished to say that living consisted in
the disciplining of primary force by form? I don't remember
whether I ever tackled the question of how man takes an
active part in the process by being aware of form, but now I
should know how to put the matter in words; I should
borrow them from Morgan who borrows them from Keats,
'I am certain of nothing but of the holiness of the Heart's
affections and the truth of Imagination.'

These things are the Spirit of Man which at the time
when I wrote I seemed to think was comprehended by the
Will. The Will is the human element, determination, which
by itself is aimless without inspiration by the divine likeness
whereby we perceive that which is not and know that it
ought to be. The Will is not the Spirit, it is the slave of the
Spirit and it is by virtue of the will's devotion to the Spirit's
divinity that man rises from being a form of life to the
status of the former and reforms of the living, aiming
always to make that which it resembles more truly and
more truly until identical with that which is not but ought
to be, that which is imagined and loved. This non-existent
is, therefore, possessed of reality in a fuller sense than is
ever possessed by existence, and the soul's imaginings more
stable, immutable and absolute than the senses' clearest
perceptions.

This is the nearest I think that we can ever get to a proof
of the existence of God. Compared with any other that has
gone before, including Descartes after which you ask, it is
good, but it is in fact a proof of the non-existence of God
and of his transcendent reality. Our struggle therefore is to

get out of existence and win freedom from the bondage of its false reality. It is not necessary to die in order to escape existence; poets and artists of all degrees are constant messengers between reality and sense. It seems as though death is the final release from bondage, but we cannot know; perhaps we may continue to exist on some other plane of sub-reality, and there once more the struggle will be renewed out of existence into life. The struggle goes on through death, and we believe that death is but the matriculation to life but whatever may be the ultimate state of affairs, this we can know with the certainty we love – wordy certainty – we cease to exist at death. We may begin a new and different existence but death ends this one for ever. The foundation of our belief is that it is the same life on both sides of death.

But this intellectual approach to the matter is the merest beginning, like being conceived. We cannot be born until the imagination has been fired and the Heart's affections enslaved and we cannot take our first breath of life until that inspiration and devotion have been tested to see whether after all it isn't just disguised existence, glands and wish fulfilment. Limp from the womb of our glorious mother, our pink little bottoms must be smacked to see whether we are cabbages or kings. Always until weaned from mother earth by death, this trial continues, always asking the same question; do you see God, or do you see just his works? do you love God or do you love just his gifts? do you believe what you know or know what you believe?

You and I, Mirren, are under test now; we have been since you first challenged me to know you and I challenged you to love. What is it we look for in each other for to love? It must be the heart's affections and sympathy of imagination, otherwise we can live only those exquisite moments of compulsory life in which existence is regenerated in children and will be bound to witness the degeneration of existence in ourselves.

Darling, I love you and want you here because I love you and because together I think we could make a pretty good best of this bondage of the flesh.

May God smile upon you and otherwise bless you for your man,
John

Russians Gain Ground in Leningrad
THE TIMES Wednesday 1 October 1941

'L' Detachment, Special Air Service Brigade
Combined Training Centre
1st October 1941

Dearest Mirren,

One day I suppose I shall become a captain, or perhaps
even a major, and then if I do particularly badly in any job
and they want to get rid of me, who knows but that there
won't be a Colonel Jock Lewes on some shelf in the military
catacomb that is headquarters. Please don't think that I
mention these high aspirations at the instigation of any
reliable hope of their fulfilment. I think of them simply as
things that may happen to any soldier, like being wounded
or given a medal; things which are almost bound to happen
to you if you remain a soldier long enough; that's why I say,
'one day I suppose I shall become a captain', or rather that's
why I say it without either a flutter of hope or a pang of
despair. But why I brought the matter up at all is different:
that was because I wanted to point out, I wanted to explain,
suggest perhaps, that if you still felt the same about the
whole thing; well, I don't know, it's just an idea that I had
the other night while reading your letters, but then they're
so old, goodness how old they are when you think how you
can change in a week, say from the absolute certainty that
carpentry is your vocation to wanting to be a train driver or

postman, or not wanting to be anything at all, but just to be left alone by an interfering world in which everyone has to be something.

Why have we got to be something? We are something already, me and you, no you and I – that's better English and politer because you come first – we are you and I already; why have we got to be something else as well? But that was the whole point about captains and majors, though it seems so silly, now that I have said all that about being things, just because your letters are old and people change their mind and themselves too, often. Yes, and themselves too, yes, now that's really what I meant; you see Mirren, you know how a rolling stone gathers no moss, and if people don't settle down sometime and be something besides just themselves to keep them settled down, well then they just keep rolling through life and don't get nice and old and mossy; well, I don't know, that has always seemed a silly proverb to me, a rolling stone gathers no moss; who wants to gather moss anyway? Moss and rust corrupt.

Is getting mossy the same as being something? Just lying still in a little cup-hollow of the ground and allowing stuff to grow on you like parasites, so that when people are what we are you can say, 'Oh we are six inches north north west from Freddie Stone and north east by east from the Mossy Stones, you know the family, frightfully stuck-up lot you know, though they've had rollers enough in their family in its time. We are also seven sixteenths of moss.' I suppose it saves a lot of trouble to be able to say what you are without giving anything of yourself away.

You're not much good at that yet, darling, or at least you weren't when I last saw you, you used to hand round great

chunks of yourself to everyone you knew, so that when
they met you they would forget about moss for a while and
think how light and bouncing meeting you made them feel,
and how beautifully you rolled, although of course they
disapproved of rolling – like people out here do of belly
rolling dancers. They suck it up like the good rich food it is
and then go home and have sort of moral indigestion about
it. You should see it, Helen; my God, it's wonderful; it's
plain carnal love naked and triumphantly unashamed, no
not unashamed, there's no question of shame, proud,
glorying and triumphant, certainly triumphant, like a chef
over an exquisite dish made of ordinary bloody meat that
any butcher could kill and cut from the same rather
unattractive animal. Out of all the attitudes and gestures of
plain ordinary fucking – I use that word because that's what
I mean – the thrust and jerk and squirm of the hips, the
parted thighs and slight sagging knees, the heaving chest,
rigid extremities, bared teeth and dilated nostrils; out of
this raw material, like nothing more than uncooked meat,
the dancer, by grace and rhythm and harmony of
movement, creates an erotic inspiration.

It can be beautiful; that is the realisation that the dancer
suddenly imparts; it should be beautiful – that is implicit in
the realisation that anything can be beautiful – and in one's
reaction to the spectacle there is very little plain gross
desire to do it. Instead there is sort of pressure in one's
breath and lifting of the heart to make of it an act of
worship, another way of saying Glory be to God, like
writing poetry or painting or doing anything well, which
means doing it beautifully.

I wonder if we'd do it well; not at first I think; it would
be too new and rich and overwhelming; it would be too

much for me at any rate, and you'd be disappointed. But
later on when we had learnt not to gulp our food we would
make a glory of it and treasure it like a good wine which
does not come to table at the bidding of the occasion, but
whom the occasion courts, striving to appear worthy of
being honoured by its appearance. What fun we could have
when we were asked out to parties, wondering whether
they would attain our special dignity or just send us home
to sleep and looking across the table with the least
millimetre of an eyebrow raised and a bland look in the eye;
um? u-huh! Or have a code: Darling, isn't this a delicious
party? means, No sleep for you tonight my love! or:
Darling, MacBeth's abroad – we could have a dog called
MacBeth; that would be extra fun –

Well, I don't know about this letter; it's a funny one, it is
really. I've said what I meant to say when I started off about
captains and Colonels, or at least very nearly said it, but I
didn't mean to be quite so, well you know, I thought that I
had better be careful what I said in case you didn't feel that
way any more. Now I have burnt my boats and either this is
in the wastepaper basket long ago or else you won't mind
much how I say the rest. Darling, don't you think we had
better get married fairly soon. Let's get married right away,
before I'm a Captain or a Colonel: no, we can't do that
because there just wouldn't be anything to live on
anywhere, much less here; but when I'm a captain, war
substantiated so they can't take it away from me again –
that takes six months from the time you become a captain –
but when I'm a real captain with lots of pay, and allowances
to scale, Will you marry me then? Darling, you know I love
you and I know I could make you so happy that you
wouldn't want to die in case Heaven wasn't as good. Just say

yes, you'll marry me when I'm a proper Captain and I won't
ask you to put it in the papers because I might never
become a captain and then people would say ha ha, or else
I might die and then they would say poor dear, and both
are horrid, I think. But if you do put it in the paper go and
tell Mother and Father first – they will be delighted – and
send me the cutting.

And if all this is a lovely dream of mine, well it has been
lovely dreaming it, and you won't mind because you know
you are beautiful and made for love and will take my dream
as an offering to your beauty. Or even if it is something
more than a dream but less than things to come, then you
will tell me sweetly because you love me, and I shall go
away from your inner chambers for a while, then come
back strongly and take you.

Darling, you know me,
 and that I love you wholely,
  my name is John

RUSSIAN SUCCESS IN MANY SECTORS
THE TIMES Monday 6 October 1941

[Although Mirren had not been silent over the months, this is the first of her letters since January that was not lost.]

Somerville
6th October 1941

My dearest John,

Your letter dated 1 October 41 arrived this morning –
and the little blue beetle, and the photograph. For the last
two I thank you with more joy than can be written or
spoken, but how can I possibly thank you for the letter in
such conventional prosaic terms, when all I want to do is
hug the wits out of you. Then you'd be so bewildered that
you'd scarcely notice we were in the train on our way to the
'Times' office to ask them to tell the world that Esmé
Miriam Barford is telling Lieutenant John Steele Lewes that
she will marry a Captain. But not all the writing and
wishing on earth can snatch you back from the east so
instead I can but write and say I love you and that I will
marry you when you come to take me to you.

I have been faithful to you, in my fashion, for many
months now . . . maybe that sounds meagre, but way in the
back of my mind, in the depths of my heart, I suppose I've
known that you've mattered more than anyone since that

day when you and I amongst the prickles of the field heard the insects hum and buzz an anthem for us; the hot sun was the warmth of the good God as he blessed us, and that same night, when I climbed out of my window to find you, was the time I truly came to you. I've tried to escape; I've wanted to escape. Last Christmas I thought of you as Paris and I decided I had escaped. But here I am, yours more sincerely each month, and with little desire or opportunity to escape. And so my love, listen to what I need to say. I know I could be happier with you than anyone I have ever met; but I know too that my love for you makes me afraid of spoiling what you so desire . . . the happiness and peace of both of us. If you think you can prevent me from ruining what should be a lovely life with you, then all is well. But there is yet one more thing. You, perhaps, are not as likely as I am to fall in love with someone else, simply because I suppose I have more opportunity of meeting people than you have. But it may yet happen to either of us, and that is one reason why I don't want to go by myself to the 'Times' just yet.

There are other reasons too, mostly selfish. I don't want people to say 'Look, there is Jock's fiancée, dancing around as usual, while Jock is fighting a battle.' I don't ever want anybody to think I'm playing with you, for I'm not. But people won't understand, when I take my pleasure in the company of others, and I will not have them being sorry for you. And just one more thing . . . I expect it's foolish vanity, but I'd feel so ashamed if the papers had to say that 'the marriage would not take place'. I should be ashamed, because that would mean that your certainty and mine proved unequal in strength to circumstance. I'd rather only our friends knew we had failed where we once were so very sure. But darling, all this doesn't mean I want to have a loophole for escape . . . I'm not merely being kind to you in saying 'yes,' nor am I deceiving myself. I know I want to marry a Captain, even though I'm still kind o' scared of not being able to make things truly good and lovely for him; that's just because I love him, I suppose.

When term is over may I go up and visit your parents and ask them if they will accept me? My own mother, who brought round your letters and the photograph this morning, is so happy to know that she may well have a Captain for a son-in-law. And Freda too – she'll be delighted because she has practically told me that I am to marry you, and she loves you dearly. John, am I being too serious? I know we may change our minds and I know that money is a problem. But please, God, please let it work out all right. You see, in nine months I should be earning my own living, and I daresay that by the time you are a Captain, and have come home, by then I expect I'll have enough florins tied up in the last silk stocking to keep myself in cotton stockings at least. And I'll have an immense store of paper handkerchiefs by then, so that the laundry bill won't be so much, and if you get a cold, then you can use my paper handkerchiefs – that would help, wouldn't it? And I'll ask for an enormous log basket for my birthday so that MacBeth can sleep in it and the baby afterwards. Let's have MacBeth and a baby too, shall we? Because then we'll have two excuses to get home quickly, and the baby will be so good and healthy that it will never wake up and interrupt our private times. Oh yes, it's sure to work out all right in the end.

Darling, I hope I shan't be sorry when you come home, because you won't recognise me. I think I must be a round pebble – you know, the kind that spins and rolls and then settles down in a tiny niche till something comes along and starts it flying and bounding again. But round pebbles are awful dangerous; they are no good as skipping stones, and though people may have a lovely time spinning it on its round surface, sometimes they lose their balance and break their necks. You will be careful won't you; maybe I'd better acquire some moss, so that I'll be a surer foothold for you.

Funny thing, moss. It grows and then one tosses it all away like confetti at a wedding, because it gets in the way of one's dancing, chokes one's laughing. But the roots are still there; the roots of knowledge and experience, and though I may make other people intoxicated and become so myself, yet one can't be utterly smooth and elusive. When you come home, you may find a shockingly mossy pebble, or you may glimpse its whiteness as it spins through the sunlight. But I hope the roots will give you a firmer handgrip, and though they may tickle and prickle the palm of your hand, it will be just a sign of new growth in the roots. Then it won't become the dry lichen whose dust gets into the eyes; nor the separate thin vivid red hairs of another kind of moss; but just the lovely warm, rich sweet-smelling moss which will have grown round my heart from the love reaching me through your finger tips as I lie in the palm of your hand. And that moss will keep me from careening around, and you won't need to grip that pebble any longer, because it will have become yours, utterly and wholly.

I don't like motionless, mossy stones; they are complacent and dull. But at least the power to grow moss does give a surer foothold; one isn't so likely to damage other people, nor to be tossed here and there for want of some grip on the smooth shiny surface of one's life.

You cuckoo, you didn't tell me you had been promoted, or maybe I just didn't understand the military term. But you have two pips in the photograph, and I've looked at your official signature in the last two letters. I'm truly glad you are a good soldier, but I wish a little that you didn't have to be good so far away. But still your last letter only took about five weeks, and now you have caught up on the term. I moved back into College on the first of October. Besides, it makes it seem as though you had just been a little bit lazy about answering the letters I have sent you this term – one can almost forget that at the beginning of October you may not have had my letters of June and July.

John, I do love your photograph; your eyes look so quizzical, but I don't like to guess what you've been doing about your mouth; was it ever really as sensuous as that? And you look so brown too. Please don't go to Russia and such places, because then we'll both have white bodies, and I'd like you to go on being brown. I'm enclosing a few photographs, and I've ordered some from Lenore; you can look at the latter when you are feeling romantic and at the former when you think you'd better be practical.

By the way, what do you suppose the Captain will suggest about his fiancée's own father at the wedding? It will be very difficult, because Hamish and Mummy won't come if my Father does, and I don't really want to ask him not to come. Have you told your parents that mine are divorced? They won't like it much, but I'll ask them if they know when next I see them. That's another reason why I feel a little shy about the paper. We can't very well say daughter of L.H. Barford and Mrs M.S. Paton, nor of Professor and Mrs Paton. Who would give me away, anyhow? But still, there is no particular hurry about that, I suppose.

Nothing much has happened during the past four days. Mike still writes his notes, but I don't see him. I even refused to go to a dance with him tonight which was a very noble effort, because a sort of a wanting-to-dance fever seems to have attacked my whole body. Oh yes, my friend Roshun and I went to see the film 'Of Mice and Men' the day before yesterday. It was very fine, but so sad. It didn't make the tears pour down the way 'All This and Heaven Too' did. Maybe the 'Mice and Men' film made one think more about the tragedy of frustrated hope, the death of dreams and illusions, whereas the other appealed directly to one's emotions and only allowed thoughts to arise in retrospect. Try and see 'Of Mice and Men' one day, if you haven't already. I'm still reading 'The Last Puritan' which I'm enjoying greatly. I'll send it on to you, for even if you have read it, you might like to look at it again. Keep it in the Ottoman Bank till you come home and then we'll put it on our bookshelf, and talk about it when we have time and leisure.

Now I must stitch my thoughts together and do a French prose. I had B+ for the last one, which is cheering considering that my other tutor has always said they were just about third class. If I could get B on my literature and essay papers then maybe they'd balance the g= of philology and I might scratch up a third, which is good enough. Do write and tell me I must work; I'm getting dreadfully idle again.

But now I truly must attend to my books. Bless you, darling, and may my fine Captain sail home with his cargo of living dreams very soon.

My love to you,
    Mirren

Somerville

It's still Friday the sixth, and I only just want to say goodnight. I've done my French and my Béroul and I've had my bath too. You know, darling, you'll have a busy time trying to shoo away my modesty when we are married. I was standing naked in front of the mirror, arching my back and trying to count my ribs, and then, just as I was patting my tummy scar and thinking how neat it was, I suddenly saw your photograph reflected in the mirror: I think I really did go pink with embarrassment!

It's odd, isn't it, the way one can be so familiar with one's own body, and yet leave other people entirely ignorant of its niceties. You are allowed to see its brown, strong throat, and you can feel the muscles of its arms and thighs. But I'm not allowed that, just because it's your body. And that's mean, because I'm quite, quite sure you don't love your own lean face as much as I do and you certainly don't want your body as much as I want its warmth and its nearness. Do you remember that time in Alice when you said something about 'don't let me do what I might regret'? Isn't it all silly . . . I know about my thighs and they don't interest me in the least. But you – you had to ask and you were afraid to know. I suspect there must be something wrong somewhere. However, I shall now wrap my nine stone of flesh and blood up in bed, and try not to sulk because I know you'd appreciate it much more than I do. Goodnight my love, but don't forget to come back to teach me how to be delicately licentious, quickly passionate and wholly, gloriously yielding and receiving. Promise you'll teach me, because other people can't; it's in your power alone. Now

Miriam is getting severe and tells Mirren she must stop
writing like this and go to bed at once. So she shall, but
they both love you, so don't think that only the vice child
needs you and wants you. All of me, every scrap of me
wants you, and will for many months past tonight.

Blessings on you – Mirren.

HITLER'S NEW OFFENSIVE TAKES SHAPE
THE TIMES Tuesday 7 October 1941

'L' Detachment, S.A.S. Brigade
Combined Training Centre
M.E.F.
7th October 1941

Darling Mirren,

I have just trimmed the wick of my lamp, and there it
stands now, brightly burning, on the deal table in my tent;
so familiar, so well remembered in all its being from those
other days when my house was lit with oil lamps, those
days which make the present what I find it to be, and make
me what other folk discover. And I come back again to the
letter you wrote on August the 14th. And now I am glad I
have written some of the letters I've sent you; now I am
glad because by then you will know how little sometimes I
resemble the impressions that chance and other meetings
have left with friends and travellers on the road and above
all with you, whom I love and desire most favourably to
impress, but shudder to deceive. But you will not be
deceived, but in you I trust and fear not to be seen by you,
for your love will forgive the blemishes and glory in
whatever is for delight. Yes, I am glad that I have written as
I did. I am not proud of the scarab-letter and yet I hope it
arrives safely, for if we are going to love each other we can't
keep little patches over the scars of operations and our

shameful parts and hope not to appear ridiculous.

I think Sparkenbroke spoke well of the act of love:
'Either it's a pleasure and a stimulus, like drinking wine; if it's
that, to hoard it and bargain for it and hedge it round with
vows and taboos is stupidity and meanness. But if it's the
spring of life itself, and to poison it is to poison the
imagination –

"Which is it?" she said.

"It is both. It is what you imagine it to be."'

Love is what you imagine it to be: I believe that, and I
have deeply shocked people by saying that I also believe
that God is what you imagine him to be. Some people can't
imagine either and must therefore borrow other people's
pictures before love or God can mean anything more to
them than thoughts about their last, next or first lover, and
pictures of Jesus or the Father.

It is not wise to be in a hurry either to begin or finish
one's picture of love, or to become impatient because the
inspiration does not come and you still can't see it as
anything more than a pleasurable process. It's much better
to be like Mary, who 'didn't see the world, as everyone else
does, in its relation to herself. It wasn't a field for her
ambition or her happiness. It was a place where you heard
and saw things – and waited.' Be patient and all will be
revealed; only believe and the ecstatic moment will come
when you see with you own inner sight the act of love
more clearly beautiful than it has ever been presented to
your sense. And in the meanwhile hear and see and wait,
and prepare the ground by interior discipline for the seed
and rain and sun of inspiration from outside.

It is admirable how permanent and stable is our
relationship companionship, at least in relation to the

incidents of living. Each night now I have come to this
letter out of my world here and read it through and added a
little and thought much and made images of you: each
night now for a week I have come here and still it seemed
so much the same visitation that to put in the dates would
be like sowing full stops after the manner of hundreds and
thousands, and that is why it seems impossible that this
should be my Christmas letter to you. Surely I shall greet
you when Christmas comes. Yes of course, but symbols are
not useless and silly just because we can sometimes do
without them: they still have all the delight of a marriage
between imagery and matter. And so I send you a symbol
with my greeting: the Christmas stocking. Bless you,
darling, be merry and love and laugh, and when the day is
over wear the stocking jauntily as a new symbol for a new
day.

I should send this letter now, but a little ago I had my
picture taken and a copy dispatched to you. I hope it
arrives; those sent to me have not. But whether it come or
no this is the sentiment that goes with it or with its brother
that shall replace it missing. It is Donne and is called 'His
Picture':

Here take my Picture; though I bid farewell,
Thine, in my heart, where my soule dwells, shall dwell.
'Tis like me now, but dead, 'twill be more
When we are shadowes both, than 'twas before.
When weather-beaten I come backe; my hand,
Perhaps with rude oares torn, or Sun beams tann'd,
My face and brest of haircloth, and my head
With cares rash sodaine stormes, being o'rspread,
My body a sack of bones, broken within,

And powders blue staines skatter'd on my skinne;
If rival fools taxe thee to have lov'd a man,
So foule, and course as, Oh, I may seem then,
This shall say what I was: and thou shalt say,
Doe his hurts reach me? doth my worth decay?
Or doe they reach his judging minde, that hee
Should now love lesse, what hee did love to see?
That which in him was fair and delicate,
Was but the milke which in loves childish state
Did nurse it: who now is growne strong enough
To feed on that, which to disus'd tasts seems tough.

Soon I won't be able to call this my letter and will have to
sign it John Donne edited and annotated by Jock. But it
isn't my letter in any case, so that's all right; it is your letter
and I only sign it to tell you who has sent it and you can
usually guess that I guess. So it doesn't matter. But it is your
letter in a very real sense. You gave me Sparkenbroke and
he gave me Andrew Marvell, and he introduced Donne to
keep me company while Andrew came from England, not
living here. And sop it is that I'm set exploring a whole new
world of life by your influence. I'm drinking up the fountain
of new spirits because you said read your Morgan, and I
listened.

And still I go on scratching away at experience just the
same and nothing makes any difference to another. A man's
experience is predestined, inevitable and inescapable, but
no one, not even God, can predict his reactions to it or
prevent his feelings. They are his life, the other just
existence, his formal introductions to the living, like me
meeting Donne and Marvell and Sparkenbroke. I could
meet them whichever way it went if I truly wished it, and

however the drum rolls and the earth shakes for me I can love you from the depth to the pinnacle of love and to extinction in you on the same condition; that I wish it truly – no, oddly enough, not that condition but another like it: that we wish to truly; for us like can join another uninvited. Marvell could have cut me dead had he wished; he is the trustee of his own legacy and may do what he will with his own; he can choose his children as he did once choose his words and however hard I tried to like him if he would not consent I could not walk with him. That we work it truly, that's the condition and that is absolute truth that there's no feigning even to ourselves. That we wish it we know, but that we should wish it truly we can only pray until we come of age and start life untrammelled by the spinster chaperone experience. Let's wish to die together into one and as a punishment we may be made to live together for ever two, except when experience withers in love's ecstacy and we glimpse one life beyond the sleep of resurgent existence.

I am the lover John.

HITLER'S NEW OFFENSIVE TAKES SHAPE
THE TIMES Tuesday 7 October 1941

Tuesday, 7th October 1941

This morning I went home to ask Hamish if he would approve of me marrying a Captain. Hamish wasn't there, but instead I read a letter of yours dated 25.9.41 which arrived at Merton Street this morning. I'm glad my letters of June and July have reached you. Those two months, and even August, were momentarily gay, but they were harsh and unkind. I'm glad you know about them. I wish too that I could tell you all that happened, but for that I shall need you near me, and above all I shall need your understanding which will accept without questioning the time when I was perhaps prodigal with my rage and impotence, my laughter, living, desiring and all those other things whose violence have made my stomach lean. I've not had to live on husks of the past, but I have hunger for peace and balance. I'll not ask you to kill the fatted calf for me when you come home; all I shall ask is that you must know me as I have been, as I was during those three months when my acquaintances were amazed at the brilliance and gaiety of my life. But if you wish, you shall know why I seemed the woman I was not. My darling, laugh with your Irish beauty, be with her, but do not love her more than you love me.

I loved fully and freely these months, but the letters which I wrote to you – didn't they bear witness of my love for you? Don't deny yourself for the memory of Mirren. Let your knowledge of her drift into your present life when you have time and space for her. But don't let her get in the way, be it of women or wine or war. Oh, just listen to Eve beguiling her lord and master! Yet she would have been sad and very lonely if Adam had not also tasted of the fruit of life. All I am trying to say is this: I think of you very often, but often too I have, and shall again give myself wholly to the business of living this my own life, which is now so distant from yours.

I know you do not, cannot let me intrude upon certain parts of your life; nor have I any wish to do. But these halls where I may not enter are austere and magnificent. You are then an ascetic lord and the warmth of love should not steal into your proud palace. But when I bar my doors to you? Well, the chambers are not very fine, nor very gracious. Some are dark and smell of books and there is little room for you in the library of my brain. Others are vast halls, thronged with people who laugh and weep; the breath of their living is hot and exciting and I am fascinated, absorbed, lost in the midst of that teeming, reeling life. Sometimes I pause to catch my wits and look round the room, wondering if I shall see Jock. For many months now he has not stood on the threshold of that hall, so, yet again, I turn my back on the door and mix again wholeheartedly with the crowd, for I know that one day, John's hand will be beneath my elbow to guide me. Till then I must be alone and yet surrounded and stimulated by the turmoil.

So you see, my love, that dwelling place of mine is not magnificent. Don't know me too much, leaving your great palace and turning to me in faithfulness. Live as you will, for you must and shall remember that I am not asking you

to be wholly mine own. What you give me, that I accept
with infinite joy.

Perhaps I'm being foolish. I think that you aren't really
like me at all. I must, or do, live for, through and by other
people. My self is in service to living and not to the soul. I
cannot pretend to have fine ambitions; I have no need to
experience the first agony of self abnegation and of
devotion to the mighty. How can I say this? I live and learn
through people; you do that too, but you have visions and
ideals which are dependent on yourself. I know what it is –
I'm earthy, full of the lust and pride of life; you are more
than that. Quite what I don't know, and anyway I have
attempted to analyse too much already. Just live as you will
and don't preserve yourself for an ideal, or rather don't
regard me as an ideal. You know I love you too for saying
that your devotion to me is unflinching. That makes me
glad and proud, but please, my love, please don't ever let
me be in the way. Seriously, you honour me too much.
That's why I feel most deeply the need for your presence
here in England. Then you would truly know me, and while
you are away you cannot help but think too well of me.
Perhaps ideally one should remain static in the mind of
another. Granted that leaves no room for development, but
at least it nullifies the danger of silliness and dreams.

Dear heart, I'm not always as afraid as this: it's just that I
don't ever ever want to disappoint you or hurt you. How
contrary indeed was Mistress Mary – and I too. Just because
I love you and want you I feel this idiotic need to shock
you, frighten you away and then, when the last shred of silk
has been ripped off my back, stand before you naked and
unashamed and so wait till you should repulse me or take
me as I am. But I'll never be able to do that, shall I, darling?

You're just a silly, blind, dreaming lover, but that doesn't seem to prevent me from thinking you are most surely the dearest and best of all lovers.

You know something – I've begun to feel uneasy about the last letter I sent concerning the Captain. In that letter where you asked if I'd say 'yes' to a Captain, you also say '. . . "one day I shall become a captain", or rather that's why I say it without either a flutter of hope or a pang of despair.' Now I did say yes to the captain, but I also forgot that the lieutenant wasn't at all sure that he ever would be a captain. That makes it kind o' complicated, doesn't it? Never mind, we'll leave it like this. My 'yes' was on account of the captain; if the lieutenant decides to keep the secret of his next promotion, or if, on becoming a captain, he laughs in retrospect at the words of the lieutenant, then Helen-Penelope won't fuss. In fact, she leaves it entirely to you to renew or retract the suggestion in your letter of the 1st of October.

My thoughts will not run smoothly this evening, I know. It's been raining continuously for the last two days and my bones and my brain are damp, almost sodden. But still I'd rather walk back from Hall through a wet dark night, than through the mind and past those black lurching trees. And it really is black tonight; I found my way by the sound of the rain. First one hears it switching against the walls of the main building, then splattering down onto the water of the tank in the lane; past the tank, and then it flicks the leaves of the trees with a surprisingly dry, brittle sound. And at last, when I hear that crispness dulled as the rain falls on the cabbage leaves I know I'm nearly back. I only have to go round the corner of the path, and when I've splashed through a mighty, far-reaching puddle, the door should be somewhere near. So it was, and once again I am safe in my room.

Today I had a cable from Bill Scriven, a friend of my friend Gavin Livingstone. Sometimes I wonder if you mind me writing to Bill and to other people abroad. It isn't as though you yourself were just one of a list of people. You are quite apart from them, and for that very reason I like to suppose that you don't mind when I welcome other people to drink from my well. Gavin thinks that I should, that every woman should, keep the waters clear and untouched, to preserve it for the one man who shall be able to drink deeply of her life. But I don't agree. I don't feel I'm being in any way unfaithful to my future husband and lover simply because I hand round the loving cup filled from my well. The cup is filled again and again, but I never lose a drop; it seems to make life richer instead. That's the only thing which makes me not so sure about marrying. As long as you are absolutely free then other people feel equally free to write to you, speak to you, behave as they will. If you are married, then inevitably a barrage is put up, and the people on the outside do feel a little shut out. That's partly why I write to Bill; I think he likes letters and I just hope you'd never feel the way Gavin does. I wouldn't care to whom you wrote, nor how often, because that is something between you and the other person. I couldn't alter your relationship with them, nor they alter our relationship. Ours might be less important or more important, but that doesn't alter the way it is.

I wonder if you'll ever meet Bill. He is not a happy man, and he is not very cultured nor very clever, except in his own sphere. But he has a wisdom born of sadness and disillusion, and I like him. I do wonder if you will ever meet him.

And now I must work. I shall have finished with these

books in seven months time – couldn't you finish your
battle by then? I love you so much, and I shall be glad when
you have finished what you must do.

Goodnight, my love, and God keep you.
Mirren

'L' Detachment, S.A.S. Bde.
C.T.C.
M.E.F.
20th October 1941

Dearest Mirren,

The journal still won't run, and so I shall not waste
energy pushing a vehicle that's meant to carry me: I'll reach
you some other way.

I've been reading through your letters that have mounted a
little blue staircase on my table during the last six weeks. There
is so much in them that I want to write about that I get the
eager bursting feeling that comes when you are filled with an
idea and you can feel it overflowing and escaping out of reach.
You so often 'say the word that I have unconsciously been
listening for, almost craving to say for myself,' that on
rereading your letters I wonder how it is I have not thanked
you for that saying and perhaps discussed it with you. Talking
of Michael Marks* you reach the idea: 'Is it imagination to

*Mirren had been seeing Michael Marks during the earlier days
of her acquaintanceship with Jock. He was later killed.

believe that we accept an inheritance of the mind?' Of course
it's imagination – the imagination in whose likeness reason
fashions the world – but it's not fantasy. How long have I been
looking for that picture! and felt the want of it without
knowing its likeness: the inheritance of the mind. My father
does not have to die for me to feel the worth of my heritage,
but when he dies I shall also feel the responsibility of
ownership. It was that phrase, read some weeks ago, its words
forgotten, its picture remaining, which prompted some verses
which I have cudgelled into a shape so little to my liking that I
hesitate to write them for you. But I will write because I want
you to see how I have accepted your picture as my own and
tried to express it in my own way with less success than your
brief question:

Inheritance

All the world is made of live men's bones,
And what we call dead substance is no more
Than colours in our eyes, and in our ears the tones
Of melody, whose forms obey the law
Which is a pattern in the life of man.

That substance lives which gives itself to life,
And fears not to attach itself to things
Which it finds beautiful, to us with care the knife
Of reason, and with love of truth words wings.
These lives are the architect's design

The world's design is drawn in mankind's visions,
In seeing beyond the point that meets the eye,
And sketching out the form of classes and divisions

Which tones of sound and colour can't imply.
Each man builds who trusts their reality.

The universe is built of what is known;
The homogeneous rock experience
Quarried by reason striving to realise in stone
Man's images of separate existence.
Each stone conforms to and reforms the plan.

Each man who's hewn or shaped or smoothed and
   polished,
Transported, fitted, mortared, laid or set
A single building stone of wisdom has accomplished
More than his task, got more than he hoped to get.
He lives in the house he's built, with the friends he made.

And each man who, in faith, has drawn a line
On the quarry wall or the picture that we live
In our thinking lives, has created more than a fair design
Or artistic pattern, given more than he hoped to give.
His bones are the world; his gift to men, his life.

I hope you won't regard my sending you verses and lines as
an indication of aspirations to the permanent status of poet.
There was a time when men appreciated the salutary effect
of the discipline of metre and rhyme on their writing and
were not ashamed to write verses without pretending to
literary immortality. Those times are past and to write
'poetry' you must be a 'poet', or want to be one, which is
worse because it is generally understood that poets can't
help it. Still a lot of things are excused in war and
poetasting is sometimes one; but I must admit I would find

it easier to do without the world's excuses or approval if I
liked my efforts better myself.

But to return to your picture of an inheritance of the
mind, do you remember this passage in 'The Fountain'? 'As
there was a physical air that men breathed in common, so
there was a spiritual air that, in the processes of thought,
they drew upon and exhaled. Some thought purified or
enriched it; other thought corrupted it; and in this
perpetual struggle there was no division of time or place or
language. Action perished; thought did not.' It's not as good
a picture as yours; it's too impersonal and is incapable of
conveying the sense of responsibility to beloved individuals
whose living mind we inherit, whose life we inherit and
perpetuate if we ourselves have heirs to our estates of
wisdom; but it's the same idea and it's true.

Michael lives in all that he gave himself to; in his
contribution to the spiritual air of thought and to its vehicle,
the language that he used; in that he enriched imagination
with his vision or gave the imagery of others the sanction of
his sympathy; in that he gave purpose to human life in his
own conception or in his understanding of others'; in that he
cleansed the spiritual air of obnoxious thought, the picture
of beauty of perverted imagery, the lamp of truth of the
smoke of insincerity. In that he gave himself in delight or
devotion to places or persons or devices, to ideas or ideals,
to his own work and the workmanship of others. In that he
handed on the legacy of life to the better for his possession.
In that he lived, he lives.

I am delightfully engaged with Quiller-Couch 'On The
Art of Reading' and have seen there – for the first time –
Knowledge and Life in their true proportions. May it never
be said of me that:

'This man decided not to live but Know.'

Now I want to enjoy life in the right way of living as
conceived by his obscene Welsh clergyman of the 17th
century: 'You will never enjoy the world aright till the sea
itself floweth in your veins, till you are clothed with the
heavens and crowned with the stars.' And also I want to live
out my fear and sloth and greed and come cleaned and pure
to you: absolved from pride and lust by the soldier's life,
and able to share with you a world to be enjoyed aright. I
think the moulds of my ideals are large enough and strong
enough to contain the molten contents of this crucible, but
whether my hand be steady enough to pour it out without
spilling it to waste is the question that I ask myself. I could
spill it all quite safely away if I wished, and doubtless get
some nice safe job on the pretext of having brains, or
language or enthusiasm or patience. But that is the point: if
this war is to be worth our whiles we must compel it to give
us what we lack and I lack courage and conscience and
humility. These I shall win by seeking them out to live and
not to know only. I know their form and have the mould of
them, now I must steadfastly take the crucible of experience
from the furnace of war and pour its searing stream until the
moulds are filled.

Today your letter arrived posted on the 1st of
September; and now I have read it and would love to be
able to go on reading it, not for the words or their sense or
even their picture, but for the whole experience of the
letter, for your dear presence. It comes softly to me out of a
dark passage like a child to its mother's bed, or the dripping
and seeping of water in a mine shaft, or a well-loved song
through a desperate mood. There is comfort, there is fear,

there is interrupted darkness, there is gentleness. And with this warm experience I shall go to bed and not answer your letter as I should, because I who ought am not just now the same as I who am.

30th October

And today comes your telegram, and I must prepare myself to wait for your letter; 'must' I say because I must wait alone and for what I know not, except that they be words with meanings and consequences, and not pictures with pleasure and associations. But am I really waiting for words? This is a tyranny to which I most unwillingly submit. Can anything you write make any difference to things as they are? And out of my life springs the knowledge that it can. You can make pictures impossible to retrieve, you can make dreams into pictures. I fear your letter and shrink from its power, weakly trying to keep what I have rather than risk it in the commerce of precision against a greater possession. But it is already committed, for I have seen and pretended to the greater and what was my courage then cannot be my cowardice now. Courage is not, as once I imagined it, a constant thing like the pillar of a vault or the stream through a mill: it is brave moments of commitment and braver moments still of meeting those commitments; it is promising oneself to life and keeping the promises. The flash of inspiration, the gallant acceptance of the challenge, the honourable running of the hazard. Courage is a hammer blow at cowardice, a fierce gust of faith, a blindfold step from jealousy to creation. And so let us have courage, you to write and I to read. Perhaps you are writing now at five to eleven on Thursday night, which is five to one on Friday morning with you. Be brave and dare to live a life in exchange for loving a memory.

I must finish this letter now, but not before sending you my love; I love you, my darling, more than my books or my home or my work. You are the life I would choose out of all the riches, to perform all things for you, perfect all things in you, pursue all being with you.

> Love is a breach in the walls, a broken gate,
> Where that comes in that shall not go again;
> Loves sells the proud citadel to Fate.

> *So:*
> Open the temple gates unto my love,
> Open them wide that she may enter in!

> Thus I wait and love you,
> 　John

> Somerville
> 23rd October 1941

Good morning, my dearest and best
Sunday the 26th

I didn't get very far with your letter, last time, did I? Never mind, today I'll write a long one, but even then it couldn't tell you how brilliantly happy I am today, and have been since Thursday. Darling, don't laugh at me, but I'm so happy I could cry. You don't know the miracle of feeling

like this, even for a brief while, after these months and
months of numbness, relieved by those odd moments I had
in London, by Gavin's kindliness and the harsh
overwhelming tide of work. Dear heavens, I haven't felt this
surging quick joy for so long, and though one always has to
pay for their glad times, it will be worth anything.

Shall I tell you the story of the last three days? On
Wednesday I did go with Gavin to the Radcliffe party, and
it was fun. There wasn't any dancing after all, but the stage
show was good in most parts, and I met so many people –
nurses, eminent doctors, medical students and so on, and
once again I became intoxicated with people. You know the
way it happens; mirth bubbles away inside one; laughter
and gay words are one's delight – oh, it was a happy,
laughing evening.

On Thursday I went home for lunch and there met
Major and Mrs Hagson? Hodgson? whose son Brian you
once knew well. It was good to hear them talking about
you; sharing their pleasure in you, and telling me news of
your friends. Brian is out in Rhodesia or somewhere, and
the H's send you their love, asking tenderly about your
moustache. The last time they saw you was that day about a
year ago, when we were lunching at the George. They
would like to see you again; they would like you to be in
England, so you see, darling, I'm one of the many who have
very selfish ideas about you and your whereabouts.

So Thursday was a lovely day, and when my tooth
throbbed it said dear-Jock – dear-Jock – dear-est – dear-est
and I was much consoled.

And then at last on Friday Hardwicke came and that has
been the best part of all. He is stationed way up at Melrose,
and we were both so starved of conversation. We talked and

argued and discussed philosophy and poetry, loving, beauty, happiness and pain and all the other eternally fascinating and incomprehensible matters. And sometimes we just stopped and smiled, for we knew there was too much to be said in too little time and that the understanding and sympathy between us was stranger than our lust for words and ideas. Oh John, I said I was love starved, that I needed man-handling, but that is only a fraction of the truth. It's no good darling, I wasn't born to be academic and scholarly; I want to know about people, about the way they think and feel, why, and what they are seeking. Hardwicke brought back to me the realisation that eighteen months ago my life was very full and so rich. You and Michael were here, you made my brain stagger with the impact of your thoughts, but it was useful and stimulating. It isn't enough to read about those people who allege they have found the answer to the questionings; their concept may be profound and valuable, but to these living people who are still searching and still learning who make life alive.

Surely you feel this passion and need to know and discover; the answer doesn't lie in our egocentric lives, but in the spirits, in the brains of all those people whose thoughts and actions make this world of ours today. Don't think I have no use for the past, because it isn't so. But somehow I must feel the pulse of the present, see to the future through the brains of others. Perhaps it is a sign of immaturity and inadequacy of my own self, but it's not enough, John; I want, I must have, other people. May the good God preserve me from having to live in some little place, barren of those women and men who search and go on searching, because their need gives them hope and faith in the wroth of their desire.

John, my love, forgive this egotistical tirade. But today these last months seem like a wild dream, full of horror and astonishment; and the happiness that has been, was welcomed primarily because it stopped one being conscious of strangeness. But now it doesn't matter. Hardwicke, with the odd touch of genius, rattled my brain and out tumbled thoughts and with them the bones of memories which have choked and barred the movement of life. Now it's teeming again, and I think you'd love me better today than you would have a week ago.

But now I must work; I'll finish this tomorrow.

27th October

This afternoon, dear Jock, I went home to show myself to Mummy in the tweeds you gave me. I feel dreadfully self-conscious in them, since they are my very first, but the general criticism of them is that they are admirable. And at home I found Mummy on the point of bicycling round with an air mail letter from you, dated 20.8.41. It arrived after the one dated the 3rd of September, and I just pray that you won't think my last letter cool and disinterested. That letter card told me that you had hoped to come home, but were not able to . . . you said it briefly, and only after reading this last letter do I realise the Cornelian conflict which was battering and bruising my dearest love. Ideals . . . they are free things, aren't they? But dear heavens, they are so hard to keep; they are destroyed so easily and their loss is more than a pity.

You've always been an idealist, and sometimes when you talked to me of them so surely and so seriously, I used to get restless. You know why, don't you. My twenty years of living had been less gracious and less kindly than your twenty-seven. Granted my ideals were more childish, less clearly defined than yours, but I worried a little because I knew mine were delicate, fragile, and you were so sure of the strength of yours. I didn't know whether that was because I was so much weaker in spirit and hope than you, or if it were because you had grown up amidst 'loving kindness' and weren't truly acquainted with those savage, cruel things which deal harshly with faith and hope.

Even now we are different in our thoughts and ways. You are being tested, not easily and not kindly. Whatever you are doing, you want to do it well, and generally, maybe, what you have been doing is what you wanted to do with your whole brain and body. But now it's a little different; you have to fight a battle whether you want to or not . . . and I think you want to fight it proudly. But John, you desire too – not only those you love, but the dignity of culture, graciousness, the quiet beauty of peaceful living. You desire those things which are not easy to find in your battle field. But since you are now compelled to face those ideals of being a good soldier, you won't fail. I don't need to say a prayer for your manliness and strength, because I know what you do will be good.

No, this isn't merely glib consolation coming from one who knows little about tests and conflicts. It comes from Mirren, born of the love she has for you. Have you forgotten a letter I wrote you, tear-stained and desperate but yet glad in the knowledge that it was you who had given me faith and hope? My greatest hope is not profound nor exalted. But I just hope that with you we may give back to the world through one living some of the greatness and goodness which has been destroyed, which is being

destroyed. That is my hope, and since you are a living part
of that ideal, I have faith in you. To be sceptical of your
own strength and power would be to mock at my own
ideal; that is not possible, for beyond the bounds of all
reason, I know that through you I have faith. No, darling,
you need no prayers said for your strength; the prayer I
have is that you and I shall live long enough to know that
we have not lived entirely in vain.

Indeed, I want you to go on being alive. Maybe we'll
never marry, but that isn't the most important thing. You'll
go on, and you will give of yourself to the world, for you
have that power. And I'll go on too. If I'm ever capable of
loving someone more than I love you, then there is no
reason why my little ideal should be wrecked. If you die
before we have had time to be together, at least I shall have
the faith and love you have given me, deep rooted and
eternal in my soul. And with that knowledge, I'll never be
defeated; I may fail to do as much as I hoped but I'll never
be defeated. And if I'm killed and you still love me as you
do, then – I don't know how you'll feel. But I do know John,
that you have given me something, and I, perhaps, to you,
that no man or god can ever destroy. We call it faith, ideals,
hope, but do we really and truly know what it is? I don't
think so, and I don't think it matters, either. But it does
matter that it is present, unforgettable, a part of my own
self.

Does it ever strike you, Jock, how odd it is that we who
have met but ten times, should matter so much to each
other? Really, we know very little about each other. I know
of your mind through your writing and speaking, and so I
learn of your steadfastness, dreams, and determinations. I
know you as a lover too, but do I know John the man who

works at the British Council? I don't know if he becomes
moody and impatient – is he intolerant and selfish? And
what do you know of Mirren? Would you suffer her
moments of gloom and could you ignore her quick, pitiless
tongue? Darling, you and I can love, but living together
and loving wouldn't be so easy for all our dreams. So
remember, I'm taking no romantic impetuous view of
marriage. I'll not propose to you next leap year, and even if
you ever do ask me to marry you, I'll not take upon myself
any vow till you have had the chance to know me truly. I
love you and sometimes when I'm feeling very lonely, I
believe I'd marry you tomorrow if you wanted me. But I
wish we'd had time to know each other properly; I'd not
want to waste a week wondering and learning about you
when you come home, but it must be. But still, you'd not
be able to marry for a little while anyway, so there will be
time enough for learning. And remember too that I'm not
asking you to belong to me; you are as free now as you
ever were, and promise, John, that you won't feel ashamed
or guilty if you ever surpass this love for me. I'd just hate to
think that you felt I had any claim on you; I don't want to
hold you . . . you shall come or go as you please, and
whatever it is, with my blessings and desire for your
contentment.

It's horrid being love starved, but it's good to know that
this hunger is born of my love for you alone, and that it can
be fulfilled by you alone.

Darling, would you forgive me if I ransacked G.H.Q. for
an adoring sugar daddy. If I flirted with him just the littlest
bit, if I tickled his fancy, maybe he'd order you home. Don't
be insatiable, please. Be nice and complacent about your
life and come home pleased with your soldiering. Couldn't

you bury all your fine ideas, and just be my nice, loving animal man. But, lordy be, I'm afraid I shouldn't want you so much if you were just a bear with little brain, so there seems to be no way out of it. Never mind, I'll keep the locks well oiled and the keys shining, and my sweet servant imagination shall whisk around and keep the palace glorious and brilliant for your homecoming. Would that do? But I can't manage all by myself; if you don't want to discourage me, go on writing and remind me that Joy Street was made to be lived in and not merely the figment of dreams. And you are to come a-visiting with me before you have time to get too many medals on your chest. They'll clank, and I'll pant agedly up the stairs, and we'll both be much too exhausted to see what's round the corner of 50 B.C. So – don't be away for too long.

But while you are away let my love breathe in through your mouth, flood in through your eyes and fill your heart so that no wee devil of disappointment has any chance at all of jumping in and snatching you away.

God bless you and keep you, because Helen, Penelope and Mirren all love you dearly.

Miriam does too, and she wants to bless you as well as God – so goodnight and blessings.

P.S. If you are in charge of a detachment aren't you a full lieutenant or something?

Dearest Mirren,

Here is some more rhyme. It's called

Parachute

All your life's been waiting for this moment
And here it is upon you and won't go
But sits and stares and wonders at the Torment
Of its presence and Time's apostasy
Who promised a short passage of this agony
That's dread, and gave it and departed in the tumult,
Leaving your life waiting down below.

And there you see in that slow movement,
Spread out in space and telescoped in time –
A baby born and bred for this sick ferment
Of apprehension, led to this precipice of fear
From true instants of happiness and dear
Minutes and seconds of remembrance,
Whose faculty for enduring was sublime.

To stand and shrink from earth below and wonder
Why ever you confided in Time's word
That moments end and one is like another.
Then suddenly to see the face of dread –
Stand by to jump – staring in signal red,
Grimly determining whatever waits down under
To squeeze what remains of life dry of what's seen and
    heard.

Green for go! Gulp! Gone! How slow it is!
The air doesn't rush and earth doesn't rise
Till you swoop into harness and know it is
Over, look up and love the white canopy
Steadfast above you, an angel in panoply
Guarding the skies.

I wonder what you'll say in your letter. I wait for it in much
the same mind as I now wait for the red and green light;
with quiet confidence and yet in awe at the greatness of the
moment. There is now more of that sickness of suspense,
but still I can't conquer the imperative urge to test again
and again the fittings of my harness, though I know full
well that I put it on aright the first time.

It's astonishing what a falling off there's been in my
writing: I don't believe that I've sent more than two letters
home in two months and to you I've not sent more than
half a dozen. And now I'm beginning to reap the harvest;
it's many days since your last letter arrived together with a
card from Christopher which I was delighted beyond
saying to receive but for which I have so far made no
adequate return. And now just as I am settled down to write
to you there comes a red warning and I must put my light
out. Goodnight my love.

12th November 1941

These letters of mine are wrung from an unwilling
preoccupation with war, which if I am to conquer and write
to you, I must have help. Help has come tonight in your
two letters written just two months ago on the 11th and
13th of September; strong generous help that makes me

ashamed of my flight from love and breaks, at least for this
moment, the tyranny of my solitude.

You have shown yourself to me tonight as a woman
whom I can love and respect, respect and love, with that
unleashing gesture of utter confidence which is the
momentary abandonment of individuality. You deal in
having to do with souls in your scheme of living, and you
have learnt the art and perfected the gifts of finding them
in the tangled mass of glands and complexes which thrust
themselves forward as the representatives of free spirits in
human intercourse. That you speak to me of Anthony and
Michael, of Hardwicke, of Harold, of your sad Irishman
and the doctor who suggested that you needed seducing, I
take as a high compliment. Whether or not you even think
of it as a gesture: but that you speak of them and of my
family and friends as you do shows me more than I would
ever have looked for in a woman before asking her to marry
me. And your picture of our relationship is what I should
have expected to result from years of living together and
some spiritual travail.

I have always been happiest and most certain that I have
been living my life when I have had to prove myself to win
respect. I have always suffered my biggest failures and
disappointments when I have been basking in the bleak
light of hero worship. It is so easy to bask in the light of
self-satisfaction supplied by the constancy of lesser spirits,
it is difficult to win respect from men and women who
respect themselves and, knowing the value of their esteem,
give it not lightly: but the most difficult piece of living is to
preserve when won and continue to deserve the respect of
free spirits freely given in admiration of an equal. Above all
I love your generous gratitude to those whose lives you

have shared and whose living has given you an image of good life. That gratitude, that wonder at the miracle wrought between you, that sense of responsibility is what the Christians meant when they spoke of praising God and thanksgiving and of love. I admire you for your determination to do something in return; much you do already by your humanity, which is the doctrine of Christianity, but your desire to do more is its true practice.

One terrible weakness has dragged down the study of psychology and psychotherapy to a status far below that which it should hold: it has been pursued by a lot of cranks, perverts and agnostics who have believed that in studying the human brain and nervous system they are laying bare the spirit and essence of man. The states of consciousness which they study are still only manifestations of the soul of man, and often not even that, but never the soul itself, but they are too proud to see that or too earthly to believe that there is anything beyond the manifestations. When they see smoke they say there's a fire, but when they see imagination they refuse to believe that anything is therein manifested. It needs enormous stores of sanity and perspicuity not to allow oneself to be deceived by the jargon of psychology and to think that because a state has been given a name all that is necessary is known about it. People don't seem to realise that the process of discovering is first to realise that we don't know, then to name the unknown and then to find out what that name means and how it is related to other names better known. Ask any would-be psychologist to tell you what a complex is and his answer when critically examined will boil down to an admission that it is a state of affairs about which little or nothing is known beyond the fact that it exists as a reasonably constant and recognisable condition of men.

If only more people like you would apply themselves to the study, not in the hope of discovering the secret of life, but from the desire to help bewildered humanity, then the progress of knowledge and humanity would not be impeded by would-be omniscients. But it is a study which must be well grounded in medical knowledge; it is already manifested by too many quacks who, like the lower orders of osteopaths, are too ready and willing to interpret every ill in terms of their own pathology. It is, in fact, a study well worth undertaking because it offers a hard and an uphill road, which is the surest guarantee that you are conquering new country and always climbing. I believe that David Winser is studying medicine with a view eventually to specialising in psychotherapy: take his advice; mine is beware of enthusiastic amateurism. I should love you to do this thing because it is something that I have often felt the urge to undertake, particularly at Oxford where I attended Dr Brown's lectures and thought much about its potentialities, and also because you are human and sane and gifted with the key to men's hearts. Tell me what you think further on this.

My darling best loved Mirren, how I wish now that I could relax with you and just be together instead of having to write surrounded by reminders of all that thrusts between us! In some quiet place, preferably our own by adoption or even property or tenancy, to see you beautiful before me and know by the surest sense that there is something fine and gentle in the world to which I am not too lowly to aspire. To desire you and to know that my desire is not unworthy or frustrated, to possess you and to know that possession does not sully, to share with you and know that in community is no loss of dignity or independence but their consummation. Should we sit and talk, or stand and kiss or lie and love to sleep, so we should live and be sure of it, and not wonder whether the sacrifice we made might not be betrayed by ignorance or vice or demagogues. And yet however little men mishandle the great sacrifice of this war, nothing that they can do or undo or leave neglected can touch the soul ennobled by its fire. Though it is an artificial fire introduced by man to wither man, yet when it touches the soul of man it is the sword of God bidding him rise ennobled. You and I, when we meet again will be different from when we parted, but this is the glory of it; we shall still be Mirren and Jock and whatever happens will be able to laugh in each other's eyes and love what we see, be blithe in the country and gay in the city and at peace with the world. We shall not let the war twist and pervert great powers, mar beauty and halt grace; we shall force from the war all that peace could not give us and return to peace triumphant and dignified, greater by the measure of our sacrifice.

Now I can write no more and will say Goodnight. The moon in not yet up but I say your rhyme, happy one, that you so gaily taught me.

God bless you darling, and preserve our love,
John

JAPAN AT WAR WITH U.S. AND BRITAIN
SEVERAL NAVAL BASES BOMBED
BRITISH GUNBOAT SUNK

NEW BATTLES IN LIBYA
MAIN TANK FORCES AT GRIPS

THE TIMES Monday 8 December 1941

14 Merton Street
Oxford
8th December 1941
[Mirren's 21st birthday]

Dearest John,

It was lovely to have your cable partly because I haven't heard from you nor written to you for some time, and partly because I didn't suspect you'd remember my holiday while you were so busy chasing the enemy. I truly will write to you soon, but the last ten days or so I have been so busy finishing off exams. I've also been busy meeting a Peter Blackiston who has been at London Hospital with brother David for the last six years. Whenever Peter comes to my room he turns your photograph down because he says you look like Douglas Fairbanks Jr, and he, Peter, gets a dreadful inferiority complex when your face stares down at him! I saw Freda on Sunday and she sends her love and a message to say that you are to come back in the summer because it's about time another reception was held in her garden. You'd better, because unless I get married soon, I with all the other spinsters, shall get tied up with the Waafs or something, and then there just wouldn't be any sense in getting married to a Captain or anyone. This is a prosaic little letter, but I hate these airgraph things. I just wanted to say that I'll write very soon to tell you that I am always your Penelope or however you will have me. God bless you – Miriam.

AMERICA DECLARES WAR ON THE AXIS
THE TIMES Friday 12 December 1941

'L' Detachment, S.A.S. Brigade
C.T.C.
M.E.F.
12th December 1941

Darling,

Had you been able to feel my longing for you in these last few days it would have dragged you hither through winds and waves by its intensity, regardless of you and all but itself, its own great emptiness. I have scratched out some scrawny lines for you: they are ill but the best I could do; and 'he who does the best he can will whiles do mair.'

To Mirren

Oh how I've needed you darling,
　　You were no luxury here
But a vital necessity calling
　　Within me for all that is dear.

You who were calling and sobbing
　　For you who are absent at home
Was my spirit in tears at the robbing
　　Of our youth of its beauty and love

Our hearts' love is fine and enduring,
   Our youth is fair but for a day,
And relentlessly falls the obscuring
   Of young flame in smouldering age.

When your image is faint and despairing
   I feel it on memory and clothes
Which I send you and thank you for wearing
   With my fingers concealed in their folds.

And so I caress you my darling
   Refuelling the ravenous fire
Whose flames would be niggardly falling
   Still consuming our youth at its pyre.

It's really a very dreary lament and I don't feel like that, but
in the streets of Cairo the other night as I walked away
from the film 'Lady Hamilton' I cried in the dark; just for a
moment tears and great baby sobs took hold of my throat
and face and wrenched away my manhood. And when I had
mastered them I went into a great shop and spent two
lovely hours choosing two pieces of cloth for you. A
flaming red velvet for Helen from America and an English
silk and cotton print for Penelope. Neither is exactly right:
in Helen's I like the cloth, but the colour I would wish a
little darker; in Penelope's I love the pattern but am not sure
how well I should like the fall of the cloth in a dress; I fear
the silk may deprive it of the gay lightness I was looking
for. But those were the nearest that were to be had to my
ideal; give them away or exchange them if they're not
going to be what I intend them for, a delight to you and to

those before whom you wear them. Because I was not
satisfied I put in two pairs of stockings: perhaps they will be
all right. Please do let me know if you have to pay duty on
them; it may be fabulous for all I know and I should feel
injured if you hid the fact and paid yourself. They should
arrive in three months time.

I sent you a cable from Shepheard's to wish you happy
birthday and to let you know that I was safe back from the
battle for a while and thought of you.

God bless you, darling, and keep you. We shall meet
while we're young and stab old time in the back with a
dagger from Joy Street, you see. Mirren, I love you. Bear
with me while I say it again. I love you, and what I can of
that love I send with the letter, but there's some that only
your lips can receive from mine; that will not mix with this
ink which is penned by your lover.

John

[23rd December, 1941]

DGXA3363 CAIRO 26 21
NTL MIRIAM BARFORD 14 MERTON STREET OXFORD

BACK TODAY WITH PULLABLE BEARD AND POSSIBLE MEDAL
OFF AGAIN TOMORROW MERRY CHRISTMAS AND ALL LOVE
DARLING

JOHN LEWES+

HEAVY FIGHTING NEAR JEDABIA
ROMMEL AT BAY
ENEMY LOSE 22 MORE TANKS
THE TIMES Wednesday 31 December 1941

Somerville College
Oxford
19th January 1942

Dearest love,

My letters have been scarce these past weeks. I've written
you so many, torn up so many that I can't remember now
what I've said and which were sent. When you have time to
answer that cable I sent the other day, then I shall tell you
why I haven't been writing. But please remember you are
my dearest and only love – don't leave me John, ever; life
wouldn't seem very purposeful without your letters to tell
me that you will bring your love home with you.

I went to see your parents to ask if they would accept
me. They welcomed me and I didn't feel uneasy or shabby
after all. The only thing is that after the way they talked
about you, so quietly, so sweetly and proudly, I wondered
all over again how I could possibly make a good life for
you; are you still willing to take the gamble? I think they
are pleased we shall be married, for they love you dearly
and at least I believe I made them understand how much
you mattered. And a sweet letter too from Elizabeth, saying
she was glad I had 'consented' to marry you. Consented

indeed! a fine way to put it, considering you've more or less
had your way with me ever since No. 2. Remember that
day when you tucked my hand in yours as we walked back
from the river? I couldn't have extracted it even if I'd
wanted to. I told David Winser about it when we had lunch
together in London and he grew quite pink in the face with
delight. You know, darling, if I weren't as sure as everyone
else is that you are a fine and gallant gentleman, I'd begin to
suspect that everyone who knows us was plotting to get me
married off to you – to save my soul or something. And you
must thank David for more or less getting me a job.

Almost before I knew what was happening he had
whisked me off to the B.B.C. with a hastily written script in
my hand. I read it in a quavering voice to a young man
surrounded by a mop of yellow hair, tea cups, telephone
wires, wastepaper baskets and secretaries, and anything else
but order. Anyway, after a lot of rushing to and fro, I made
a recording to be broadcast to Canada and the U.S.A. I
talked about the slums, and because they liked my voice
and the way I said things I've been offered a job for
broadcasting when Schools are over. It's not definite yet
and the matter hasn't been seriously discussed. But it seems
that women with microphone voices are rare and they said
mine was too good to be true. So with luck I shall yet get a
job in June all right. It would be fun if you were working for
the British Council and I for the B.B.C. We could have a
minute flat in London and if we both had a job, maybe we
could afford to have a baby sooner than if I were just sitting
around waiting for you to come back from the office.

I had some more photographs taken by a man who 'spots'
for British film producers. He approved of my face and
asked if he might carry around a copy of a photograph and

show it to the producers. I had a wire the other day saying, 'You are urged to make film tests. Please communicate for further information.' I've written to say I can't do anything about it for another two months at least and though the novelty of having a test would be fun, I don't much like the idea of film work. Not at the moment anyway, because I suspect an awful lot of people will have to do a great deal more about fighting before this war is over. The copies of the photographs haven't arrived yet; shall I send you one when they do? By the way, do you suppose you could send another copy of that photograph of yourself. Christopher is very special about you, but very proud, and I think he rather wants to show you to the Barford relations whom I never see.

Is this an odd thing to ask? Even if we don't really tell the papers soon, please may I wear a ring for you from you? Freda gave me one, but it doesn't have quite the right feeling about it. I don't wear it on the proper finger because it's rather like pretending. You could guess the size, if you remember that my hands are not slim and tiny. Not a blue stone – otherwise you choose – and not a yellow one either. If you'd rather wait till you come home, it will be all right.

I wish I could remember if I had sent any of those letters. Yours of November 11th arrived the first week of this month, and of course your Christmas cable has come too; but I've told you that already. I was waiting for that particular letter of yours. You see I was wanting you to understand what I was trying to say, and I wasn't sure if you would.

I had a touch of 'flu just before term started and the remains are clinging to me like a hobgoblin. And, dear

goodness, but it is cold. It's snowing hard now, the flakes
swirling around in the clutch and the toss of the wind. It
was lovely at first, thick and soft. But the sleet has come
and the thin rain and at night everything is frozen over; I've
taken enough exercise staggering around in this ice to last
me for many months now. And the ambulances are having a
tremendous party. They go skidding about collecting the
battered bodies of rash cyclists and willy-nilly skating
pedestrians. The odd thing about snow is that it makes one
feel shut in – do you know what I mean? One almost wants
to get out of the room and into that swirling frozen air. And
rain is so different; you feel you've shut out the rain, that it
can't reach you. Maybe it's because heavy falling snow
obscures the vision so much more – I don't think I much
like this shut-in feeling.

But apart from the snow this term is no different from the
last. The same faces, the same sorts of essays, tutorials,
conversations and none of it very stimulating. The food is a
little worse and the scanty fire ration has been cut down a
little more. Yet what does it matter – it can't go on like this
for ever and the time we've had before minor discomforts
and the time we shall have when these discomforts are
eased will be so much greater than these few odd months.

Somerville is becoming more and more aware of war –
remarkable. We've been asked to help cut down the need
for domestic staff, so we wake up, sweep the common
rooms, take duty in the porter's lodge, dig cabbage patches
and put in roughly about 6 or 8 hours a week doing
'voluntary' work. It's rather tiresome, but at least it does
make a change.

I wish to goodness I could see the news reel of you in a
bomber. Darling, I'm sure your parachute must be very safe.

I think they are made out of our silk stockings and rubber corsets and they come to you with so much love that they are bound to be perfect. Do you suppose that you could get the V.C. please? Then you just would have to come home and thank the king for thanking you; I'm sure that's much more important than Randolph Churchill's return 'on duty'. There was a photograph of him kissing his wife and I was so cross because they say he beats her awfully hard – and so naturally I'd appreciate a kiss from you more than she did from him!

This is a slight letter but it will be all right again soon. If only God would let you answer that cable, I'd be so happy. And please God, let you come home soon; life doesn't have much sense to it without you and your letters. It's very nearly a year since I last saw you – on the 23rd of this month. It seems longer than that, doesn't it?

John, how could I reach your mind across these leagues of sea and desert? Somehow you've got to know, now, at once, how important it is that you should send a cable. Look, darling, you don't want me to be bony and grey-haired, do you? Well, I've lost almost two pounds since January 5th and if I don't hear from you pretty soon I shall be so ugly; circles under my eyes and scraggy around the ribs, and you know you wouldn't like that. So be good and tell me you love me very soon. You always have my love and all I can do now is to ask the Almighty Powers to be merciful and to keep you safe and free.

Yours ever,
Mirren

[23rd Jan 1942]

530 7.10 LIVERPOOL OHMS IMPORTANT 52 -
IMPORTANT - A H LEWES ESQ 8 TUDOR COURT
CASTLEWAY HANWORTH MIDDLESEX=

DEEPLY REGRET TO INFORM YOU OF REPORT RECEIVED FROM
MIDDLE EAST THAT LIEUT J S LEWES WELSH GUARDS WAS
KILLED IN ACTION ON 30TH DECEMBER 1941 THE ARMY
COUNCIL DESIRE TO OFFER YOU THEIR SINCERE SYMPATHY =
UNDER-SECRETARY OF STATE FOR WAR +

50 Bryanston Court
George Street, W1
26th January 1942

My dearest Mirren,

   It isn't for lack of thinking of you that I haven't written
these days. You have been very much in my thoughts just as
I had been thinking of Jock every day since the offensive
started and fearing what you might hear as I imagined he
was on particularly dangerous work. My darling, I feel so
sad, and it doesn't seem that there is anything I can say to
help. The world is so full of sorrow and suffering these days
that sometimes one wonders how it can be borne. However
bitter the sorrow, it is better to have known someone so
fine than for your paths not to have met – and much
happier for him than if he hadn't known you; remember
that.

I rang up the flat on Sunday night in case you were staying here, but perhaps you spent that night with Jock's parents. How are they?

Uncle Hal had to come to London today so I came with him as Auntie Blanche is expected here later in the week. She has a bad throat & I believe she is in bed at present so I hope that the moving of the furniture may be postponed and that I can go back with Uncle Hal. The house is much warmer than this flat! It will probably be a job getting back – we were snowed up last week and part of the bathroom ceiling fell through, leaving Mary Howells clutching a board in the attic to prevent herself falling through! Mice came into the house and I was wakened by one pulling my hair!

How are you getting on with your work? Do you understand the old French any better? You will have to read for all you are worth to get a good degree. Maybe easier said than done, but have a shot at it.

I really don't suppose you have any time for a letter but

Private M.P. Howells
        Company B, Platoon 3
            15 A.T.S.
                Aldermaston Court
                    Nr Reading

would doubtless be glad of a letter during the early stages of being in the A.T.S. What grim weather in which to start.

We love you so much and think of you such a lot,
    Auntie Esmé

[7th March 1942]

499 120 SANS ORIGINE 25

NLT MISS BARFORD SOMERVILLE COLLEGE OXFORD

CABLE RE JOHN LEWES RECEIVED THREE WEEKS AGO MADE
ENQUIRY NO REPLY YET WILL CABLE ANY NEWS LOVE =
SCRIVEN +

[24th April 1942]

74 C 28 SANS ORIGINE PLN 16

NLT M BARFORD 14 MERTONST OXFORD =

JOCK LEWES WILL NOT RETURN HOME DEEP SYMPATHY = BILL
SCRIVEN + 14 +

EPILOGUE

Jock never received any of the letters Mirren sent after 1st October 1941. Eventually they were returned to her, and, like the one shown here, were saved.

Two weeks after learning of Jock's death, Mirren wrote to his brother David.

Somerville College
Oxford
8th February 1942

My dear David,

Thank you so much for your letter, and above all thank you for saying I may write. It is a letter which will probably displease you, because it will show you that I'm not really courageous at all. My mind knows what to do about living: the faith and the knowledge Jock gave me is still alive and will be alive as long as there is breath in my body. But I'm scared, David, so scared. You see, it was easy looking forward to a life with Jock. He has pulled me together in so many ways, and with him to give me strength I know beyond all doubt that somehow we could have given back to this world of ours, even a little of the good which is being destroyed each instant. Life can be so harsh and so bitter, but till now I've always known how to accept that part of it and fashion it into a weapon with which to fight for and with this business of living.

 But now, it's all so bewildering. You know, for months after I met Jock for the second time, I tried to escape from him. I rushed around with other people and told myself over and over again that Jock was fun but that he didn't really much matter. Do you know why? I was frightened of him. He seemed to ask nothing of me and yet in spite of myself, each time I wrote, or saw him, I wanted to give him everything I had. I'd never trusted anyone, nor believed in anyone and yet Jock – I don't know why really, or how, but knowing him and being with him seemed to charm all the shabbiness and mistrust out of me and I felt helpless. He never asked for my trust or belief and yet I couldn't help but yield it to him. And I was most truly frightened, because it didn't seem possible that a man could be as gay and as wise, as strong and as tender as he. I was frightened of being let down with a terrific bang, frightened of letting myself love him because I didn't believe so supreme and great a thing could happen to me, and not be ruined and destroyed.

But it wasn't any good. I loved him very much; he knew it and because he gave me faith, not only in himself, but in living and dying too, he became not only the flesh and blood I loved and desired, but the very Flame of life itself. It was like being born again; he was inside me, around me. I couldn't do all the little, shabby, easy things because I should have been ashamed before him. I used to wonder how I could ever be fine enough and clear and dear enough to be worthy of him. I loved him so much that I was still scared of myself, because I didn't want to spoil life for him and make him bitter and sad. And yet I knew in the depths of my being that it would be all right; that just the loving him and being with him would have prevented me from spoiling things.

And now? With him the Flame seems to have died too. Everything is so thin and cold and empty and David, I'm not brave. The part of me which used to feel, doesn't feel any more. I don't know where the warmth and spontaneous pleasure of seeing and hearing, thinking and even just being has gone to. Some times it seems as though the emptiness were filled with the surging of great winds, howling seas, and wings, huge strongly beating wings. At those times one doesn't feel sad or suicidal, but just expectant. It is so vast and strong that one feels one will be smothered, or one's brain crushed beneath the tide. It's an odd feeling, just as though one weren't to be allowed to breathe and live more than a second longer. And when I find I really am still alive, then the wondering starts. I wonder how and when, why and how the world will ever make sense again. We who have loved Jock have accepted so much from him. I wrote to him about death and the people who were left behind, and he understood when I said we received our inheritance of the mind or the spirit, from the dead. It is so, David, and that which Jock has given us is most rare and fine. And it's our responsibility, not just to accept that inheritance, but to perpetuate it. I don't know what happens after death, and I don't think it really matters very much. We are primarily concerned with living and the what-has-happened-to-Jock-now? is of the least importance.

We have to go on living and for the purpose, I at least am sure, of giving back to life the good and the noble, gracious things, to replace the shabbiness and the unworthiness. If Jock had lived, he could have done that in a greater measure than you or I ever might have done, simply because he himself was a finer person. But he wasn't allowed to live, and yet he has given of himself freely and generously to those who know him. I know that I at least have accepted a good deal from him and I know that the surest way to annihilate Jock perpetually would be to ignore that responsibility or to keep the knowledge and memory of him neatly smothered up beneath a welter of

trivialities. David, I still can't escape from him. I'm no
Galatea to his Pygmalion, but what I know to be good and
true in him, what I love in him, has become a part of my
way of being. Whatever happens, though I never think of
him consciously from one year to another, is that
something of his, from him, has fused and become one with
my very life.

That doesn't sound problematical nor distressing and it
isn't. But maybe I'm not so clever at moulding circumstances
into weapons after all. There is no flame any longer, and I
don't know how to make life like that which Jock would
have wished. This is a very egocentric letter, but I'm writing
partly to get things straightened out for myself and not just
for your edification. It may sound very as though I were
very prodigal, but I've lived so much through and because
of other people. I've wanted to know the way they've
thought and felt and as I've learnt from them, so I've been
able to use that knowledge to understand other people
later. And even just the loving, the affection – not the way I
felt about Jock – that too seemed to make things warmer
and happier. He once said I possessed a sort of loving cup
and that I handed great draughts around to people. He
liked that and so did I, because it was good to know people
were happy. But now – all of that has been stilled and
pounded to dust. Maybe it won't last, but people and just
living don't matter much. And you see, if that goes on, then
I'm not being the way he wanted not only me, but other
people to be too. You know, most truly alive and not scared
of misery and happiness, experience, laughter and sweat
and all the other movements of brain and body which make
the pattern of life brilliant and vital.

Does this sort of bitterness and deadness inside me go

away, David? I have to love people, and I don't know how
to any more; I have to marry and I don't think I want to
very much. And yet if I don't wake up again, I'm not really
me, and I'll not be able to hand round to the world not just
the loving cup, but the brilliance and the white fine flame
that Jock gave me. Have you the faintest idea what I'm
talking about? Probably not, because you just don't know
the way my thoughts wander and you must have guessed
that the clock has just struck 1.45 a.m.

Yet I am sure of two things. The flesh and the blood of
Jock is dead, and that hurts the people who knew him. But
there is something left, and it shall give me the strength, all
of us the strength to go on being and living the way Jock
helped us to understand was most worth while. And
secondly – I swear before the Powers that are, that if I never
affronted Jock while he lived I'll give him no cause now to
turn away in shame for my weakness and failure. I'll not let
that happen; somehow I won't let it happen, for if it should,
how then could I see you and your parents again without
feeling I had betrayed Jock.

So dear David, don't concern yourself about me. I'll have
dozens of children and you can be godfather or whoosh out
their adenoids for them – or do both. Take this letter for
what it is worth and remember I was writing it to me as well
as to you, so the questions don't really have to be answered
at all. And talking of letters – some of Jock's were mostly
concerned with his philosophy and not of living, so maybe
you'd like to read them some day.

I'm glad you found those words of Jock to be important;
they matter to me very much too.

Goodnight – good morning, and God bless you for
being as you are.

My love to you,
Mirren

P.S. Don't let your parents know that I visit the wind filled regions occasionally, because I expect they are feeling kind o' tired. You're tired too, but don't forget I fell for your broad shoulders and fine kilt, so maybe you can bear the weight of eight pages as firmly and easily as a spangle of confetti on your bonny blond head!

M.

A year after Jock's death, Mirren was a Lance Corporal in a British Army Intelligence unit.

c/o Mrs Sanigor
237 London Road
Bedford
4th March 1943

My dear Mrs Lewes,

I have been wanting to write to you for a long time, and have even delayed thanking you so very much for Jock's photograph. All this, ungracious though it seems, because I couldn't bring myself to write before I had made up my mind about something.

To me, you and Mr Lewes will always be Mother and Father. And what need I say of Jock; you both must know how much I loved him; how much in a way I still do love him. But the memory of him has ceased to hurt as it did; somehow it's an almost friendly, warming memory and the word dead ceases to hold any fear and bitterness. It's taken a long time for all this to happen to me, but I had to let it happen before I could begin to live whole-heartedly again.

A little while ago I said I would marry an American doctor called Dick Wise. He has known all about Jock, and it was to Dick I turned when I felt some times that I should never, never be able to stop grieving deeply, cruelly for Jock. And now I understand that I love Dick. He has a depth of understanding, a generosity of mind and spirit and a tenderness which are most rare. I'm not being foolish. I'm not just turning to Dick because he afforded a means of escape. It is he who really taught me how to value Jock, how to love him and be eternally grateful to him in a way which isn't contorted by emotion.

I wish you could meet Dick; he is a good deal older than I am – thirty-four. But he is very unspoiled, quiet on the whole, but can be as gay and as nonsensical as anyone.

It's odd, you know; I never felt that I could possibly want to marry anyone. But there is a deep and firm relationship between Dick and myself and he is a good man. I believe, most sincerely, that we shall make a fine thing of our marriage, and with Dick I shall be able to reach closer to those high standards of living which Jock inspired into anyone who ever knew him. And I am so happy with Dick, so much at peace now, and so untroubled – eager to be married and to build a fine life between us.

After the war, I shall go back to America with him, but he loves England and wants our children to regard England as their home just as much as America, so I shan't feel too stranded. We are going to call our first son Christopher John – do you like that? If I can extract a photograph from Dick, I will send one to you.

I hope you will both be pleased about Dick and me, and don't think 'so soon?'. You see, in a way it has been too long. I tried so desperately hard to behave and think the way Jock would have wanted me to, but I just felt utterly dismayed, defrauded of something the reason for which I couldn't understand. But now I understand just how enriched I am by having known Jock so well, and if I should ever make a good thing of this business of living, it is because Jock is my friend, philosopher, and guide.

Please tell Elizabeth and David and tell them too that I am very happy.

> My love to you both,
> from, your 'daughter'
> Mirren

Mirren Barford and C. Richard Wise were married on 18th June 1943.

AFTERWORD

The manner of Jock Lewes' passing was as tragic as any soldier's death. On 30th December 1941, after destroying two aircraft on the ground at Nofilia aerodrome, Jock Lewes' party was attacked by a lone ME110 fighter. Jock was hit in the thigh and despite prompt medical attention the wound was fatal because the femoral artery had been severed. He was buried by his patrol about twenty miles south-east of Nofilia. Jim Almonds, one of the 'Tobruk Four' who had joined 'L' Detachment with Jock, records the following in his diary.

On the move this morning travelling north-west to pick up Mr. Fraser and party. 10.00 am., sighted lone Messerschmitt 110 Fighter heading our way. Kept still in hope he would not see us. He passed right overhead and was going away, everyone breathing a sigh of relief, when one wing dropped and round he came. Circled us very low and then attacked, armed with four machine guns forward and two cannon. He gave us a hell of a time not to mention the guns in his tail. A sharp fight followed and we gave as good as we got. His second burst got our truck but did not hurt anyone or set us on fire. It soon became obvious that it was only a matter of time before we should all be killed if we stayed with the trucks so we left and got behind a rock. Mr. Lewes had been wounded in the leg . . . for a time we played ring a roses with it round the rock, three members of the LRDG, Bob Lilley and myself .We had that plane beat, it took him some minutes to get round the rock but we could do it in a few strides and his rear gunner must have been killed earlier in the engagement, the cannon were out of action.

A later entry in Jim's diary records:

> I thought of Jock, one of the bravest men I have ever met,
> an officer and a gentleman, lying out there in the desert
> barely covered with sand. No one will stop by his grave or
> pay homage to a brave heart that has ceased to beat – not
> even a stone marks the spot.

The loss of Jock Lewes was a savage blow to David Stirling,
who is quoted directly:

> I'd taken stock of my position over the last few days. Jock
> Lewes' death was tragic. Apart from losing a trusted friend,
> I knew I was going to miss his very fine brain. Jock had
> become fully sold on the idea of small patrols after the last
> operations and I had intended to ask him to take over all
> recruiting, rear administration and training. I think he
> would have objected strongly because he was such a fine
> front-line soldier and leader; but in the end he'd have done
> it to perfection.

Stirling paid his own tribute to Jock in a letter to his father:

> 20 Nov 42
> No 1 SAS Regt
> Kabrit
> M.E.F.
>
> Dear Mr Lewes
> I hardly know how to begin this letter. Any form of expla-
> nation is so inadequate as to be not worth while
> presenting.

Jock could far more genuinely claim to be the founder of the SAS than I.

He may have told you that we both served in the same Commando. In June 1941, after a series of abortive operations, Jock became impatient at the methods and poor training arrangements of the Middle East Commandos. He realised that the facilities for operating the large and clumsily organised Commando were insufficient in the Middle East at that time, so he applied and got permission to detach a section from the unit, and to train it on the lines required to enable it to cover an operation which he himself had planned. Although this operation was never executed owing to lack of decision at the top, there was never any doubt that it would have been successful. The whole conception, the thoroughness with which he trained the men and the beautiful simplicity of his plan seemed to eliminate the chance of failure.

After this operation was postponed, I think three times, Jock was included in a detachment of our Commando which went up to Tobruk. Although not in command of this force, he soon, by virtue of his astonishing qualities of leadership, determination, and skill in all field craft, established himself as the crack patrol commander in his sector of the Tobruk perimeter. So good was he that on one occasion a Brigadier responsible for another sector of the perimeter requested General Morehead that Jock should be loaned to carry out a vital mission in his area. I have frequently heard it said that in this period, Jock earned a DSO.

When Jock was fighting in Tobruk the rest of our Commando was disbanded. After this had taken place, I worked on a proposal that a unit should be formed to cover the undoubted operational opportunities of the Commando unit of a size that was consistent with very limited naval and air force facilities. This proposal was largely based on Jock's ideas and was merely an application of them on a unit basis. Later, ME instructed me to go ahead and form a unit on the lines of Jock's ideas. Inevitably, the first officer whom I applied for was Jock. In fact, I built the unit around him.

There is no doubt that any success the unit had achieved up to the time of Jock's death and after it, was, and is, almost wholly due to Jock's work. Our training programmes and methods are, and always will be, based on the syllabuses he produced for us. They must show the extent of his influence.

Jock was killed while returning from an operation against Nofilia aerodrome by straffing from German fighter aircraft. He was hit high up in the leg by a cannon shell which apparently cut the main artery. The truck in which he was travelling also carried the medical orderly and his equipment so that Jock had almost instant attention by a trained professional. He remained conscious and continued to give instructions to his men until he died fifteen minutes later. He was buried twenty miles inland South East of Nofilia. On our next operation I hope it will be possible to visit the spot where Jock is buried and to build a permanent cairn to mark the place.

In five or six weeks time I hope to be returning to England for a five-weeks visit. If I may get in touch with you on my arrival I will be able to give a much more complete account of Jock.

Yours sincerely,
David Stirling

In retrospect, and this has been admitted by key Generals and politicians of the time, the actions of the SAS in Africa, the Aegean, Italy, France and Germany did much to shorten the war. Apart from the direct destruction of men and material they tied up countless numbers of German and Italian soldiers and spread fear behind the enemy lines.

It cannot be said that without Lewes the SAS would never have been formed, for it was an idea waiting to be realised. But, it can be said with the greatest of certainty that without Lewes the unit would never have gained professional status so quickly and efficiently. Further, there is little doubt, from an examination of the records and many interviews that Jock, had he survived, would have gone on to command the SAS after Stirling's capture.

APPENDIX

EX-SYDNEY BOY CONCEIVED FAMOUS 'SECRET ARMY'

THE SYDNEY MORNING HERALD,
Saturday 6 January 1945

By a Staff Correspondent

Three years after his death in action the full story has been
officially released of the young Guards officer who conceived
the idea and devised the training curtain of what has been
described as 'Britain's most romantic, most daring and most
secret army' – the S.A.S. (Special Air Service), an ambiguous
name chosen originally to confound enemy intelligence.

He was Lieutenant John Steele Lewes, and Australia has
special reason to be proud of him, for he grew up in Sydney,
and was educated at the King's School, Parramatta. His
mother was a Sydney woman.

Australians of the Ninth Division, A.I.F., will remember
him for exploits in Tobruk, where, in a company of thousands
of brave men, he earned the reputation of the most successful patrol leader in the garrison.

Lewes was born in Calcutta, and came to Australia as a
baby. After matriculating at the King's School, he went to
Oxford, where a comparatively small incident indicated his
calibre. Oxford for 14 years had regularly lost the Boat Race
to Cambridge. Lewes became president of the Rowing Club,
and so drove and inspired his crew that that year, contrary to

everybody's expectations, Oxford 'staged a comeback', and won.

After graduating, Lewes joined the British Council, and worked for a considerable time in Berlin. When war broke out he joined the Welsh Guards, and later went out to the Middle East in a commando unit. A fellow-officer, writing to Lewes's father after his death, said: 'Jock could far more genuinely claim to be the founder of the S.A.S. than I. In June 1941, after a series of abortive operations, Jock became impatient at the methods and poor training arrangements of the Middle East commandos.

'He realised that the facilities for operating the large and clumsily organised commando were insufficient in the Middle East at that time, so he applied and got permission to detach a section from the unit, and to train it on the lines required to enable it to cover an operation which he himself had planned.

'Later, Middle East instructed me to go ahead and form a unit on the lines of Jock's ideas. Inevitably, the first officer I applied for was Jock. In fact, I built the unit around him. There is no doubt that any success the unit had achieved up to the time of Jock's death, and after it, was, and is, almost wholly due to Jock's work. Our training programmes and methods are, and always will be, based on the syllabuses he produced for us.'

This officer's faith and drive sold his idea to the Eighth Army, and he and Lewes started a school in the desert called 'Stirling's Rest Camp', where the first 77 volunteers, including at least one Australian, were assembled and put through a curriculum of training devised by Lewes.

The foundations which a man had to possess were these: He must be a qualified parachutist; he must be an expert with all kinds of small arms, and well practised in close combat; he must have more than average skill in navigation; he must be tough enough to jump off a truck going at 30 m.p.h. and enduring enough to march 100 miles with a heavy pack. Above all, it was the school's aim to produce individualists. Each man must be able to face any contingency, and make decisions alone.

DESERT OPERATION

His first operations were in the desert, where, fed and equipped by the secret patrols of the famous Long Range Desert Group, they sometimes remained behind the enemy lines for two months at a time, operating against airfields and lines of communications. They were chosen by Montgomery to break through the German lines and link the First and Eighth Armies in Tunisia. They destroyed coastal batteries to pave the way for the invasion of Sicily. When Italy was invaded S.A.S. squadrons ranged up and down the peninsula, wreaking havoc behind the enemy lines.

But the S.A.S.'s biggest job was in the invasion of France. Dropped by parachute behind the German lines, they worked with the Maquis to create confusion in the enemy rear. It has been stated: 'It was largely due to the panic and chaos wrought deep behind the enemy lines that the triumphant advance of General Patton's Third Army on Paris was possible.'

Jock Lewes did not live to see the triumphant vindication of his idea. He was killed by a cannon shell from a German fighter on 30 December 1941, while returning from an operation against Nofilia aerodrome, Libya. He was aged 27 years when he died.